Seeking Common

Seeking Common Ground

Latinx and Latin American Theatre and Performance

Edited by
TREVOR BOFFONE, TERESA MARRERO, and CHANTAL RODRIGUEZ

LONDON · NEW YORK · OXFORD · NEW DELHI · SYDNEY

METHUEN DRAMA
Bloomsbury Publishing Plc
50 Bedford Square, London, WC1B 3DP, UK
1385 Broadway, New York, NY 10018, USA
29 Earlsfort Terrace, Dublin 2, Ireland

BLOOMSBURY, METHUEN DRAMA and the Methuen Drama logo are
trademarks of Bloomsbury Publishing Plc

First published in Great Britain 2022

Cover design: Rebecca Heselton
Cover art: Herbert Siguenza

A catalogue record for this book is available from the British Library.

A catalog record for this book is available from the Library of Congress.

ISBN: HB: 978-1-3502-3021-7
        PB: 978-1-3502-3020-0
        ePDF: 978-1-3502-3022-4
        eBook: 978-1-3502-3023-1

Typeset by RefineCatch Limited, Bungay, Suffolk
Printed and bound in Great Britain

To find out more about our authors and books visit www.bloomsbury.com
and sign up for our newsletters.

This book is dedicated to the incomparable Diane Rodriguez
(June 22, 1951–April 10, 2020). Her artistry, vision, and fierce advocacy
for artists across the globe left an indelible mark on our field and in our hearts.

Contents

Foreword

Our Common Ground: *Viajes teatrales por las Américas*

Carlos Morton

Contrary to what some xenophobic politicians say, those who reside in the United States are not the only ones who have the "right" to call themselves "Americans." From Alaska to Argentina we are all *Americanos*. The only one true "natives" are the indigenous people, the rest of us are recent immigrants. The Encuentro de las Américas held November 2–19, 2017 in El Pueblo de Nuestra Señora la Reina de los Ángeles del Río de Porciúncula demonstrated that we share a common ground, featuring plays created by Americans from different regions of the United States (California, Texas, New York, Puerto Rico), but also from Canada, Mexico, Cuba, Colombia, and Peru.

Latin American *teatristas* convened their first continental/hemispheric gathering in 1968 at Manizales, Colombia including the US-based Bread and Puppet Theater. In 1970 El Teatro Campesino (ETC) began collaborating with Los Mascarones, a Mexico City-based theater that were also present at the first Chicano Festival in Fresno, California, 1970. That same year Los Mascarones director Mariano Leyva together with Luis Valdez and Jorge Huerta founded El Teatro Nacional de Aztlán (TENAZ), a national network of Chicano theater groups. Los Mascarones toured the United States on and off during 1970–4, and ETC reciprocated by visiting Mexico. The two groups had a common purpose: a search for identity and culture, especially the indigenous roots of Mexicans and Chicanos.

During the 1970s ETC also traveled to Europe and in 1973 British theatre director Peter Brook and his Paris-based company participated in an experimental workshop with El Teatro Campesino in San Juan Bautista. The joke was that ETC was becoming so "worldly" they should change their name to "El Teatro Cappuccino." Valdez borrowed freely from Mexican folklore, history, and iconography, and championed a binational message like the Mayan concept "In Lak'ech" (*tú eres mi otro yo*). When asked to define *Teatro* he described it "as a cross between Cantinflas and Brecht."

In 1974 the first *Encuentro* of the Américas took place in Mexico City with the Quinto Festival de los Teatros Chicanos sponsored by the government of then President Luis Echeverría. Theatre companies from California included ETC, the San Francisco Mime Troupe, and El Teatro de la Esperanza, but also Su Teatro (Denver) and Teatro de los Barrios (San Antonio). The Mexican side featured many *teatros populares* (i.e., working class) like Los Marcarones (Cuernavaca) and Los Zopilotes (San Luis Potosí). Also present were groups from Central America, Cuba, Colombia, Paraguay, and Venezuela. The slogan was "Somos Uno Porque América Es Una" and over 700 "cultural workers" were in attendance including important directors like Augusto Boal, Santiago García, and Enrique Buenaventura.

Most of the performances took place in venues in and around Mexico City, but also at Teotihuacán and El Tajin, important archaeological sites. The first Encuentro, a seminal event in *Teatro* history, wasn't without its polemics. Arguments between South American Marxists and New Age Chicanos ensued. According to Mexican researcher

(INBA) Julio Cesar Lopez Cabrera in the journal *Tiempo Laberinto* Augusto Boal and Enrique Buenaventura strongly critiqued ETC and Los Mascarones. They condemned the quest for identity and culture as a "dangerous romantic tendency, anti-historical, and a marked departure from concrete reality." In other words, the Marxists believed that theater should serve the people and be a medium for revolution, especially in the United States.

In 1981 the Cuban government followed up with an important Encuentro in 1981 in La Habana, inviting Chicano, Nuyorican, and progressive Cuban *teatristas* from the USA to a two-week theater festival. Besides me, José Luis Valenzuela, Evelina Fernández, Herbert Siguenza, and Marvin Feliz Camillio were in attendance. (Luis Valdez had gone to Cuba in 1964, and inspired by the Cuban revolution, returned to the Bay Area to kick-start ETC.)

A third Encuentro took place in 1983 in Nicaragua during the US-backed Contra insurgency against the ruling Sandinista government. I recall going to the front lines where *teatro* troupes entertained the troops. Along for the ride were researchers like Beatriz Rizk (Colombia), and artists like Cecilia Vega (El Salvador) and Oscar Ciccone (Argentina). In our fervid imaginations, we felt like *Internacionalistas* in the same spirit as the Lincoln Brigades during the Spanish Civil War.

In the 1980s Oscar Ciccone and Cecilia Vega persuaded Joseph Papp to institute the Festival Latino at the New York Shakespeare Festival. Papp also started a Latino Playwriting Contest that gave opportunities to US-based playwrights like Eduardo Gallardo and me, and produced Latino plays in New York. The Festival brought in famous actors like Mexican Fernando Allende and Argentinian director Norma Aleandro to the Big Apple. Papp even flew in entire companies like El Laboratorio de Teatro Campesino e Indígena de Tabasco who performed an equestrian version of *Bodas de Sangre* in the Catskills in 1985.

The networking and cross-pollination continues. In 2016 a group of Southern California artists including Josefina López, Bill Virchis, and Rickerby Hinds traveled to La Habana, Cuba to participate in a theater festival sponsored by Casa de las Americas. Encounters like this and the latest manifestation of Encuentro de las Américas 2017 is part of a long continuum. It reminds us of our commonality on this soil we call "America."

An interlude with the Latino Theater Company

The Latino Theater Company welcomes you with open arms and hearts to make our home your home. Those of us with origins in Mexico, Latin America, and the Caribbean and live in a country we call America can sometimes forget that America is not a country, but a continent. We often view our ancestry through a lens of nostalgia and romanticize our Latin American roots. So it's ironic that our own country, the United States, can too often make our community feel that this country is not ours to share, and brands us as unwanted criminals. Los Angeles in the twenty-first century is one of the most culturally diverse cities in the world. 51 percent of the city is Latino. Outside of Mexico City, it is the largest Mexican city in the world. Outside of El Salvador, it has the largest Salvadoran population in the world. More people speak Spanish than English in Los Angeles today, yet California's official language is English. It is important to come together now, in this politically polarized age where viewing someone who is not of our own race, political affiliation, religion, sexual orientation as "the enemy" has become the norm.

> (Excerpt from the Encuentro de las Américas Manifesto, delivered
> by José Luis Valenzuela on November 9, 2017
> as part of the opening ceremonies of the 2017
> Latinx Theatre Commons International Convening)

In the fall of 2020, as this volume was being prepared for publication, the members of the Latino Theater Company were invited to reflect on the Encuentro de las Américas. Below are excerpts, in their own words, about the impetus and goals of the event.

José Luis Valenzuela (Artistic Director): The Encuentros were part of the Latino Theater Company's five-year plan in relationship to Latino theater in the United States, and the role that we would play over the course of those years. In 2014, the question we posed to ourselves and the field was "Who are we?" In 2017 the question was "Where do we come from?" and the final Encuentro (delayed due to the COVID-19 pandemic) would ask, "Where are we going?" These were the pillars of our artistic inquiry and the Encuentro de las Américas was the second part of it, exploring where we come from— Latin America. It was important to us to explore the roots, historical and theatrical, which inform our artistic and cultural relationship to Latin America. It was also very important for us to create these events in order to alter the narrative of the American theater. In traditional festivals, artists usually perform their work and that's it. For us, it was crucial that the Encuentro include a required viewing schedule so that artists could watch each other's work, attend panels, and work in artistic devising sessions in order to share their methodologies. We also wanted to disrupt the idea of a single curator for a festival, and bring an ensemble-based, artist/practitioner analysis to the organization of the gatherings.

Evelina Fernández (Resident Playwright and Associate Artistic Director): After the success of Encuentro 2014 we thought it was important to expand the experience beyond the US to include Latinx artists throughout the continent. In the tradition of the original Chicano Theatre Festivals in the 1960s and 1970s when there was intentional collaboration, learning, and inspiration between Chicano Theatres and groups and maestros from Mexico and Latin America, we hoped that we could facilitate a similar experience. We considered it an honor to be able to produce and welcome all of the artists and all of the work into our home, the Los Angeles Theatre Center. The diversity in artistic process, aesthetic and theatrical language and approach was inspiring and gave us great hope for future sharing and collaboration. Besides the shows themselves, the collective creating that took place throughout the festival's devising sessions with the performing artists from different companies working together created an environment of "*compañerismo*," a commonality of struggle and, yes, even love. An unforgettable experience for sure!

Sal Lopez (Associate Artistic Director): It was an exciting prospect to have Latino artists from across multiple borders convening in the same place receiving each other's work; congregating on a daily basis socially and professionally embracing the diverse and commonality of passion for the theater. It was important for us as a company because it would provide an opportunity to study, admire, collaborate, and inspire one another. To know there are other artists around the country and the world with whom we can be in community with is affirming and empowering. It was necessary because for us to host such an ambitious undertaking would help establish our place in the theater community, our staying power, and legitimize our continuing struggle not just to survive, but to be bold.

Geoffrey Rivas (Associate Artistic Director): Part of our mission at the Los Angeles Theatre Center is the pursuit of artistic excellence and the Encuentro created a way of exploring artistic standards and theatrical approaches across the Americas. We wanted to establish a measuring bar to consider our aesthetics alongside other companies and artists. In that same vein, we were committed to fostering new relationships between artists and companies and to provide a space where established relationships could be deepened and renewed so that these explorations about artistic excellence could be sustained over time.

Lucy Rodriguez (Associate Artistic Director): To grow we must have new experiences. And while the concept of having a theater festival is not new, the specific combination of those people, that work, in that particular time was new and exciting. We also wanted to learn how artists in other countries get produced, what kind of financial support is available to them, etc. It was also important to us to invite artists at all levels of their careers; it has been very rewarding to see intergenerational networking happen at these festivals. The Encuentro de las Américas provided a great forum for international connections to be made.

Acknowledgments

This book would not exist without the visionary leadership of José Luis Valenzuela and the members of the Latino Theater Company—Evelina Fernández, Sal Lopez, Geoffrey Rivas, and Lucy Rodriguez. Their efforts to produce the 2017 Encuentro de las Américas festival exemplify their mission as the stewards of the Los Angeles Theatre Center—to provide a world-class arts center for those pursuing artistic excellence; a laboratory where both tradition and innovation are honored and honed; a place where the convergence of people, cultures, and ideas contribute to the future. We honor the immense work of the administrative and technical staff of the Los Angeles Theatre Center for making the festival not only a reality, but a success. We extend our deepest thanks to the playwrights, directors, actors, dramaturgs, designers, producers, technicians, and all contributors who breathed life into these productions and made the Los Angeles Theatre Center a site of international artistic exchange for a few weeks in 2017. Additionally, we are grateful to Herbert Siguenza for creating this book's cover art that so beautifully captures both the spirit of the festival and aims of this book.

We are indebted to the immeasurable support we have received from the Latinx Theatre Commons (LTC), a flagship program of HowlRound. The LTC has mobilized a powerful network of US Latinx theater makers that are transforming the narrative of the American theater. The Encuentro de las Américas and this anthology are just two examples of the breadth of this work.

We extend special thanks to former LTC producer Abigail Vega and current LTC producer Armando Huipe for their support of this project. Moreover, we give thanks to our team at Methuen Drama/Bloomsbury Academic who have been a joy to work with. Our editor, Dom O'Hanlon, has been an enthusiastic supporter of the project from day one; we are thrilled to have this project in his hands.

This anthology has been made possible through generous funding from the Andrew W. Mellon Foundation and the Latinx Theatre Commons.

"Sensory Strategies" Panel was previously published in *Theater*, Volume 49.1, Duke University Press, 2019.

Introduction

Trevor Boffone, Teresa Marrero, and Chantal Rodriguez

On Saturday morning, November 11, 2017 the three of us co-editors and festival attendees slowly made our way with coffee in hand to the Los Angeles Theatre Center's Theatre 4, an intimate blackbox space that had been transformed into rural Colombia. As the doors to the theater opened, we were met with the sounds of drums and Afro-Caribbean rhythms and a host of characters plucked right out of August Strindberg's classic *Miss Julie*, who were greeting spectators at the door, pouring shots of rum, and dancing on stage. Any thoughts of having to see *another* adaptation of *Miss Julie*, much less at 10:00 a.m. on a Saturday, quickly dissipated as members of Vueltas Bravas' production of *Miss Julia* broke down all barriers and, quite literally, invited us into the circle. While we were all physically in Los Angeles, the feeling was that of a big street party in Colombia. Difference—be it cultural, linguistic, gender, class, or race—did not keep us apart in this space. In Theatre 4, we were all united in community, dancing, laughing, smiling, and ultimately experiencing the beauty and power of live theater together at the Encuentro de las Américas International Theatre Festival.

From November 2 to 19, 2017, the Latino Theater Company, operators of the Los Angeles Theatre Center (LATC), in association with the Latinx Theatre Commons (LTC), produced the Encuentro de las Américas, an international festival and convening of theater artists and scholars from across the Americas. Building off of the success of the US-focused Encuentro 2014, the 2017 Encuentro de las Américas featured fourteen theater companies from Latin America, the United States, and Canada, a micro-festival with an additional twelve Los Angeles-based companies, film screenings, concerts, and an international convening of artists, theater makers, and scholars from across the Americas. Members of the LTC Steering Committee served on the festival selection committee and produced the first International LTC Convening during the middle weekend of the festival (November 9–12).[1]

An encuentro is an encounter, a meeting, a gathering, a place to come together to build community. The Spanish word also signifies a discovery. Encuentro de las Américas was just that: an encounter between artists that have been separated by national, political, and linguistic barriers for centuries. The result? A discovery in which US Latinx and Latin American artists could engage in artistic exchange and identify areas of congruity. At the center of this encuentro was the notion of common ground, a concept that also anchors this collection. In putting these works in conversation with one another, our goal is to continue a conversation that addresses what common ground may exist among theater artists across the Americas, such as divergent experiences of colonization, the limits of language, and a history of modern-day economic and cultural colonialization by the US. As such, this book considers the ways in which disparate cultures, identities, and art-making methods complicate the idea of common ground. And, while certainly fruitful, the coming together of artists from the Hemispheric Americas brings with it the complications that have historically strained the relationship between the United States and the rest of the Americas. To this end, Encuentro de las Américas and the work that follows question this utopian vision of commonality.

Seeking Common Ground: Latinx and Latin American Theatre and Performance responds to these topics by foregrounding a plurality of voices to unpack the complexities of common ground. This collection asks, what types of forms, aesthetics, and themes were activated in the works in the festival? What kinds of conversations did each performance generate? And, perhaps most importantly, what can we learn from this international experience as theater workers in the contested political climate of the early twenty-first century?

As individuals living at different intersections, each contributor to this volume not only came to Encuentro 2017 with a unique standpoint, but left Los Angeles with a deeper relationship with and understanding of other theater artists and scholars from the Americas. Ultimately, this volume demonstrates how Encuentro de las Américas was not just a theater festival, but a strategic, public event that proudly proclaimed that artistic dialogue and exchange between US Latinx and Latin American theater artists is part of our history and must be a part of our future as well.

The Latinx Theatre Commons: Three Years of the Commons-Based Approach (2014–17)

The Encuentro de las Américas is the second in a proposed three-part cycle of Encuentro festivals produced by the Latino Theater Company. Led by artistic director José Luis Valenzuela, the ensemble has been together for over thirty years with individual roots deep within the Chicano Theatre Movement. In 2011, while on tour for the first time as an ensemble, the company was reinvigorated by their engagement with artists and audiences across the country and they were determined to support what they felt was a crucial absence in the field of Latinx Theater—the ability to see one another's work and discuss it openly. Without direct engagement with Latinx work, Latinx artists and audiences must often rely on problematic and biased criticism which fails to understand the work in its own cultural context. Additionally, rather than wait for regional theaters to include more Latinx work in their seasons, the company yearned to revitalize a national network that would support artistic exchange among Latinx companies. Soon after their tour, the Latino Theater Company began to plan of a series of Encuentros. The first would be a national Latinx theater festival—Encuentro 2014. The second would be an international festival with Latinx and Latin American artists from across the Americas—Encuentro de las Américas 2017. The third would be a global festival without a specific focus on Latinx or Latin American work—Encuentro Global.[2]

The momentum created by Encuentro 2014 was almost immediately apparent. In terms of the Encuentro artists, a revitalized network of national Latinx theater artists and companies emerged as a result. Some of the 2014 productions that engaged this network include: the presentation of Caborca Theatre's *Zoetrope* Part I and II at Pregones Theater (January 2015); About Production's *Properties of Silence* at the Carrie Hamilton Theater at the Pasadena Playhouse (March 2015); Rubén González's *La Esquinita, U.S.A.* at Pregones Theater (December 2015), Aurora Theater (July 2016), and Su Teatro Cultural Performing Arts Center which also included Rickerby Hinds' *Dreamscape* (April 2016); the Latino Theater Company's *Premeditation* was presented at Arts Emerson in Boston in the spring of 2016 and was accompanied by

Marissa Chibas' *Daughter of a Cuban Revolutionary;* and both José Torres-Tama's *Aliens, Immigrants, and Other Evildoers* and Theatre Mitu's *Juarez: A Documentary Mythology* have toured throughout the country since 2014.[3] The festival's influence on the artists was indeed palpable and demonstrated the ways in which reinvigorating a national network of Latinx theater makers can support the wider dissemination of Latinx work in the US American Theatre.

While the 2014 festival artists received an undeniable boost, the Latinx Theatre Commons itself dually benefited from the momentum generated by the festival, and in particular the national convening weekend of November 6–9, 2014. As Encuentro 2014 was the LTC's first fully public event, it cemented the organization on the national theater map, leading the LTC to grow in unexpected ways.[4] This growth was rooted not only in the momentum generated by the Encuentro 2014 festival and the national convening, but also in the confidence gained by executing such large-scale events. Following the 2014 convening, the LTC hosted eleven in-person gatherings in Chicago, Dallas, Seattle, and New York City before returning to Los Angeles for the second Encuentro in 2017.

In service of the pillar of scholarship, *Café Onda*, an online gathering space for community, sourced contributions as well as feedback and now exists as part of HowlRound Journal. Additionally, the LTC also supported the publication of *Encuentro: Latinx Performance for the New American Theater* with Northwestern University Press (2019), in order to document the historic festival and extend its reach. In a similar vein, the El Fuego Initiative facilitated the world premiere of new plays featured in the 2015 Carnaval of Latina/o New Work at The Theatre School at DePaul University. In early 2015, theaters across the country were approached about securing productions for every playwright featured at the Carnaval. This historic initiative started with twelve theaters committing in less than a day, which soon expanded to eighteen, and comprises nationally recognized theaters in Los Angeles, New York City, Washington DC, and elsewhere. In addition to supporting productions of these new works, the El Fuego Initiative also supported scholarship by pairing each production with a scholar of Latinx theater who would document the piece through their scholarship.

With each of these initiatives, the conversations among LTC Steering Committee members, Latinx artists, companies, and audiences deepened and informed future programming. According to theater scholars Maria Enriquez and Christopher Goodson, these initiatives "create a mobile, collaborative network that illuminates, challenges, and redefines American theater through the presence of an active Latinx theatre collective."[5] Given these premises, many scholars, such as Teresa Marrero, understand the LTC as one of "the most important movement of the new millennium."[6] It provides a national presence for the Latinx theater movement, which largely had been without a cohesive organized structure since TENAZ (Teatro Nacional de Aztlán) shuttered in the early 1990s.

Notably, while there has been growth, critical feedback—both from within the group itself and also from Latinx artists who have resisted participation in the LTC and its events—has revealed long-standing issues which compelled the LTC to engage in core work focused on equity, diversity, and inclusion (EDI).[7] Questions regarding inclusivity and representation were significant during the 2014 Encuentro, and while its goals were to provide a snapshot of contemporary Latinx theater, including its various methodologies and aesthetics, a large focus also became whose voices were missing from the conversation. The 2017 Encuentro de las Américas certainly did highlight a wider range of voices and aesthetics practices through its transnational focus. The core values of the 2017 festival were: cross-cultural collaboration, exchange of methodologies, openness to risk, and inclusive dialogue. In tandem with José Luis Valenzuela's vision for a festival of theater artists from across the Américas, the LTC saw the convening as an opportunity to (re)build bridges and relationships. Aside from the annual Miami Hispanic International Theater Festival, regular opportunities for collaboration between US Latinx and Latin American theater artists are few and far between on US soil. With the increasingly hostile stances on immigration and international relations with Latin America that the United States has historically adopted building relationships is not always easy.

While the festival aimed to find commonalities across a multitude of borders, it also proved that common ground may also be fragile. For example, as the LTC's first international convening, the Encuentro 2017 convening intended to be fully bilingual in English and Spanish. Large group sessions featured live interpretation by LTC volunteers and every production included supertitles in its counterpart language. Noticeably, this was a utopian vision. Supertitles were often placed in awkward places or at times lagged behind the performance itself, making it difficult to fully follow the action of the performance. The gargantuan task of live interpretation by non-professional volunteers also led to challenges, and calls for an approach to language justice that includes sign language and indigenous languages.

In terms of race, Encuentro 2017 spurred much discussion about Afro-Latinidad, as well as the issue of anti-blackness both within the US Latinx community and in Latin America. Moreover, the idea that race and racism are only issues in the United States was frequently voiced by Latin American artists, who have dealt with different systems of power created by the legacy of colonialism such as colorism. Whereas US-based artists appeared to share some common discourse around issues of race, Latin American artists had a different framework for understanding racial tensions. Indeed, there was little, if any, common ground in this respect.[8]

Common Ground: Towards a Theory of Commonality Across the Americas

To best understand the impetus for an international gathering based on the premise of finding common ground and embracing a collective voice, one must first examine the very notion of common ground. With this in mind, our understanding of common ground is informed by theories from Benedict Anderson, Juan Flores, José Esteban Muñoz, and Roberto Esposito. Ultimately, these theories demonstrate the complexities of commonality and how, while some things may be shared across national borders, there are many aspects of community that are simply not legible across markers of difference. While Encuentro 2017 aimed to create a space to tease out the notion of common ground, in the end, it left us questioning the assumption of a natural or essential connection between US Latinx and Latin American artists.

The notion of commonality or common ground is rooted in the notion of socially constructed, or imagined, communities to use Benedict Anderson's term. Anderson uses the term imagined communities "because the members of even the smallest nation will never know most of their fellow-members, meet them, or even hear of them, yet in the minds of each lives the image of their communion."[9] In *The Nation and Its Fragments*, Partha Chatterjee critiques this universalized version of nation by questioning whose standpoint is being represented. One's or a group's positionality is embedded within its relative placement within a given socioeconomic structure. In other words, the positionality of the imagining, or the "imagined community," is marked within a socioeconomic—and we would add racial and linguistic—structures.[10]

Even so, the idea of community often foregrounds the very things that bind people together. For example, in the field of public health, MacQueen et al. conclude that:

> A common definition of community emerged as a group of people with diverse characteristics who are linked by social ties, share common perspectives, and engage in joint action in geographical locations or settings. The participants differed in the emphasis they placed on particular elements of the definition. Community was defined similarly but experienced differently by people with diverse backgrounds.[11]

Thus, while the notion of community embodies utopic elements of sameness, we experience it differently. Offering a perspective informed by Latinx Studies, in *From Bomba to Hip-Hop: Puerto Rican Culture and Latino Identity*, Juan Flores expresses that the concept and the very makeup of the term *comunidad*, or community, harkens back to two terms:

> *Comunidad*: the Spanish word, even more clearly than the English, calls to mind two of the key terms—*común* and *unidad*—in the conceptualization of this notoriously elusive idea. What do we have in "common," and what makes for our unity? It is important to note that though the two terms point in the same semantic direction they are not synonymous, and their apparent coupling in the same word, *comunidad*, is not a redundancy. For while *común* refers to sharing—that is, those aspects in the cultures of the various constitutive groups that overlap—the sense of *unidad* is that which bonds the groups above and beyond the diverse particular commonalities.[12]

In "The Latino Imaginary," Flores adds that in communities: "'*común*' stands for the community in itself, while '*unidad*' refers to the community for itself, the way that it conceives of, imagines itself."[13] This connection based on commonality and unity increases the possibilities for collaborative theater and social change. Echoing these thoughts, philosopher Roberto Esposito posits that "what is common is that which unites the ethnic, territorial, and spiritual property of every one of its members. They have in common what is most properly their own; they are the owners of what is common to them."[14] The idea of "common" is ingrained in accessibility.[15] In addition, the Latin origin of "*munus*" refers to duty, gift, or obligation. Therefore, as Esposito demonstrates, "The subjects of community are united by an 'obligation.'"[16] These subjects cede individuality in order to become affiliated with the group and fulfill these obligations to the community.

The shared sense of common ground among US Latinx artists can be traced to the condition of "feeling brown," or feeling like a problem in a society that values whiteness. In "'Chico, what does it feel like to be a problem?' The Transmission of Brownness," cultural theorist and performance studies scholar José Esteban Muñoz argues that identity is a problematic term when it is applied to Latinx communities because they do not adhere to monolithic definitions of race, nationality, language, or other traditional markers of difference. In this manner, Latinx identity in and of itself is problematic. By feeling like a problem, various Latinx communities find a link that functions to help them belong within a society that openly and frequently discriminates against them. People of color's feelings are what they have in common and what unites them, *lo común* and *la unidad*. According to Muñoz:

> Feeling Brown is feeling together in difference. Feeling Brown is an "apartness together" through sharing the status of being a problem. [. . .] Brownness is a value through negation, the negation projected onto it by a racist public sphere that devalues the particularity of non-Anglo Americans.[17]

"Feeling Brown" is in conversation with Turner's notion of communitas if we look at both phenomena as the communal pleasure of sharing common experiences.[18] It is necessary that these individuals come together under the confines of a collective to construct a mode of belonging achieved through the concept of community. In this way, community is not just one of location and belonging, but what José Muñoz calls dislocation and unbelonging. This community is formed as much around what is common and what unites community members as it is about difference.

In light of Flores, Esposito, and Muñoz's assertions, it is clear that community is ingrained, both etymologically and philosophically, in an idea of collectivity. Yet, what happens when the idea of collectivity, or common ground, is built on shaky terrain? What happens when a group of theater makers and scholars convene to seek common ground without a shared analysis around race, gender, and class? While the festival artists spent three weeks building community and exchanging artistic methodologies, the convening added over 100 new voices and topics to the dialogue. These conversations were at once challenging and invigorating, and are rooted in a history of artistic exchange between US and Latin American artists.

Intercultural Exchange between US Latinx and Latin American Artists

The origins of contemporary artists from the United States and Latin America using theater as a site of intercultural exchange along the Americas' North–South axis can be traced to the early days of Chicana/o—and later Latinx—theater festivals. Central to this movement was TENAZ, which produced festivals from 1971 to 1992. Since the genesis of the Latinx Theatre Commons, parallels have been drawn to TENAZ, which served as an umbrella organization of the Chicano Theatre Movement from the 1970s to the 1990s. The missions of these two groups are radically different. TENAZ was focused on a revolutionary alternative to the exclusionary practices of commercial theater, whereas the LTC works to update the narrative about Latinx theater in the new millennium and to increase access for artists of color in the wider field of not-for-profit theater. To this end, the desire to connect Latinx theater makers through festivals and convenings has been central to both TENAZ and the LTC.

As the central organizer of Chicano Theatre festivals until the 1990s, TENAZ worked to activate these events in service of their overarching goals—to establish communication between *teatros*, to provide a means for the sharing of materials, and to establish recurring training workshops. The role of criticism and feedback was also essential to the festival process, and each production in these festivals was given a specific forum to hear responses from the other artists. Regarded as a field-changing festival, El Quinto Festival de los Teatros Chicanos: Primer Encuentro Latinoamericano (The Fifth Chicano Theatre Festival: First Latin American Encounter) was held in Mexico City in 1974. According to the TENAZ festival committee, the journey of Chicano teatros to Mexico "is an acto becoming mito. A political act becoming myth. Teatro becoming ritual. It is a journey into the very heart of unity."[19] This was more than a festival; rather, it was framed as a spiritual homecoming. As described by Jorge Huerta, its impact was profound:

> This massive undertaking began with ceremonies and performances at the pyramids of Teotihuacán, outside México City and culminated two weeks later at the pyramids of Tajín, in Veracruz, México. Many of the Chicanas/os had never been to México City, and their limited Spanish sometimes kept them from fully expressing their observations and feelings. It was a culture clash of major proportions as the working-class teatro members were exposed to, and contrasted with, major theatre companies and internationally known Latin American directors, and playwrights. Many of the Mexican, Central, South, and Latin Americans were fascinated by the Chicanas/os living *en la barriga del monstruo* (in the belly of the monster) in the United States, while said "monster" was running rampant in their countries—supporting repression and violence of all kinds in order to support American interests.[20]

The idea of unity between all oppressed peoples of the Américas was at the core of the festival's ideology. "Un continente, una cultura (one continent, one culture)" declared the festival committee, and forty-three years later the Latino Theater Company and the Latinx Theatre Commons called on Encuentro de las Américas participants to embrace their collective voice.[21] As Huerta argues, "a theatre festival is the natural manifestation of the collective desire to celebrate a people's history, myths, hopes, and dreams; to share ideas and quite simply to be renewed in one's mission as cultural workers. In the case of Latina/o theatre, there is also the desire to question the status-quo."[22]

But even the idealistic notions of continental unity proposed by TENAZ ran into trouble. The now infamous Quinto Festival de los Teatros Chicanos in 1974, whose ideology hinged on the notion of aesthetic compassion, was intended to be a pilgrimage of conversion whose goal was for Chicanas/os and Mexicans to (re)connect through a single vision of social justice and a united racial identity rooted in Amerindian mythologies and the notion of Aztlán as the Chicano motherland (Gómez).[23] In *The Revolutionary Imaginations of Greater Mexico: Chicana/o Radicalism, Solidarity Politics & Latin American Social Movements*, Alan Eladio Gómez documents the festival's ideal that "*Somos uno porque América es una*" (We are one because America is one), a philosophy that ran into ideological, political, and economic problems.[24] Rooted in Chicano nationalism, this was viewed from the Latin American leftist movements as naive, and from the Mexican left as puerile. This landmark event, nevertheless, managed to bring together more than 300 performances in two weeks from Latin America and the US.[25] Thus, while TENAZ historically marks the first ambitious theatrical encuentro among the Americas, there, too, ideological differences emerged.

Even so, the legacy of TENAZ has informed Latinx theater making since its inception, creating an ecosystem that has encouraged international exchange between the Américas. Since the 1990s there has been a proliferation of theatrical activity along the North–South axis, such as the exchanges fostered by the Hemispheric Institute of Performance and Politics, at New York University with the work of Chicano performer and theoretician Guillermo Gómez-Peña, the feminist work of lesbian Mexican actor and now senator of the Mexican national legislature Jesusa Rodríguez and her partner Liliana Felipe, one of Latin America's foremost singers and composers, the collectively devised experimental work of the Peruvian group Grupo Cultural Yuyachkani, and the work of Highland Chiapas's all-indigenous woman's theater group FOMMA (Fortaleza de la Mujer Maya), to name but a few.[26]

Given its continued longevity, the International Hispanic Theatre Festival in Miami has been an important site to stage Latin American work in the US since 1985. Even so, these festivals have not fully foregrounded intersections and points of exchange across national borders that Encuentro 2017 intended to address, nor have they discussed the possible challenges of these intersections. The same was the case with the University of Kansas's US-based festivals and symposia which hosted Latin American and Latinx theater artists from 1982 to 1990. The festival was organized by George Woodyard, founder and editor of the University of Kansas's *Latin American Theater Review*. With its focus on both Latin American and US Latinx theater, *Latin American Theater Review* remains the only one of its kind in US academic journals. *GESTOS*, another pivotal publication foregrounding theater from Latin America, the United States, and Spain, was published by the University of California, Irvine, founded and directed for twenty-five years by Prof. Juan Villegas, is now defunct. Both of these publications and their contributors have historically documented the South/North theatrical connections.

On the North to South axis, it is germane to note that very little if any Chicano or Latinx plays are read, much less produced in Latin America's major theater capitals such as Mexico, Cuba, Chile, Colombia, and Argentina. Exceptions are El Teatro Campesino's Mexico City production of *Zoot Suit* in 2010 and some of Caridad Svich's adaptations, such as Isabel Allende's *La Casa de los Espíritos*, and the Lark's Mexico–United States Playwright Exchange, which was founded in 2006. Similarly, very few Latin American plays make their way to US professional, regional theaters either in Spanish or in translation.[27] US non-profit theaters that have fostered Spanish-language theater such as GALA Hispanic Theatre in Washington, DC, Teatro Avante in Miami, Aguijón Theater in Chicago, Teatro Rodante Puertorriqueño and Repertorio Español in New York City, the Bilingual Foundation for the Arts, Frida Kahlo Theatre, 24th Street Theatre in Los Angeles, and Teatro Dallas in Texas produce works in Spanish, usually with English supertitles.[28]

It is noteworthy to mention the fact that professional Latin American stages have traditionally looked towards European theatre for models and often produce French, German, and Italian works in Spanish translation, particularly in commercial theatres located in the capital cities. On the other hand, Latin American popular or grassroots theater movements spawned from the 1960s onward grew into what is commonly known as the New Latin American theater—which followed the decolonization practices from Brazilian Paolo Freire's *Pedagogy of the Oppressed* and Augusto Boal's *Theatre of the Oppressed*—to engage in devised work and collective creation.[29] This is to note that, other than the recent growth of international musical blockbusters, the US has had little influence on the aesthetics and theatrical practices of and by Latin American artists, with the possible exception of New York City's La MaMa Experimental Theatre Club founded in 1961 by Ellen Stewart. The lack of mutual familiarity between the various aesthetics became apparent during the 2017 Encuentro de las Américas; namely, the recognition that, despite the good will to foment unity, there were areas of tensions that needed to be recognized. Even so, as the site for the first international convening of the LTC, the Encuentro de las Américas festival aspired to form a hemispheric connection with Latin American artists, but could that connection be found through drama? If the Quinto Festival de los Teatros Chicanos in Mexico City was considered a homecoming for Chicano artists, what would Latin American artists find in coming to Los Angeles to share their work?

Encuentro de las Américas International Theatre Festival: An Overview

The values of the 2017 Encuentro were to promote the following: cross-cultural collaboration, exchange of methodologies, openness to risk, and inclusive dialogue.[30] These values not only informed how the selection committee chose the participating productions, but also guided the various conversations that occurred throughout the convening weekend.[31] In addition to productions by seven US-based Latinx theater companies, artists from Canada, Colombia, Cuba, Mexico, and Peru were in residence at the LATC for three weeks.[32] Productions in the 2017 Encuentro de las Américas included:

- *10 Millones*, Argos Teatro—Havana, Cuba
- *Broken Tailbone*, Nightswimming & Carmen Aguirre—Toronto, Canada
- *Conjunto Blues*, Guadalupe Cultural Arts Center—San Antonio, TX
- *Deferred Action*, Cara Mía Theatre Co.—Dallas, TX
- *Dementia*, Latino Theater Company—Los Angeles, CA
- *El Apagón/The Blackout*, Pregones Theater—the Bronx, New York
- *Las Mariposas Saltan al Vacío*, Compañía Nacional de las Artes—Bogotá, Colombia
- *La razón blindada*, 24th Street Theatre—Los Angeles, CA
- *Latin Standards*, Marga Gómez—San Francisco, CA
- *Miss Julia*, Vueltas Bravas—Bogotá, Colombia
- *Quemar las naves. El viaje de Emma*, Organización Secreta Teatro—Mexico City, Mexico
- *Ropa Íntima*, Ébano Teatro—Lima, Peru

- *Culture Clash: An American Odyssey*, Culture Clash—Los Angeles, CA
- *WET: A DACAmented Journey*, Alex Alpharaoh—Los Angeles, CA

These productions ran in repertory in five spaces at the LATC for three weeks, with the middle weekend seeing the 2017 LTC International Convening bring over 150 artists and scholars to Los Angeles not only to see the work, but more importantly to discuss aesthetics and the possibilities of cross-cultural collaboration with festival artists. The Encuentro de las Américas festival also included a micro-festival entitled *Patas Arriba* (Upside Down). Framed as an "LA Anthology," the micro-festival featured the work of twelve LA-based theater artists, staged in non-conventional areas of the cavernous Los Angeles Theatre Center. During the Convening weekend, the LTC engaged participants in guided conversations about aesthetics both in the United States and abroad, themed panels and roundtables, opportunities for relationship building and networking, group meals, and post-show parties. As they did in 2014, the Latino Theater Company and the Latinx Theatre Commons partnered to offer a Creative Producing Fellowship component to the festival, to provide opportunities for leadership training that broadens the pool of arts workers ready to take on key leadership positions. The 2017 Encuentro de las Américas Creative Producing Fellows included Israel López, Ammy Ontiveros, Diana Romo, Cris Swartz, and Ramon Vargas.

Encuentro 2017 marked the first effort by the LTC to build bridges between US-based Latinx and Latin American theater artists. After national and regional convenings in Boston, Los Angeles, Chicago, Dallas, Seattle, and New York City, the moment was ripe to facilitate a dialogue between artists in the United States, Canada, and Latin America. While each convening has had a specific aim, whether to engage with the local community, address national field-wide concerns, or to foster new play development, the International Convening at the Encuentro de las Américas aimed to find commonality and solidarity between artists from disparate places in the Américas.

As playwright Georgina Escobar notes in "The Composition of Latinx Aesthetics," the "compositional movement of the LTC [. . .] is not only taking form, but is encouraging other movements—modeled and inspired by the LTC."[33] Escobar explains how, while the commons-based approach may appear easy or a given, "It has taken work and plenty of careful listening for us to find moments of harmony [. . .] to form the strong tenants that may support the movement for years to come."[34] In many ways, the Encuentro de las Américas was an act of careful listening as artists from across different borders sought to find the "moments of harmony" that Escobar speaks of. Of importance is to highlight the momentary; that is, the impermanent nature of commonality, one that is constantly shifting. To do this, many of the conversations at the convening were guided by the following questions: What has kept us apart for the last fifty years, and how do we come back together? How do we engender a more equitable exchange between Latinx and Latin American artists? What is our common ground across our borders? What are we doing differently? And, perhaps most importantly, as an art form reliant on collaboration: what can we do together that we cannot do separately?[35]

The LTC uses a commons-based approach to build community and foster an ecosystem that supports tangible, widespread social change. While in Los Angeles, Encuentro artists shared their work and methodologies with other theater makers. The goal was as simple as it was nuanced: to create a shared, multidimensional understanding of the field, from Argentina to Canada. In line with the LTC and HowlRound's values, the convening weekend was rooted in the commons-based approach, or a philosophical method that "stands in contrast to the enclosure and privatization of knowledge, but more importantly it creates opportunities for new ways of conceptualizing possibilities through collaborations using existing infrastructures."[36] In this way, the LTC used the commons-based approach to extend its reach across the Américas by assembling participants to collectively experience and discuss the performances, aesthetics, and methodologies outside of the typical Eurocentric artistic lens often privileged in mainstream theater making in the United States. The festival, therefore, sought to find commonalities between Latinx and Latin American artists—while respecting differences—to forge opportunities for future collaborations, and to devise a space in which artists from across the Americas could build bridges. To this end, the Encuentro de las Américas incited necessary conversations across borders—both physical and not—that have separated various artistic communities. For decades, these boundaries, such as cultural misunderstanding, discriminatory and oppressive immigration laws, nationalistic mindsets, and the everlasting effects of colonialism, have separated the theater community across the Américas.

Encuentro de las Américas: The Anthology

From its inception, scholarship has been one of the main pillars of the Latinx Theatre Commons. The LTC Steering Committee fully supported the publication of *Encuentro: Latinx Performance for the New American Theater*, and continues to do so with the present volume.[37] The guiding principles for selecting what is in this anthology are multiple; however, this book aspires to generate a multidimensional conversation about common ground, without neglecting differences, and to document the Encuentro de las Américas festival. As such, this book is divided into four sections, each focusing on a different aspect of common themes explored between US Latinx and Latin American artists in the festival: gender and sexuality, class, politics, and autobiography. While these four topics guide a section, the conversations within each section are not limited to them. As representative works by Latinx and Latin American theater makers, these plays are intersectional by nature, always foregrounding the relationships between how certain identity markers affect other ones. In this way, while we use *Dementia* as the anchor play for the section on gender and sexuality, it would be impossible to truly discuss this play without a nuanced conversation about class, the State, and the political moment that led to the systematic erasure of Latinx bodies during the height of the Aids epidemic. Moreover, as Chantal Rodriguez explains in her overview of the play, *Dementia* is inspired by true events which pay homage to the very roots of the Latino Theater Company's ensemble.

To best capture the plurality of voices present at Encuentro 2017, every production is featured in some way in this anthology. Moreover, the theme of common ground coalesces through a multiplicity of voices and formats. This includes full playscripts, profiles and interviews with Encuentro artists, and brief snapshots. Each section is anchored by a representative play. While each playscript that we selected stands alone in its own way, this decision was also influenced by a variety of other factors. Some plays have previously been published (*Ropa Íntima* and *El Apagón*, for instance). Others rely heavily on music, design and, embodied elements and, as such, would not transfer well to print format (*El viaje de Emma* and *Broken Tailbone*, for example). Moreover, we were limited to plays that were ready to be published in English, despite in some cases being performed in Spanish at the festival. While some of the texts are not being published in their full format, we believe that the profiles, interviews, and snapshots to follow fully capture the essence of these works and encourage the reader to seek out more information about these artists.

The first section, "Traversing Boundaries of Gender and Sexuality," focuses on the nuances of gender and sexuality. Noticeably, this was one of the main themes that was missing from Encuentro 2014. In light of this, the Encuentro 2017 selection committee accounted for issues of gender parity and stories that represented a multiplicity of sexual identities. As this volume demonstrates, the results were varied, both in execution and in reception. Even so, works by Evelina Fernández, José Milían, and Rocío Carrillo Reyes exposed the ways in which gender is constructed across national borders, ultimately revealing that the very notions of gender and sexuality are blurry when viewed outside of their original cultural context. While we may have a common-ground understanding of topics such as gender identity and feminism in the United States, these works revealed the ways in which these issues are, in fact, regional at times.

For the Latino Theater Company and Compañía Nacional de las Artes, this conversation was driven by reviving two plays focusing on the height of the Aids epidemic. The Latino Theater Company's production of *Dementia* by Evelina Fernández focuses on Moe, a victim of the 1990s Aids epidemic who is about to die. Under the direction of José Luis Valenzuela, the centrality of Moe's deathbed around which old wounds—like favorite oldies songs—bring both joy and pathos. Moe, played by company member Sal Lopez in a tour de force turn, meets Death, who comes in the guise of a torch-singing drag queen. This play is an important part of the Latino Theater Company's repertoire as well as the history of Latinx theater as it stages an example of the relationship between Latinidad, homosexuality, and Aids. While Aids was one of the leading causes of death among Latinas/os in the early 1990s, it was rarely articulated in the dominant culture.[38] On a similar thematic line, Colombia's Compañía Nacional de las Artes presented *Las mariposas saltan al vacío* (*Butterflies Jump to the Abyss*) by José Milían and directed by Jorge Cao. *Mariposas* was a visual spectacle that captured the intimate story of a community of people who were institutionalized for various reasons, most prevalent of which was their proximity to the 1990s Aids epidemic. The production offered a plethora of perspectives on love, betrayal, promiscuity, ignorance, joy, and, ultimately, the power of forgiveness. While some festival-goers found the material dated (as was the case with *Dementia*), the play shed light on an international epidemic that placed the issues of queer men in a historical context.

While *Dementia* and *Mariposas* primarily focused on male victims of the Aids epidemic, Mexico City's Organización Secreta Teatro shifted the focus to women to highlight the relationship between gender, sexuality, and history. Headed by writer-director Rocío Carrillo, the company presented an interdisciplinary, collectively created piece, *Quemar las naves. El viaje de Emma* (*Burning the Bridges, Emma's Voyage*), which was a decidedly feminist retelling of Homer's *The Odyssey*. Foregrounding Emma's exploration towards independence following the death of her husband, the production notably featured almost no spoken word. Rather, Emma's journey was dramatized through movement, ritual performance, and imagery. The performance was a lush visual feast orchestrated to the ambient sounds generated by the actors, a live percussionist, and a magical musical score matched by an epic, larger than life scenic, visual, and costume design. Even so, some US-based festival-goers found the staging of the semi-nude female body problematic effectively revealing a disparity between US and Latin American understandings of feminism and the representational practices of nakedness.

The second section, "Staging Transnational Realities of Race, Ethnicity, and Class," foregrounds key underpinnings of Latin American society and therefore how they affect diasporic communities in the US. *Ropa Íntima*, *Miss Julia*, and *El Apagón* highlight the ways in which race and class interact, and how identities are lived in these intersections. As opposed to other companies that offered original works, Lima, Peru's Ébano Teatro instead produced *Ropa Íntima*, a Spanish-language translation of Lynn Nottage's award-winning *Intimate Apparel* (2005). The play was translated into Spanish by Marianella Pantoja and featured direction by Miguel Pastor. Ébano Teatro was founded in 2014 and claims to be the only theater company in Peru dedicated to addressing its Afro-Peruvian population. Staging a well-known play by an African-American playwright in translation is part of the company's repertoire, yet some of the convening participants were left hungry to see an original work that is more closely aligned with Peru's own Afro-descendant communities. Even so, Nottage's work took on new meaning in a Peruvian setting, effectively demonstrating the universality of protagonist Esther's journey to empowerment. As Ébano Teatro demonstrated, conversations on the intersections of class and race can cross national borders as Nottage's play went from a decidedly North American context to one that spoke to the challenges facing Peru's marginalized Afro-descendant population.

In a similar vein, Vueltas Bravas from Colombia used a classic play as its point of departure. Their production of *Miss Julia*, based on August Strindberg's 1888 naturalistic classic *Miss Julie*, and adapted by J.Ed. Araiza with direction by Lorenzo Montanini, turns naturalism on its head not only by tropicalizing the setting to a rural Colombian midsummer night's dream, but also by deconstructing the very representational naturalism of the original text. This adaptation and translation into colloquial Colombian Spanish and formal English opened with a party-like ambiance welcoming of the audience into the theatrical space. The live percussive sounds of drums, together with offerings of shots of rum and regional Afro-Colombian rhythms prepared the space for the subsequent ritualistic destruction between Miss Julia and Juan, her servant, much to the dismay of his wife, the household cook.

Situating similar conversations about the working class in the Bronx, New York, Pregones Theater presented *El Apagón* (*The Blackout*), which hinges on the historic city-wide blackout of 1965. Based on a short story by José Luis González and adapted to the stage by Alvan Colón-Lespier, Jorge B. Merced, and Rosalba Rolón, who also directed, it features the company's musical ensemble. This piece exemplified what Pregones does best: the use of popular rhythms of Puerto Rican music to harmonize with stellar acting and great storytelling, provoking the audience to feel like they are attending a 1960s block party even while seated in a theatrical setting. The storyline is simple: a working-class Puerto Rican man wants to get home in time for the birth of his child. He must overcome the city-wide blackout, which leaves him stuck underground in the subway in Brooklyn, while trying to make his way all the up to El Barrio in East Harlem in the dark. Using a narrative style much like that of *10 Millones*, this story unfolds in the spectator's imagination through oral storytelling.

Section Three, "The State, Politics, and Lived Experience," shifts the focus to the relationship between the State, politics, and the individual. Plays by David Lozano, Culture Clash, Carlos Celdrán, and Arístides Vargas speak to how policies enforced by the State can have detrimental effects on the lived experiences of Latinx and Latin Americans. Demonstrating the negative aftermath of immigration legislation, revolution, and the legacy of xenophobic leadership, these plays reveal the cloudiness that their characters face. Oftentimes, there is no happy ending as these problems are still being faced by peoples throughout the Americas.

The politics of immigration in the United States are front and center with Dallas, Texas's Cara Mía Theatre Company, who came to the table with its hard-hitting and highly polished political piece *Deferred Action,* the second part of a trilogy on immigration. Co-written by the company's artistic director David Lozano (who also directed) and Lee Trull, the play tells the story of Javi, an undocumented DACA (Deferred Action for Childhood Arrivals) recipient from El Salvador. *Deferred Action* is a finely tuned bird's eye view of the political ins and outs between the Democratic and Republican Parties in 2016, right before a fictional presidential election that ousted the incumbent political party from office. Created by consulting North Texas DREAMers and Salvadoran immigrants in the area, *Deferred Action* stands out as a unique union of ethnographic research and dramaturgical choices. While some may object to the ending in which Javi the DREAMer sells out to the Republican Party, this play dishes out hard-hitting political realism in a way that urged audiences to think.

Continuing the conversation about sociopolitical issues in the United States, Los Angeles-based Culture Clash's *Culture Clash: An American Odyssey* highlighted the group's popularity as a now-legendary and iconoclastic Chicano cultural producer to speak to current issues facing the US Latinx community. While the original members are José Antonio Burciaga, Marga Gómez, Monica Palacios, Richard Montoya, Ric Salinas, and Herbert Siguenza, the company has done its main body of work with the latter three. Under the direction of Robert Beltran, Culture Clash's show mixed new pieces with segments from older comedic sketches, some of which have aged better than others. For instance, problematic issues arose around the portrayal of a transgender woman fielding questions about gender affirmation surgery.

While US-based companies Cara Mía and Culture Clash examined issues pertaining to immigration, Latin American artists explored the effects of dictatorships and revolutions within the home country. Argos Teatro's production of *10 Millones (10 Million)* is an autobiographical testament by playwright, director, and scenic designer Carlos Celdrán of the deep divides evoked by the Cuban Revolution of 1959. A young man comes of age during the fervor of the first years of the Revolution, only to find at what cost to his family. The main characters, the young man, the father, the mother, and another man, sometimes address each other, but most often direct themselves to the audience narrating what often seems to be an apology (in the classical sense of the word as a self-defense). *10 Millones* is an emotional piece that resonates with anyone who has had to separate from loved ones and their country of origin for political reasons. Ultimately, Celdrán's play speaks to the plight of those who face difficult family choices in the face of revolution and state-sanctioned repression. This play was presented in Spanish during Encuentro; the company provided the English-language version that appears in this volume.

Taking similar thematic content and infusing it with classic literature, Los Angeles-based 24th Street Theatre presented their production of *La razón blindada* ("Armored Reason"), written and directed by Argentine playwright Arístides Vargas. Vargas found inspiration from Cervantes's *El Quixote*, Franz Kafka's *The Truth About Sancho Panza*, and testimonies from political prisoners held in Rawson Prison during The Dirty War in Argentina in the 1970s. Reprising their roles as political prisoners, actors Jesús Castaños-Chima and Tony Durá, the duo can only interact with each other for one hour per week. Moreover, they must remain seated; they can never stand. To pass the time, they entertain each other with stories of Don Quixote and Sancho Panza, ultimately revealing the ways in which theater can transport us even amid oppressive surroundings.

Section Four, "Music and Autobiographical Performance," highlights autobiographical voices from the festival—privileging the work of solo performers Carmen Aguirre, Alex Alpharaoh, Marga Gómez, and Nicolás Valdez—to expand on the notion of the personal as political. In these shows, each playwright-cum-performer meditates on their own life experiences to unpack how the intersections of race, ethnicity, and immigration have formed their cultural identities. Indeed, even though these works examine individual experiences, they are, in fact, universal stories. Indeed, while *Conjunto Blues*, *Broken Tailbone*, *Latin Standards*, and *WET: A DACAmented Journey* all focus on a particular family, they are stories that speak to US Latinx and Latin American communities from Chile to Canada.

Conjunto Blues by Nicolás Valdez captures the legacy of conjunto music in South Texas. Presented by the Guadalupe Cultural Arts Center in San Antonio, *Conjunto Blues* follows the story of El Músico who takes the audience not only through a journey of self-reflection, but the expression of cultural identity. The autobiographical play draws from playwright and performer Nicolás R. Valdez's life growing up in Texas. Under the direction of Rubén C. González, the play riffs off of Valdez's memories of how Tejanos have used conjunto music as a form of resistance for generations. In the same vein, Carmen Aguirre's *Broken Tailbone* meditates on her life experiences growing up in Canada's Latinx dance halls. Indeed, the use of music and dance have been tools of resistance and community-building for Latin American immigrants in Canada. Produced by Nightswimming, *Broken Tailbone* is structured as a Latin dance lesson. As such, Aguirre is front and center leading the audience through an immersive dance lesson which is grounded in her own experiences confronting cultural stereotypes as a Chilean immigrant in Vancouver.

Infusing comedy and music, stand-up comic and actor Marga Gómez's *Latin Standards* pays homage to her father, the late Willy Chevalier, a comedian, producer, songwriter, and prominent figure in the golden era of New York's Latino variety shows. Gómez meditates on perseverance and addiction to creativity passed down from immigrant father to lesbian daughter. Also including musical elements, in particular hip hop, Alex Alpharaoh's *WET: A DACAmented Journey* is a one-man piece written and performed by Alpharaoh. Directed by Kevin Comartin, *WET* tells the autobiographical tale of Alpharaoh, a thirty-something-year-old DREAMer who has lived his whole life in the United States undocumented. Echoing *Deferred Action*, the piece's emotional desperation is anchored on the aftermath of the 2016 presidential election and the Trump regime's anti-immigrant policies. Lingering on his own undocumented status despite having lived in the US since he was three months old, Alpharaoh's performance troubles the idea of fluidity across Americas' borders, effectively demonstrating how the notion of common ground is complicated by the United States' increasingly xenophobic laws and views towards the Latinx community.

Conclusion

Indeed, this festival offered a plethora of differences in aesthetic as well as thematic choices. Using the Encuentro de las Américas as a model, the playscripts, interviews, profiles, and snapshots all foreground the ways in which assumptions of commonality affect how we communicate with each other across borders and cultures. Disparate peoples from across the Americas—including Latin Americans, US and Canadian Latinx peoples—still maintain common ground around the notion of "togetherness" that is shared. Despite the utopian notion of unity, this volume demonstrates a genuine longing for communication between Latin Americans and the US Latinx community.

As long-standing steering and advisory committee members within the LTC, and participants in the festival, we the co-editors recognize our own racial and class privileges, including our US citizenship, and our bilingual Spanish and English access, among other markers. Our hope is that this collection will serve as another living document to a seminal moment in Latinx, Latin American, and United States theater histories. Indeed, despite the limitations and challenges of common ground, the festival spoke to the yearning to be connected that theater makers from across the Americas feel. By featuring a plurality of voices and perspectives—in addition to a diversity of formats—*Seeking Common Ground* casts a wider net than *Encuentro: Latinx Performance for the New American Theater*, effectively being more rigorous in the inclusion of the festival artists. The works herein are a testament to the wide range and artistic sophistication of Latin American and Latinx theater and performance, not to mention the power harnessed through commons-based collaborations across borders.

While we may never know the lasting results of some of the main questions posed by the convening, one thing was apparent: there is power in critical mass. At LTC convenings, people have connected on a deeper level simply by having shared experiences in addition to shared interests. In Los Angeles, Latinx and Latin American theater had room to live and breathe without having to justify its existence. This is how a movement grows. Creating a space for theater makers of color to gather in the United States is a radical act. At Encuentro 2017, Latinx and Latin American theater were *not* marginalized. They were centered. There was a space for critical engagement and reflection. There was an opportunity to discuss aesthetics and community engagement. Most importantly, Encuentro de las Américas created a space for a transnational conversation to continue.

Notes

1. Established in 2012, the Latinx Theatre Commons is led by a volunteer Steering Committee comprising artists, advocates, and scholars. The LTC has a paid full-time producer that facilitates the Steering Committee's work. The LTC "joins theatre artists, scholars, and students both virtually and in-person through an effective, volunteer-basis model that creates opportunities for theatre practitioners of all ages, races, and gender identities, while advancing the state of Latinx theatre in the United States" (Marrero). In partnership with HowlRound, the goals are "to transform the narrative of the American theatre, to amplify the visibility of Latina/o/x performance making, and to champion equity through advocacy, art making, convening, and scholarship" ("Latinx Theatre Commons"). For more on the LTC, see *The Latina/o Theatre Commons: A Narrative Report* by Brian Eugenio Herrera, "The Latinx Theatre Commons: A Commons-based Approached Movement" by Teresa Marrero, and *Encuentro: Latinx Performance for the New American Theater* edited by Trevor Boffone, Teresa Marrero, and Chantal Rodriguez.
2. Chantal Rodriguez, "Is One Octopus Enough?" *Theater*, Volume 49.1, Duke University Press, 2019.
3. For a detailed overview of the 2014 Encuentro Festival and its impact, see *Encuentro: Latinx Theater and Performance for the New American Theater*, edited by Trevor Boffone, Teresa Marrero, and Chantal Rodriguez.
4. While the 2013 Boston Convening was the LTC's first national event, due to limited capacity and budget, the event was by invitation only. This was met with significant critique from members of the Latinx theatre community who viewed the inception of the LTC as elitist and exclusionary.
5. Maria Enriquez and Christopher Goodson, "Latinx Theatre Commons Seattle Convening: Latinx Theatre in Unexpected Places," *Theatre Topics*, 27, no. 1 (2017): E-21–E-29.
6. Teresa Marrero, "The Latinx Theatre Commons: A Commons-based Approach Movement," *Theatre Topics*, 27, no. 1 (2017), E-11–E-19.
7. One of the most public signals of this work is the shift from the use of "Latina|o" to "Latinx" in the organization's name. After much debate and discussion, in January 2017, the LTC formally changed its name. In a statement published on HowlRound, the LTC Steering Committee stated, "This change signals the beginning of our work toward being radically inclusive of those who do not identify as either 'a' (female) or 'o' (male). The 'x' includes everyone: those who identify as 'a,' those who identify as 'o,' and everyone beyond and between." The LTC's analysis of radical inclusivity also led to an urgent need to require anti-racism training for all Steering Committee members. In 2018, the LTC facilitated training with the People's Institute for Survival and Beyond.
8. For example, one interesting intersection was seen in Ébano Teatro's body of work which culls the plays of black US playwrights like August Wilson and Lynn Nottage to explore the Afro-Peruvian experience. Moreover, 24th Street Theatre's production of *La razón blindada*, played on the Wednesday evening prior to the formal convening's start date of Thursday. While many conveners missed the production entirely, word quickly spread about the production's use of gestural blackface, which Grace Davila López addresses in her snapshot in this anthology.
9. Benedict Anderson, *Reflections on the Origins and Spread of Nationalism* (London: Verso, 2006): 6.
10. Partha Chatterjee, *The Nation and Its Fragments: Colonial and Postcolonial Histories* (Princeton, NJ: Princeton University Press, 1993): 5.
11. K. M. MacQueen, et al., "What Is Community? An Evidence-Based Definition for Participatory Public Health," *American Journal of Public Health*, 91, no. 12 (2001): 1929–38.

12. Juan Flores, *From Bomba to Hip-Hop: Puerto Rican Culture and Latino Identity* (New York: Columbia University Press, 2000): 193.
13. Ibid., 185.
14. Roberto Esposito, *Communitas: The Origin and Destiny of Community* (Palo Alto, CA: Stanford University Press, 2010): 3.
15. Ibid., 3.
16. Ibid., 6.
17. José Esteban Muñoz, "'Chico, what does it feel like to be a problem?' The Transmission of Brownness," *A Companion to Latina/o Studies*, edited by Juan Flores and Renato Rosaldo (Malden, MA: Blackwell Publishing, 2007): 444–5.
18. L. B. Turner (ed.), *Communitas: The Anthropology of Collective Joy* (New York: Palgrave Macmillan, 2012): 2.
19. TENAZ Festival Committee, "El Quinto Festival de los Teatros Chicanos. Un continente, Una cultura," *Chicano Theater Magazine* 3, Spring (1974).
20. Jorge Huerta, "Encuentro 2014: Moving Forward, Never Forgetting the Past," HowlRound, November 2, 2014.
21. Portions of this section of the Introduction were previously published in "Is One Octopus Enough? A Reflection on the 2017 Encuentro de las Américas" by Chantal Rodriguez. *Theater*, Volume 49.1, Duke University Press, 2019.
22. Ibid.
23. Alan Eladio Gómez, *The Revolutionary Imaginations of Greater Mexico: Chicana/o Radicalism, Solidarity Politics & Latin American Social Movements* (Austin, TX: University of Texas Press, 2016).
24. Ibid., 102.
25. The San Francisco Mime Troupe also participated in the festival.
26. In the field of performance studies, the Hemispheric Institute of Performance and Politics at NYU has organized biennial encuentros since 2000. Part performance festival and part academic conference, these encuentros bring together between 500 and 700 participants, and take place in a different site in the Américas with a specifically anti-colonial framework for engagement.
27. Notable examples in the twenty-first century include productions of Latin American plays at the Goodman Theatre, Writers Theater, Two River Theatre, The Public Theatre, Kirk Douglas Theatre, and Woolly Mammoth Theatre. Even so, productions of Latin American plays at these theatres are few and far between.
28. The 24th Street Theatre in Los Angeles, and presenter of one of the productions to be later discussed, is another that currently presents works in Spanish only.
29. In terms of collective creation, representative groups include Colombian Enrique Buenaventura's Teatro Experimental de Cali, Teatro La Candelaria founded in Bogotá in 1966 (Santiago García), and Yuyachkani—a Quechua indigenous word meaning "I am thinking, I am remembering"—founded in Lima, Peru 1971.
30. "How a Commons Becomes a Selection Committee," by Abigail Vega, http://howlround. com/How-a-Commons-Becomes-a%20Selection-Committee.
31. The festival selection committee included the five members of the Latino Theater Company (José Luis Valenzuela, Evelina Fernández, Lucy Rodriguez, Geoff Rivas, and Sal Lopez), and six members of the Steering Committee for the LTC (Jose Carrasquillo, Adriana Gaviria, Jamie Gahlon, Richard Perez, Anthony Rodriguez, and Chantal Rodriguez). The selection committee was listed publicly in the festival application and on the LTC's website.
32. For more on the selection process, see Vega, "How a Commons Becomes a Selection Committee." https://howlround.com/how-commons-becomes-selection-committee

33. Georgina Escobar, "The Composition of Latinx Aesthetics," *Café Onda: Journal of the Latinx Theatre Commons*, August 23, 2017.
34. Ibid.
35. "From the Latinx Theatre Commons Steering Committee," Encuentro de las Américas festival program (2017): 3.
36. Teresa Marrero, "The Latinx Theatre Commons: A Commons-based Approach Movement," *Theatre Topics* 27, no. 1 (2017).
37. Aside from supporting the dissemination of these books, the LTC provided honorariums to every artist and scholar included in the two volumes.
38. David Román and Alberto Sandoval, "Caught in the Web: Latinidad, AIDS, and Allegory in Kiss of the Spider Woman, the Musical," *American Literature*, 67, no. 3 (1995): 559.

Works Cited

Anderson, Benedict. *Reflections on the Origins and Spread of Nationalism*. London: Verso, 2006.

Chatterjee, Partha, *The Nation and Its Fragments: Colonial and Postcolonial Histories*. Princeton, NJ: Princeton University Press, 1993.

Escobar, Georgina. "The Composition of Latinx Aesthetics." *Café Onda: Journal of the Latinx Theatre Commons*. August 23, 2017. http://howlround.com/the-composition-of-latinx-aesthetics. Accessed December 10, 2017.

Esposito, Roberto. *Communitas: The Origin and Destiny of Community*. Palo Alto, CA: Stanford University Press, 2010.

Flores, Juan. *From Bomba to Hip-Hop: Puerto Rican Culture and Latino Identity*. New York: Columbia University Press, 2000.

Gómez, Alan Eladio. *The Revolutionary Imaginations of Greater Mexico: Chicana/o Radicalism, Solidarity Politics & Latin American Social Movements*. Austin, TX: University of Texas Press, 2016.

Huerta, Jorge. "Encuentro 2014: Moving Forward, Never Forgetting the Past." HowlRound, November 2, 2014. http://howlround.com/encuentro-2014-moving-forward-never-forgetting-the-past.

MacQueen, K. M., McLellan, E., Metzger, D. S., Kegeles, S., Strauss, R. P., Scotti, R., . . . Trotter, R. T. "What Is Community? An Evidence-Based Definition for Participatory Public Health." *American Journal of Public Health*, 91, no. 12 (2001): 1929–38.

Marrero, Teresa. "The Latinx Theatre Commons: A Commons-based Approach Movement." *Theatre Topics*, 27, no. 1 (2017): E-11–E-19.

Muñoz, José Esteban. "'Chico, what does it feel like to be a problem?' The Transmission of Brownness." *A Companion to Latina/o Studies*. Ed. Juan Flores and Renato Rosaldo. Malden, MA: Blackwell Publishing, 2007, 441–51.

Rodriguez, Chantal. "Is One Octopus Enough: A Reflection on the 2017 Encuentro de las Américas Festival?" *Theater*, Volume 49.1, Duke University Press, 2019.

Román, David and Alberto Sandoval. "Caught in the Web: Latinidad, Aids, and Allegory in Kiss of the Spider Woman, the Musical." *American Literature*, 67, No. 3 (1995).

TENAZ Festival Committee. "El Quinto Festival de los Teatros Chicanos. Un continente, Una cultura." *Chicano Theater Magazine*, 3, Spring (1974).

Turner, Edit L. B. *Communitas: The Anthropology of Collective Joy*. New York: Palgrave Macmillan, 2012.

Section One

Traversing Boundaries of Gender and Sexuality

Dementia

Evelina Fernández

Latino Theater Company—Los Angeles, California

1 Latino Theater Company's *Dementia*, Los Angeles Theatre Center, 2010.
Photo: Christopher Ash.

Critical Introduction
Chantal Rodriguez

The Latino Theater Company has a storied history in the trajectory of Latinx theater in the United States and in Los Angeles. The members of the company include Artistic Director José Luis Valenzuela, Resident Playwright and Associate Artistic Director Evelina Fernández, and ensemble members and Associate Artistic Directors Sal Lopez, Geoffrey Rivas, and Lucy Rodriguez.[1] For over thirty-five years they have developed an ensemble-based artistic practice committed to the creation of thought-provoking theater.

Originally conceived as the Latino Theater Lab in 1985, the company developed new work under the auspices of the Los Angeles Theatre Center (LATC), then under the leadership of Bill Bushnell and Diane White. After the LATC closed in 1991, Center Theatre Group (CTG) agreed to become the fiscal receiver for the Lab, and CTG's

Artistic Director Gordon Davidson invited Valenzuela to develop and direct the Latino Theatre Initiative at the Mark Taper Forum.[2] By 1995, the Lab had formally become the Latino Theater Company, and they left CTG so they could run a small community theater house at Plaza de la Raza Cultural Arts Center in Lincoln Park where they created their first season of Latinx plays. Eager to produce work on a larger scale and with equity contracts, the company soon returned to the LATC, then being run by the City of Los Angeles, where they produced Evelina Fernández's *Luminarias* in the 1996–7 season. After several years developing *Luminarias* into a film, working professionally in television and film, and further honing their aesthetic, the company returned to the LATC in 2002, with *Dementia*, one of the first Latinx plays to directly deal with homosexuality and Aids.[3]

As Geoffrey Rivas recalls, *Dementia* was the production that put the company on the map. Not only did it garner the prestigious GLAAD Award for Outstanding Theater Production in Los Angeles as well as four Ovation Award nominations, it marked the company's return to the LATC and also their staying power as a professional company committed to the development of new work.[4] Soon after, the company was encouraged to apply to run the LATC and in 2006, after a three-year struggle, they were awarded a twenty-year lease from the City of Los Angeles to operate the historic building. As the stewards of the LATC, the Latino Theater Company's mission is "to provide a world-class arts center for those pursuing artistic excellence; a laboratory where both tradition and innovation are honored and honed; a place where the convergence of people, cultures, and ideas contribute to the future."[5] The 2014 and 2017 Encuentros were envisioned as part of this mission, and offered as a gift to the field as well as to the city of Los Angeles.

As the producers and hosts of the Encuentro de las Américas, the company decided to produce a revival of *Dementia* as its programmatic offering for the festival so that they could re-examine their roots as a company, given the inciting question for the festival, "Where do we come from?" The play is not only an important one in their professional history, but also in their personal lives as well. Loosely based on true events, the play is informed by the life and death of José Guadalupe Saucedo, an acclaimed Chicano actor, director, and theater manager. Saucedo was a founding member of the historic Chicano theater El Teatro de la Esperanza in Santa Barbara where he worked closely with Valenzuela and Fernández. He would go on to be the best man at their wedding, and godfather to their son. Saucedo's ties to the Latino Theater Company extended to the Los Angeles theater scene as well, and they collaborated on many projects. In 1991, Saucedo became the first Latino to be named associate artist at the Mark Taper Forum and he was very vocal about his plans to partner with Valenzuela on future endeavors.[6] Sadly, Saucedo died on October 3, 1995 at the age of forty-two, due to complications from Aids.

Commissioned by CTG's Latino Theatre Initiative, then under the leadership of Luis Alfaro and Diane Rodriguez, Evelina Fernández pitched three ideas and *Dementia* was selected. She began writing the play in 1999, and developed it with the company members through rigorous workshops and readings. The world premiere was staged at the LATC in 2002, co-sponsored by The Wall—Las Memorias project, a non-profit HIV/Aids community education organization. The play explores topics that were then (and may still be) taboo in the Latinx community including homosexuality, Aids, teen pregnancy, and euthanasia, through the Latino Theater Company's signature style—a blend of music, movement, and text, along with their impeccable comedic timing.

While Moe, short for Moises, slowly succumbs to Aids in his family's East LA home, he summons his best friends for a "going away for good party" so that he can have one last chance to truly live out loud, and in drag. Moe's hospice nurse is his teenage niece Tamara who is unwed and pregnant. As Moe slips in and out of lucidness, his alter ego and muse, a torch-singing drag queen named Lupe, pushes him to confront his truth and to die without regret. She declares, "We have to work on the end, it's all about the exit you know." Inspired by and featuring the music of famed Cuban singer La Lupe, the music and choreography in *Dementia* punctuates the narrative with universal themes of frustrated love and the desire to live life unapologetically.

As Moe's friends arrive, both Tamara and the audience learn how entangled their histories are. All of the characters in this play are flawed and must confront their own issues along with their grief. Eddie and Alice's marriage is on the brink of failure due to infidelity, Moe's flamboyant childhood friend Martin struggles with his own shame, not of being gay but of being Mexican, and Tamara's future is woefully uncertain as she awaits the birth of her child. Meanwhile, Moe's plans are halted by the sudden appearance of his ex-wife Raquel. Moe's dress goes back into the closet, and everyone's skeletons begin to come out. While the play centers Moe, it is ultimately an allegory on the value of living one's truth and being able to give and receive unconditional love.

In this regard, one of the most important parts of the play for the company was to specifically name that Moe was dying of Aids so that the play itself could work against the shame that impacted so many families during the Aids crisis. In a particularly poignant monologue Moe states ". . . do you know how many of us got married, had kids, did what we were supposed to do? Do you know how many of us are still pretending? Fathers, grandfathers, brothers, living their lives for everyone except themselves; still dying of 'cancer' or 'pneumonia' because their families are ashamed to say they died of Aids?!" Another impactful aspect of the original production is the way that it brought both Chicano and diverse queer audiences to see the company's work, and with that came the possibility of mutual recognition and hopefully continuing dialogue.

When *Dementia* was revived in 2010 as part of the LATC's Spring Season it went through a significant aesthetic evolution, as the dementia inhabiting Moe's mind further informed the design of the show. Most notably, Christopher Ash's surreal set was marked by massive headless bodies which framed the playing space. According to director, José Luis Valenzuela, the set was meant to reflect the fact that in the 1990s Aids had no face in the Latino community because of the taboo, shame, and lack of national response to the crisis.[7] The cast also welcomed Ralph Cole as Lupe, originally played by Richard Coca, and Esperanza America to the role of Tamara, originally played by Tonantzín Esparza. This cast, and the new set, was then reunited for the 2017 revival at the Encuentro de las Américas.

Reflecting on the reception of the play in 2017, the company noted how much society had progressed in each staging of the play with regard to the visibility, advocacy, and activism of the LGBTQ community. Sal Lopez noted that when the play was first staged in 2002 there were some family members he didn't feel comfortable inviting because he didn't think they could enjoy the show given its themes. By the time it was produced in 2010, his entire extended family attended the production, and by 2017 members of his own family had come out themselves.[8] As Evelina Fernández noted, by the time the play was produced at the Encuentro it was clear it had become a period piece.

For the most part, the Latinx Theatre Commons conveners agreed with Fernández's assessment. While they were undeniably impressed by the Latino Theater Company's signature and expertly crafted theatrical style, there was often a generational divide regarding the play's reception. This was amplified by considering *Dementia* in dialogue with the festival offering from Compañía Nacional de las Artes (Colombia), *Las Mariposas Saltan al Vacío*. *Mariposas* is set against the backdrop of Cuba's imposed containment of people with HIV and Aids in the 1980s, and also vacillates between fantasy and fiction. Given the level of nuance in contemporary culture regarding our understanding of gender expression and sexuality, many considered the plays dated and longed for contemporary queer representations that were not associated with tragic death. At the same time, the revival of these plays also conveys that while the height of the Aids epidemic is behind us, its stigma may not be. Moreover, there remains an urgent need to support the queer and trans community in the US and Latin America given the continued violence that they face simply for living their truth. Ultimately, the plays acted as a means of theatrical and historical documentation, while the audience responses served as a call to action for the amplification of contemporary queer narratives to combat the homophobia and transphobia that persists globally.

The next expression of *Dementia* will be seen in the Latino Theater Company's film *Moe* which is currently in post-production. Through each of its iterations, including this book, *Dementia* honors Moe's final wish, "I wanna cruise," as his story and its lessons reach the minds and hearts of multigenerational and even international audiences.

Notes

1 The original ensemble included the late Lupe Ontiveros, legendary actor, activist, and arts advocate.
2 For a comprehensive history of the Latino Theater Initiative please see Rodriguez, Chantal. *The Latino Theatre Initiative/Center Theatre Group papers, 1980–2005*. Los Angeles, UCLA Chicano Studies Research Center Press, 2011.
3 For a detailed history of the Latino Theater Company see "Latino Theater Company: How we grew and why" by Jose Luis Valenzuela. *American Theater Magazine*, November 21, 2016. https://www.americantheatre.org/2016/11/21/latino-theater-company-how-we-grew-and-why/
4 Conversation with the Latino Theater Company about *Dementia*. October 28, 2020. https://www.youtube.com/watch?v=Cl_kVJX6a-I
5 About the Latino Theater Company. Los Angeles Theatre Center website https://latinotheaterco.wixsite.com/ltc-archive
6 Koehler, Robert. "Jose Saucedo: As the first ever Latino associate artist at the Taper, the L.A. native hopes to enrich the multicultural mix." Los Angeles Times, February 3, 1991.
7 Conversation with the Latino Theater Company about *Dementia*. October 28, 2020. https://www.youtube.com/watch?v=Cl_kVJX6a-I
8 Ibid.

Dementia

Evelina Fernández

Production History

Dementia received its world premiere in 2002 at the Los Angeles Theatre Center, directed by José Luis Valenzuela, produced by Latino Theater Company. The Latino Theater Company revived the show at the Los Angeles Theatre Center in 2010, and in 2017 at the Encuentro de las Américas. *Dementia* won a 2002 GLAAD Media Award for Best Theater Production and was a Los Angeles Times Critic's Choice.

Characters

Lupe
Tamara
Therapist, *played by Lupe*
Alice
Martin
Raquel
Eddie

Setting: Los Angeles, California 1990s.

Moe's bedroom

Alice & Eddie's

Moe's imagination

Act One

Prologue

Empty stage. Music plays and the ensemble rolls in a vanity, a dresser, chairs fly in, and then a bed is rolled in with a skeleton of a man laying in it. Oxygen tank flies in, a mask is placed on his face. Lights come up on a beautiful torch singer, **Lupe**, *in a sexy evening gown. She is dark, with big hair, heavy make-up. She has a heavy accent.*

Lupe   Are ju ready?

She reaches for a small cushion with a syringe and bottle on it. She hands it to a young girl on the stage. The girl takes it and injects fluid into the IV tube. **Lupe** *motions and the man in the bed takes a deep breath.*

The girl, **Tamara**, *sixteen, speaks.*

Tamara   I don't know nothing. I never been nowhere. Never learned nothing. Can't do nothing. Now, I'm gonna have a baby. What can I do? I guess I could get on welfare, but then they'd probably make me go to school or work in an office or something and I don't know how to do that.

Lupe   What about the boy?

Lights up on **Alice**, *forties, sitting across from her therapist, who sits in the shadows.*

Alice   He didn't fit in with the other kids. He was different . . . He was gentle . . . I always try to look for the good in the kids at my school. That's why I became a teacher and then a principal. Because in the end, that's what they are, kids . . . Some are more damaged than others. He wasn't damaged.

Lupe   What are your thoughts?

Lights up on **Martin**, *young-looking for his age of forty, thick-rimmed glasses, sits in a chair, legs crossed, hands folded on his lap. He sits across from his therapist who sits in the shadows.*

Martin   Sex. Sex, sex, sex, sex, sex. That's all I think about sometimes. While I'm driving in my car, cutting someone's hair, while I'm taking a shit. All I think about is going into a bar and picking up a stranger I can . . . well, you know.

Lights up on **Raquel**, *a woman in her forties, lying on a couch in a dimly lit therapist's office, wearing sunglasses and smoking a cigarette. Her face is well-lit, but the therapist can only be heard from the shadows.*

Raquel   I want a baby. I'll pay for one. I'll pay someone to have one. I'll adopt one. I've contemplated stealing one. I've contemplated killing for one. I had every test, tried every remedy; saw *curanderas*, went through artificial insemination, in-vitro cycles and I couldn't conceive. I'm desperate.

Lights up on **Eddie**, *fortyish, good looking, dressed in black. He speaks to his therapist in the shadows.*

Eddie   I can't believe she did this to me. I can't forgive her, I can't. How could she, after all these years? I can't get it out of my mind. I think about it all the time I keep imagining her . . . I go over and over it in my mind. I can't stop thinking about it.

Tamara   I can't really work in an office cuz I can't type and I can't really read that good. I don't know how to spell and I never worked in an office before so I don't know what I could do in an office. I wish my boyfriend loved me so we could get married. But, then he'd probably want me to cook and clean and I don't know how to do that.

Martin   I hate who I was. This Chicano thing? Please! Get over it! I don't even tell people I'm . . . Mexican. I mean, what would be the point? What do I have to be proud of?

Alice   He didn't belong there. That's what he said to me. He said that he always felt like God had been careless.

Raquel   It isn't fair! My sister is a lousy mother and she has five kids and won't give me one! I've thought about killing my sister so that I can keep the kids. But, I don't want five. I just want one! My husband thinks I'm insane.

Lupe   How is the relationship?

Eddie   The relationship is . . . strained. We can't make love. I don't know what she wants from me.

Martin   Teenage Mexican mothers on welfare. Mexicans in gangs. Mexicans in prison. Sweaty Mexicans working in the fields, in the yards, on their cars.

Tamara   I guess I could learn how to cook. But I don't know who would teach me how cuz my mom's not talking to me cuz I'm pregnant.

Alice   I don't have children . . . by choice.

Martin   Mexicans bussing tables. Mexicans wearing tacky clothes. Mexicans with gold teeth.

Lupe   What happened to him?

Alice   He was shot. He died . . . It had a profound effect on me.

Martin   Mexicans with heavy accents. Mexicans with dyed blonde hair. Mexicans on the beach, in the summer, fully clothed.

Tamara   I guess I could clean the house. I don't really know how, but I guess I could try.

Raquel   Sometimes, I think God is punishing me.

Lupe   What for?

Alice   For what I did.

Raquel   I was pregnant once. A long time ago. I ended the pregnancy. Sometimes . . .

Lupe   Yes?

Raquel   I'm not sure that . . .

Alice   I love my husband.

Eddie   I feel betrayed . . . He's my best friend. Who can I talk to?

Lupe   Where are you living now?

Tamara   At my grandma's. I'm helping her take care of my uncle Moe.

Martin   Why did this happen to him and not to me?

Alice   I want to tell him how and why it happened, but he doesn't want to talk. He says it's an inconvenient time . . .

Lupe   Because?

Alice   . . . his best friend is . . .

Lupe   . . . dying.

Martin   . . . of Aids.

Eddie   I think he wants to say goodbye.

Alice   I don't want to face death again.

Martin   I don't want to see him die.

Raquel   There's only one man I've ever really loved.

Lupe   Who is he? What's his name?

Raquel (*she can barely say it*)   Moises . . . Moe.

Lupe (*sings*)

   Funny how a lonely day
   Can make a person say
   What good is my life?
   Funny how an aching heart
   Can make me stop to say
   What good is my life?
   Funny how I often seem to pick
   And find another dream
   In my life
   'Til I look around and see
   This great big thing is part
   Of me
   And my life.

   This is my life
   Today, tomorrow for love will
   Come and find me
   For that's the way I was

Born to be
This is me
This is me
This is my life
And I don't give a damn for lost emotion
There's such a lot of love
I've got to give
Let me live
Please, let me live!

Scene One

The song ends. Applause. **Lupe** *bows.*

Lupe   Gracias . . . (*Heavy accent.*) Thank you berry much . . . (*She blows kisses.*) Gracias.

Moe *applauds. As he gets out of bed, his Aids-ravaged body is a vision to behold.*

Moe   Bravo! Bravisimo! That was fabulous, darling. Simply fabulous!

Lupe   Ay gracias, mi amor!

Moe   You are so beautiful.

Lupe   Do you really think so?

Moe   Yes, and talented.

Lupe (*she smiles a sly smile*)   Thank you . . . My dress?

Moe   Gorgeous.

Lupe   My moves?

She sways her hips.

Moe   Oh, so sensuous . . .

Lupe   Do my leeps look . . .?

Moe   . . . Delicious. Just like Marilyn Monroe.

Lupe   Ay, no! Maybe . . . Tina Turner or Eartha Kitt, pero Marilyn Monroe? (*She pouts.*) You might as well call me ugly!

Moe   Sorry . . . (*She continues to pout.*) Come here. (*She goes to him and sits on the bed next to him.* **Moe** *touches her face and consoles her.*) I loved everything you did. What you do takes talent, grace, style. It takes . . .

Lupe (*in her man's voice*)   Huevos.

She is a drag queen.

Moe   Exactly! I could never do that.

Lupe   We have to work on the end. It's all about the exit, you know?

Moe   Yeah, I know . . . They never remember the beginning or the middle, they only remember the end.

Lupe   You can have a great performance, but if the end is no good . . .

Moe   It has to be brilliant! Unforgettable . . . We have to work on it . . . (*His head falls back on the pillow. He begins to breathe hard.*) We'll work on it. Don't worry, the show will be fabulous. They'll love it.

Lupe   And then?

Moe   And then . . . And then . . . we'll go cruising. Down the boulevard. The boooolevard! I wanna cruise where the women wear bright spandex and don't care about the imperfections of their bodies because beauty isn't in the skin but deep, deep down in the corazon de melon, baby. Deep, deep down in the heart of East Los and Montebello, and Pico Rivera and everywhere else where there's a brown town . . . Cruising down the boulevard. In a big shiny Riviera with an eight-track tape player playing War:

(*He sings.*)

"The world is a ghetto . . ." Or Malo playing "Suavecito, mi Linda, Suavecito . . ." I wanna cruise the boulevard before the bars went up. Before 1970 and the Silver Dollar tragedy. Before the pigs put the fear of the law into us by clubbing our naive heads. Before they sent our sons and brothers to fight a senseless war and leave East LA for the first and last time . . . I wanna cruise the boulevard when we could— without being harassed for wanting to meet each other on the boulevard. I wanna cruise where old men and women would go to the *mandado* carrying their *verduras* in their plastic handbags from Mexico. Señoras in their cotton dresses and viejitos in their khakis, pendeltons and *chanclas*, taking off their fedora hats to wipe their brows.

Scene Two

The telephone rings. **Tamara** *answers it.*

Tamara   Hello? I already told you. I don't want to talk to you. I found out you're cheating on me and she's pregnant too! You need to get clipped!

Moe *sits up in his bed.*

Moe   Tamara! Tamara!

Tamara   I gotta go. My uncle's calling me. (*She hangs up and goes to* **Moe**.) Uncle Moe! Uncle Moe!

Moe (*confused*)   Huh?

Tamara   You okay? You're burning up again. She puts a damp towel to his head.

Moe   I . . . Yeah, I'm okay.

Tamara   You were tripping again.

She checks his oxygen tank.

Moe   Yeah . . .

Tamara   Where'd you go, huh?

Moe   For a test run, tu sabes.

He begins to cough. She puts the oxygen mask to his face.

Tamara (*referring to his IV bottle*)   Do you need to be hooked up?

Moe   Yeah . . . With a man . . . eh . . .

Tamara *laughs.*

Tamara   You're crazy . . .

Moe (*he sings Patsy Cline*)

Crazy. Crazy for living without you.

(*He falls silent.*)

Tamara   Are you scared, Uncle Moe?

Moe   Huh?

Tamara   You know . . . of dying . . .

Moe (*sings*)

First I was afraid
I was petrified
To think that I would have to live without you by my side.

(*He breathes hard. He whispers.*) I'm scared shitless, baby.

(*Silence.* **Tamara** *tries to put his oxygen mask on him.*) I don't want it yet. Get me my black silk underwear. I have to get dressed. (*She gives him a look.*) I'm having a party, remember?

Tamara   Are you sure, Uncle Moe? You've been going in and out of your . . . You know . . .

Moe (*sings*)

I'm coming out
I want the world to know
Got to let it show.

Tamara *laughs.*

Tamara   You never came out.

Moe   I didn't wanna burden anybody. I wanted to keep them guessing.

Tamara   Everybody knows, Uncle Moe . . .

Moe (*mocking* **Tamara**)   "Everybody knows, Uncle Moe . . ." You don't know shit! (**Moe** *gets ugly.*) You don't know where I've been or what I've done or whom I did it with. I've been places you can't even imagine and done things you don't even want to imagine with people you couldn't even imagine.

Tamara   You're right. And I don't think I want to.

Moe (*back to normal*)   Actually, it's a going away party. (*Laughs.*) A going away for good party! It's a party for my friends, in my honor. They've all been so wonderful. I feel obligated. I hate to feel obligated.

Tamara *puts her hand underneath the sheet. They both know the routine. He holds up the sheet, she pulls off his diaper. She cleans him with a towel. She goes to the dresser and goes through his underwear: all colors, tiny bikinis, thongs. She takes out a thong with a little red devil on the crotch. She laughs.*

Tamara   Did you really wear these?

Moe   Yes . . . (*He sighs.*) But nobody saw them. (*She takes out some black, silk boxers with green chili peppers on them. She holds them up.*) Dem da' ones. (*She smiles and goes to him. He pulls up the sheet and she slips on the underwear.*) I hope I don't shit.

Tamara   You won't. You just did.

Moe   It is better to give than to receive. Whoever made up that bullshit was right. Because when you receive you have to be grateful to others. But if you give others have to be grateful to you. Understand?

Tamara   Does that mean you have to be grateful to me?

Moe   I don't think so. But the main reason I am having a party is because I like to party! (*He sings.*) Do a little dance, make a little love. Get down tonight. Hand me the phone.

Tamara *hands* **Moe** *the phone and he dials.*

Scene Three

Lights up on **Eddie** *and* **Alice** *in bed. The phone rings. They both look at the phone with dread. Finally,* **Eddie** *answers.*

Eddie   Hello?

Moe (*into the phone*)   Eddie? It's me, your compadre.

Eddie   Hey, Moe. How's it going?

Moe   Do you have the things I asked you to bring?

Eddie (*hesitates*)   Yeah.

Moe   Good. Don't forget the crown. Let me talk to Alice.

Eddie *hands the phone to* **Alice.**

Alice   Hello?

Moe   Alice? Hi. Remember the dress you wore to the opening night of *Blood Wedding*? The black one?

Alice   Uh huh.

Moe   Can you bring it with you?

Alice   The dress?

Moe   Yeah and bring the shoes and accessories to match, okay?

Alice   Okay.

Moe   Thanks, computa! We're gonna "boogie, oogie, oogie til we just can't boogie no more." Okay, bye.

He hangs up. **Alice** *holds on to the phone.*

Alice   This is insane, Eddie. He can't have a party now.

Eddie   When then?

Alice   Later.

Eddie   Later?

Alice   When he gets better.

Eddie *gives* **Alice** *a look.*

Eddie   He's not gonna get better, Alice.

Alice   How do you know that? What a pessimist you've become.

Eddie (*sarcastic*)   Yeah, okay, I'm a pessimist.

Alice   I'm sorry . . .

Eddie   I don't wanna talk about it.

Alice   I mean about Moe.

Eddie   He's gonna die. Today, tomorrow. We had so many plans. So many dreams. We were gonna create a great theater; do great plays. I would write and he would direct. Grow old and wise. Become maestros. (*Pause.*) He's the only one I can call when I'm confused . . . He's the only one I trust to judge my work. I know I should be thinking about him and how he's feeling and all I can think about is what am I going to do without him.

Alice   He could get better, Eddie.

Eddie   He weighs ninety pounds.

Alice   But, he's only five foot seven.

Eddie *gives her a look.*

Eddie   He hasn't eaten in weeks.

Alice   But, he could get better. He could get better, Eddie, he could.

Eddie   He could. If he could eat. If the blisters in his mouth and his throat would allow him to chew and swallow some food. He could, Alice, if he would stop all his vices. But what would Moe be without his vices?

Alice   Oh, God, I hate this!

Eddie   He wants to have a party, Alice. There's no way I can tell him no. I've never told him no. Moe parties. He always has and he always will even if it kills him. He wants to have a party. We have to go.

Alice   I'm sorry . . .

Eddie   Alice, please stop saying you're sorry.

Pause.

Alice   I'm sorry. (**Eddie** *gives her a look.*) For saying I'm sorry, I mean.

Scene Four

Moe *is lying on the bed with his eyes closed, covered with a sheet.* **Martin** *sits next to* **Moe** *on a small chair, holding* **Moe**'s *hand. He stares at* **Moe** *for a long moment.*

Martin   Look at you. So thin, so frail. I think that if I squeeze your hand tight your skin will tear open, it's so thin. Your skin is so dry and flaky. Not the shiny brown skin that you used to have. You had beautiful brown, taut skin. Remember when we'd go to the nude beach? (**Moe** *nods with his eyes shut.*) And you'd peel off your clothes and run into the ocean. Your brown penis swinging from side to side.

Moe (*eyes still shut*)   Long, brown penis . . .

Martin   Yeah, yeah, yours was always bigger than mine.

Moe (*eyes still shut*)   But you used yours more.

They laugh.

Martin   That's for sure. (*Silence.*) How did this happen, Moe?

Moe *play-acts. He tosses his head from side to side.*

Moe   I don't know, I don't know. I sat on a toilet seat. I swear I did, mother . . . I swear!

Martin   You were never promiscuous. You didn't sleep around. Sure you had crushes on Chemo or Chulo and Chato or whoever the Mexican flavor of your month was. Always straight, always someone who would never be with you. But, you never did anything about it. They were all crushes . . . infatuations.

Moe *opens his eyes. He bangs his head with his fists.*

Moe   Martin, please . . . shut up!

Martin   I'm sorry . . . (*He strokes* **Moe**'s *head.*) Look at you. Your hair. I told you I'd buzz it for you so that it won't be so obvious that it's falling out. Look at you,

Moe. (**Moe** *begins to cough.* **Martin** *puts a glass of water to his mouth.* **Moe** *drinks.*) Better?

Moe *nods.*

Moe   My mind keeps going places without me wanting it to. I get the feeling, though, that I'm gonna take off soon. You know . . . on my journey.

Martin   Oh, Moe . . .

Moe   Shut up and let me talk! I don't necessarily want to go, but my quality of life, well, look at it.

He looks around his room.

Martin   It sucks, huh?

Moe   Sucks? It doesn't suck. It's fucked.

Martin   I know.

Moe   Remember, you're in charge of pulling the plug . . . (**Martin** *looks away.*)

Moe I know it's a horrible burden on you, Martin, and I'm sorry, but I know you're the only one who'll do it. The others . . . Eddie, he'll never do it. He never knows when to end anything. I mean, look at his plays. And Alice, well, she's too emotional.

Martin (*emotional*)   I know . . .

Moe   She wouldn't be able to live with herself afterward, wondering if somehow I was gonna "get better." So, it's up to you, Martin . . .

Martin   Okay, Moe . . .

Moe   And don't pull it before it's time either, cabron.

They laugh. **Moe** *breathes hard. He reaches for the oxygen mask.*

Martin   Then don't piss me off.

Moe   I have an exit plan B.

He breathes in the oxygen.

Scene Five

Tamara *enters.*

Moe   Oh, my God. Look, an angel . . . Do you see her? She's beautiful. She has beautiful white wings and a golden aura surrounds her very . . . uh oh. What's this? She's got something in her belly. Could it be that she swallowed those watermelon seeds after she was warned not to. Or has she been fooling around with that big, strong, fine-looking archangel with the big, long staff. I have to admit he's very attractive and I would've preferred it if he'd been interested in me but by the looks of it he was much more interested in this beautiful creature that stands before me. What is your name, my little angel?

Tamara (*she rolls her eyes*)   It's me, Uncle Moe.

Moe *snaps back into reality.*

Moe   Oh, hi mija.

Tamara *sees* **Martin**.

Tamara   Hi, Martin.

Martin *is surprised to see* **Tamara**.

Martin   Hi. I didn't know you were . . . with child.

Tamara *checks* **Moe**'*s tank.*

Tamara   Yeah. Shit happens.

Martin   What'd your mama say about it?

Tamara   She's pulling the "tough love" thing. That's why I'm here.

Martin   What are you gonna do?

Tamara (*shrugs*)   I don't know.

Moe   It's okay, baby . . .

He embraces **Tamara** *and* **Martin** *rolls his eyes.*

Martin   Who's the . . . donor?

Moe   Oh, that ugly . . . I mean . . . unattractive cholo-looking guy . . .

Martin   Him?

Tamara   Uh huh . . . But, it's over. (*To* **Moe**.) You really think he's ugly?

Moe   Well, he's not really my type.

Martin   Yes, he is. Straight, cholo, totally unresponsive.

Moe   You don't even know my type, Martin! (*To* **Tamara**.) Did I ever tell you about the guy I loved?

Tamara   Oh, yeah. What was his name?

Martin   EliASS!

Moe   Elias. He was so fine . . . He loved me. I know he did. He wanted me. But it was one of those impossible loves, you know. Sometimes love does not conquer all. Sometimes we have "issues" that cannot be resolved. He left because he couldn't bear to love me. Not a night goes by when I don't think of him before I go to sleep.

Tamara   What ever happened to him?

Martin   He ran away with a cult.

Tamara *laughs.*

Tamara   No, for reals.

Moe   He did.

Tamara   You mean like "Heaven's Gate"?

Moe   No, like he traveled up a river in Egypt. (**Tamara** *looks confused.*) De-Nile?

Martin   Whatever . . .

Tamara   Man, Uncle Moe. Your friends are so weird.

Moe   Come here, baby. (**Tamara** *goes to him and puts her head on his chest.*) You're gonna have a beautiful child.

Tamara (*convincing herself*)   Yeah . . .

Martin   You better be ready to feed it, change its caca.

Moe   She already knows how to do that. She's been taking care of me, remember? (*He cries like a baby.*) Wah! Wah! And if it's a boy you're gonna name him . . .?

Tamara   I don't know.

He smacks her on the head.

Moe   Moises . . .

Tamara   Oh, yeah.

Moe   And if it's a girl?

Tamara   What's that name you like?

Moe   Paloma . . .

Tamara   Paloma. Dove, right?

Martin   Like the soap?

Moe   No, like the bird of peace, pendejo. Go on, mija . . . And you're gonna teach her? (*She shrugs.*) All the good things about life and love and she'll be a leader of the Chicano movement and she'll fight against the oppression of our people. (**Moe** *goes off.*) "I had a dream that all brown people came together and realized their power. I had a dream that we had a million man march and no one showed up. My eyes have seen the Glory of the coming of the revolution, baby!"

Tamara   Uncle Moe . . .

Martin *pleads.*

Martin   Moe . . . Moe, please, stop!

Moe *falls back on his bed, exhausted.*

Moe   Ay . . . (*He falls back on the pillow and closes his eyes for a moment. He reaches for his oxygen mask and puts it to his face.* **Moe** *reaches for* **Martin**. *He breathes like Darth Vader.*) "Luke, I am your father . . ."

Martin *is horrified.*

Scene Six

Eddie *and* **Alice** *poke in their heads.*

Alice   Hieee . . .

Martin   He's gone. He's losing his mind . . .

They go to the bed and kiss him.

Alice   You look, nice, compadre.

Moe (*eyes closed*)   Mentirosa.

Alice   Well, your color's good . . .

Moe   Too bad I'm not a TV. (*He opens his eyes and sits up.*) I already took a bath. Help me get dressed. Did you bring the dress? (**Alice** *lays the dress bag on a chair. He throws off his sheet.* **Martin**, **Eddie**, *and* **Alice** *react to the sight of his emaciated body. He is wearing a "No On 187—Deport Pete Wilson" T-shirt.*) Look I'm wearing my silk boxers. You never know when you're gonna get a little action.

Martin *looks at the dress bag.*

Martin   What's that?

Alice   A dress.

Moe   For "moi."

Martin   Are you crazy?

Moe   Did you bring the makeup?

Martin   He's on his deathbed. Is everyone in denial here? The man is dying of Aids! Hello?

Eddie   So, he wants to wear a dress. What's the big deal?

Martin   He also wants to do drugs and have sex.

Moe   Hello!

Martin   Does that mean we're gonna let him! Look at him. He'll look like Diana Ross for Christ's sake!

Moe (*sings like Diana Ross*)   "I'm coming out . . ."

Martin   This is grotesque, it's, it's . . .

Moe   It's Buñuel!

Martin *puts out his hands.*

Martin   Can we pray?

Moe   No! (*Everyone slowly grabs hands.* **Moe** *refuses.*) No, I don't want to pray . . .

Martin (*prays*)   Dear Lord. Give us the strength to overcome this challenge. We put ourselves in your hands, dear Lord . . .

Moe *yawns.*

Moe   Boring . . .

Martin   Give Moe the guidance to put his spirit in your hands . . .

Moe *sighs.*

Moe   Oh, please . . .

Martin (*to* **Eddie**)   Go on . . .

Eddie   What?

Martin   Pray.

Eddie   Uh . . .

Moe   Yeah, right. He doesn't know how to pray. Go ahead, Eddie, try to pray.

Eddie (*caught off guard*)   Thank you God for giving us this . . . daily, uh, I mean this day . . .

Martin *gives* **Eddie** *a "Are you serious?" look.* **Alice** *begins to laugh. They all get the giggles.*

Moe   I told you!

Martin   Can't you guys be serious about anything?

Moe   Can't you not be serious about anything?

Martin *drops hands.*

Martin   Forget it.

Eddie   Oh, come on Martin. He was kidding . . .

Martin   No, he wasn't. It bothers him that I've found peace in the Lord and that he's still a troubled spirit . . .

Moe   Yeah, yeah, yeah . . . Can we put the music on now?

Martin   No, we cannot!

Moe   Eddie, put on the music. (**Eddie** *looks at* **Alice** *and* **Martin**.) Eddie, put it on!

Eddie *goes to put on the music.*

Martin   You wanna be responsible for his death, go ahead.

Eddie *turns on the music.* **Lupe** *begins to sing an Aretha song.*

Lupe (*sings*)

> Looking out on the morning rain . . .
> I used to feel so uninspired . . .

Martin   Oh, God. It's an Aretha fest.

Moe   Did I tell you I'm working on a show? A one man . . . uh woman show. (*To* **Eddie**.) Eddie, it's great. It's about a singer. A tortured torch singer with an incredible voice. But she's real you know and so full of passion and love for life! She sings from her soul. Her innermost being goes into every song. You know what I mean, Eddie?

Eddie   Yeah . . .

Moe   But her only downfall is . . .

Eddie   A man . . .

Moe   No, her downfall is . . . her insatiable desire for love . . .

Eddie   That's great, Moe.

Moe   Isn't it? And there are all these characters in her life, you know, (*he laughs*) and they all have issues! But, I'm having problems with the end.

Eddie   Why's that?

Moe   I don't know. I haven't found . . . that thing . . . you know . . . that moment . . . that . . .

He looks to **Eddie**.

Eddie   . . . revelation?

Moe   Exactly, that, that . . . holy moment. I haven't found it! Because you know, Eddie, the end has to be . . .

Eddie   . . . unforgettable. It has to be . . .

Moe   . . . awesome. (*Pause.*) I gotta take my pills. Alice, get me my pills.

Alice *brings the medication bottle.* **Moe** *fumbles with it.*

Eddie   Here, I can open that for you.

Moe   Thanks. What color are those?

Eddie   Yellow.

Moe   Those are the right ones. (**Eddie** *opens the jar and* **Moe** *takes the pills. He smiles.*) I like these. They get me high. Hand me that bag, comadre. (**Alice** *hands* **Moe** *a bag.*) Party favors. (**Moe** *takes out some weed and begins to roll a joint.*) Anyway, I want you guys to see some of my new show tonight. Later, though, after we've got a little buzz, lost some of our fucked-up inhibitions. We'll party a while and then I wanna go cruising. Whittier Boulevard all the way, baby!

He puts the joint to his mouth.

Martin   Moe . . . You'll die.

Moe   It's medicinal. For my appetite.

Martin   Yeah, right.

Moe   It's from the Cannabis Resource Center! (**Moe** *lights the joint.*) Leave me alone, Martin.

Martin   No.

He takes the joint away from **Moe***.*

Moe   Get the fuck out of my face!

He takes the joint back and takes a hit. He begins to cough hard. He gasps for air. **Eddie** *and* **Alice** *lie him on the bed.* **Eddie** *puts* **Moe***'s oxygen mask on him.* **Moe** *closes his eyes as he breathes hard.*

Scene Seven

All that is heard is **Moe***'s breathing when* **Lupe** *appears out of the darkness.*

Lupe (*referring to* **Martin**)   What is "her" problem?

Moe *removes the mask.*

Moe   He thinks I'm gonna die.

Lupe   So? What's the big deal? They are kind of pathetic, your friends, no?

Moe   No! They're not. They are the people I love most. They love me. They'll miss me. It'll hurt them not to have me in their lives.

Lupe   Who are you kidding? You think they want you around the way you are? You shit in your pants. You pee. You wear diapers. You need to be changed like a baby. Nobody wants to take care of you, Moises. Nobody.

Moe   Tamara does.

Lupe   Tamara. What does she know? Nothing! Let's go! Let's get the hell out of this place, Moises. It's full of idiots!

Moe   But I love these idiots and there are things I have to take care of. Things I have to do.

Lupe   Andale, Moises. Vamonos. Let's go on the ride of your life. Where there's no pain, just light, just love . . .

Moe *breaks out of his trance.*

Moe   No, I can't. There are things I have to do. Eddie, Alice, Martin . . . It's all unfinished. It's all unfinished . . .

Scene Eight

Martin, **Eddie,** *and* **Alice** *sit next to* **Moe**'*s bed.* **Alice** *looks terrified.*

Alice   Is he breathing?

Eddie *checks.*

Eddie   Yeah. His medication must've kicked in.

Martin   Thank God. (*He begins to cry.*) I don't know what to do anymore. He's driving his mother crazy. He doesn't want to wear clothes. (*He whispers.*) The other night, his mother was in bed . . . and he tried to get into bed with her . . . naked.

Alice   He's delusional. Half here and half there. He obviously didn't know what he was doing . . .

Eddie   But isn't there something beautiful about that? Something primal?

Martin *looks at him like he's nuts.*

Martin   No, there isn't! And don't go put it in one of your plays, either! I'm so sick of you putting our lives on the stage!

Eddie   What are you talking about?

Martin   I'm talking about you getting all of your material from real life!

Eddie   Where am I supposed to get it?

Martin   Try your imagination.

Eddie   The characters in my life are much more bizarre and demented than anything I could ever imagine.

Martin   Are you referring to me?

Eddie   Maybe.

Alice   Excuse me! This is about Moe, not us! Where is his mom, anyway?

Martin   On a religious retreat.

Eddie   Why would she leave when Moe is so sick?

Martin   She has her spiritual needs, too.

Alice   So, who's taking care of him?

Martin   Tamara.

Alice   Tamara?

Martin   Thank you! But, it's so typical. His family is so full of shit. Talk about dysfunctional . . .

Eddie   Oh, come on, Martin . . .

Martin   Oh, excuse me. I forgot. I'm the only one that speaks the truth around here. My best friend is killing himself and I'm hurting, okay? We're all hurting and none of us know what to do about it. Let's be honest here!

Eddie   Could somebody tell me what's so fucking good about being honest?

Alice   What do you mean?

Eddie   I mean, maybe it's better not to tell the truth . . . sometimes.

Alice   Are you referring to us?

Eddie   I didn't say that.

Alice   I wouldn't have been able live with myself, Eddie.

Eddie   So, you were honest and you feel better about it? That's what it's about, isn't it, Alice? You feeling "okay" about yourself?

Martin   What are we talking about, guys?

Alice   No! It's about being honest, Eddie!

Eddie   Honesty can be brutal, Alice! Honesty fucking hurts!

Martin   I'm feeling excluded.

Alice   I'm sorry!

Eddie   What do you want me to do what, Alice? Thank you for your honesty and strength of character?

Martin   Would somebody tell me what the hell we're talking about here?

Eddie   Nothing!

He exits.

Martin   How rude!

Moe *wakes up.*

Moe   Eddie?

Eddie *goes to* **Moe**.

Eddie   Yeah, Moe?

Moe   I'm ready.

Eddie   What?

Moe *grabs* **Eddie** by *the collar. He plays the martyr.*

Moe   Help me, Eddie. I have things to say, things to do, I still have dreams and ideas formulating in my brain. (*Pause.*) Help me, Eddie. Help me . . .

Eddie   What, Moe? What do you want me to do?

Moe *pulls* **Eddie** *close.*

Moe (*whispers in his ear*)   Help me put on the dress.

Eddie *looks around at* **Alice, Martin,** *and* **Tamara**.

Martin   What did he say? (**Eddie** *picks up the dress bag and begins to take it out.*) What are you doing, Eddie? Don't do it. (*He begins to cry.*) Please don't do it. He doesn't know what he's saying . . .

Eddie *looks at* **Martin**.

Eddie   Maybe he doesn't, Martin. But maybe he does. Maybe this is his very last wish and we won't let him have it? How would you like to be in his situation? Huh?

Martin   I would never be in his situation. He's in this situation because he was careless. Because he didn't take care of himself!

Eddie   Fuck you, Martin!

Alice   Eddie!

Eddie   Don't you judge him. Don't any of you judge him. He never judged you. (**Martin** *sits in a corner and cries.* **Eddie** *looks at* **Tamara** *and* **Alice**.) Now, are you gonna help me or not?

Silence. **Alice** *looks at* **Eddie** *and* **Tamara**. *She nods "Yes."* **Tamara** *removes the sheet.*

Tamara   Are you sure you want this, Uncle Moe?

Moe   I'm sure, baby.

Tamara   Okay, then . . . (*She laughs.*) You are so crazy . . . (**Tamara** *directs* **Eddie** *and* **Alice**.) Now, let's pull off your T-shirt, Uncle Moe. Careful.

Moe *holds up his arms and she gently pulls off his T-shirt. He is a skeleton. They help him into the dress, which fits rather loose.*

Moe   Do you think I should stuff my tits? (*They zip him up.* **Tamara** *gets some underwear from his drawer and stuffs his tits.*) Now, for the makeup . . . Not too heavy. I want to look natural. Well, as natural as possible. Do you remember when I had a natural?

Alice *begins to apply the makeup.*

Alice   Yeah. Eddie had one too.

Moe   Yeah, but my natural was natural. He had a fake natural.

Tamara   What's a natural?

Tamara *looks confused.*

Moe   You had to be there.

Tamara *puts a wig on* **Moe**. *It's all messed up.*

Tamara   This thing needs work.

She tries to fix the wig with her fingers. **Martin** *rolls his eyes.*

Martin   Here. I'll do it.

He takes a comb and begins to tease the wig.

Moe (*smiles*)   Thanks . . .

Tamara *polishes his fingernails while* **Lupe** *sings soulfully.*

Lupe (*sings*)

> Te vi partir ayer por esa puerta
> Te dije adiós con pena mi alma muerta
> y tu escucha bien si vuelves a mi puerta
> que yo no te abriré para que . . .

Scene Nine

Raquel *is lying on the therapist's couch, wearing sunglasses, and smoking a cigarette.*

Raquel   You know I've always thought of myself as a good, forgiving person. I mean, I see a dead dog in the street and my heart aches. I always give a large donation at mass. I don't lie, usually. I don't steal or cheat. I consider myself a good, decent, honest person. Except for when it comes to Moe. It's been fifteen years since he left me and still I go over in my mind over and over and over what I want to say to him the next time I see him. And I think of the cruelest, most hurtful things and still, I don't think that they are hurtful enough. I've wished him the worse. I've willed him to suffer. And now he's dying . . .

Lupe   Have you ever considered forgiving him?

Raquel (*taken aback*)   Forgiving him?

Lupe   I think you need to see him.

Raquel   See him?

Lupe   You need to either tell him how much you hate him or you have to forgive him. You decide. But, you can't hold on to this forever.

Raquel *removes her sunglasses and looks at her therapist.*

Lupe (*sings*)

    Si vuelves tu
    me tienes que querer
    Me tienes que llorar
    Me tienes que adorar
    Si vuelves tu
    la vida no ha de ser
    Lo que contigo fue
    Cuando estabas aquí
    No será igual
    Si vuelves tu . . .

Scene Ten

Lights up on **Moe**. *He is dressed in drag.* **Martin** *is working on his wig.* **Alice** *is polishing his toenails. The phone rings.* **Tamara** *answers.*

Tamara   Hello?

Raquel (*offstage*)   Hello?

Tamara (*with attitude*)   Yeah?

Raquel (*offstage*)   Who am I speaking with?

Tamara   Who do you wanna talk to? If this is Smiley's bitch . . .

Raquel (*offstage*)   I'm sorry . . . I must have the wrong number. I'm looking for Moises. Moises Cisneros . . .

Tamara   Oh. Hold on. Who's calling?

Raquel (*offstage*)   Raquel.

Tamara *hands* **Moe** *the phone.*

Tamara   It's for you. Some woman named Raquel?

Moe   Raquel?

Martin   Rachel?

Eddie   Raquel?

Alice   Really?

Tamara   Who's that?

Moe *loses it.*

Moe   Ah, la bruja!

Martin   His wife.

Moe   The weech, the weech! La pinche bruja que me hecho la sal! Help! Help!

Tamara   He has a wife?

Eddie   Moises, answer the phone.

Moe   No! No! I can't. I don't know what to say to her! Tell her I'm indisposed. Tell her I've disappeared. Tell her I'm not the person she used to know. Tell her!

Martin   Cut the shit, Moe! Now answer the damn phone!

Moe *stops, takes a breath, then takes the phone and in the sweetest voice possible says.*

Moe   Hello.

Raquel (*offstage*)   Hi, Moises. It's me, Raquel.

Moe   Oh, Hi, Raquel. How are you?

Raquel (*offstage*)   I'm fine, Moe. How are you? I heard you were sick.

Moe   Well, I . . .

Raquel (*offstage*)   I have to see you, Moises.

Moe   See me? When?

Raquel (*offstage*)   Now.

Moe   Now? I have company, actually.

Silence.

Raquel (*offstage*)   I need to see you, Moises. Please . . . Moises, please . . .

Pause.

Moe   Okay.

Raquel (*offstage*)   I'm around half an hour away. I'll call you when I get to the East Side.

He hangs up the phone.

Moe   She put the guilt trip on me! (*In a panic.*) She's coming over!

Alice   Does she know you're . . . not well?

Moe   She said, "she heard."

Martin   I told you, you should have told her.

Moe (*mocking* **Martin**)   "I told you, you should've told her." I haven't seen or talked to her in fifteen years. Why should I tell her?

Martin   Because she was your wife!

Moe *Was* my wife. Meaning she is no longer my wife. She is my ex-wife. Meaning past tense like you're tense and you're making me tense. Rachel and I have nothing to share anymore. I can't let her see me like this!

Alice Compadre, you're sick. There's nothing you can do . . .

Moe I mean in this dress! Take it off!

Tamara *goes to take off the dress.*

Tamara What happened to coming out?

Moe In front of my wife? Are you crazy?

Lupe *appears.*

Lupe Cabrona! Cobarde!

Moe I know. I'm sorry . . . (*He pulls off the wig.*) (*To* **Eddie**.) Come here. Help me. Give me some clothes. (*To* **Alice**.) Comadre, fix my hair. (**Eddie** *helps him sit up. They pull off the dress. It hurts him.*) Ow, ow, ow . . . (*They stop, afraid to hurt him more. The dress is stuck over his head, with his arms in the air. They don't know what do.*) (*Silence.*) Take the fucking thing off! (*They do, very slowly.* **Alice** *strokes his hair with her hand. A big chunk falls out. She looks at it.* **Moe** *takes it out of her hand and sticks it underneath the pillow.*) Take off the makeup. (*They put cream on his face and take it off with a wet rag.*) (*When they are done.*) How do I look?

He looks like La Muerte.

Alice (*she lies*) Great!

Moe Eddie?

Eddie You look fine, Moe.

Moe Tamara?

Tamara I don't know.

Moe Martin?

Martin Like a calavera with a tan!

Moe *looks at* **Lupe**.

Lupe Ju look like sheet!

Moe What the hell. She probably looks like "sheet" herself. After fifteen years how good can she look? She's middle-aged for Christ's sake. I'm sure her arms are flabby and her thighs are cellu . . . cellulit . . . tious.

Martin I've heard she looks absolutely fabulous.

Moe Oh, she would. She would! She would look fabulous, just to get back at me! Just to get back at me . . . for . . . For . . . For . . . for . . . for . . . for . . . for . . .

He begins to gasp for air. He has chills. **Tamara** *touches him.*

Tamara I gotta get his fever back down.

He is shivering.

Moe For . . . fffffff . . . fffffff . . . fffff . . .

Eddie Moe? Compadre?

Scene Eleven

Lupe *appears.*

Lupe To get back at you for what?

Moe Fffff . . . For what I did.

Lupe Who is this. . . . person?

Moe My wife. Remember I told you about her. She's the one I hurt. I hurt her.

Lupe So, apologize.

Moe I did.

Lupe Then what are you afraid of?

Moe The truth.

Lupe Hearing it or telling it?

Moe Both. I don't like to hear it because it usually hurts too much. And I don't like to tell it because of the same reason.

Lupe Did you lie to her?

Moe No. I just never told her the truth. The whole truth . . .

Lupe And nothing but the truth?

Moe So help me God! I think she might have found out, but not from me. And so I'm afraid she's come to tell me bad things. Things that are hurtful. And I deserve it, I do. She loved me. I think she loved me.

Lupe But you didn't love her?

Moe Oh, yes, I loved her. I loved her very much. But I fell in love with somebody else . . .

Lupe Elias?

Moe Yes. But I never told her. When she found out I liked men . . . She called me names . . .

Lupe (*indignant*) Like what?

Moe   Puto, fag . . .

Lupe   Maricón?

Moe   Yes!

Lupe   That beech!

Moe   She was hurt, that's all. She wanted to hurt me. I can't blame her. I pulled her life out from under her.

Lupe   That is no excuse! She should get a life!

Moe   I thought she had. She met a nice guy. They got married. But when she called I heard that "tone" in her voice. That tone that used to make my insides ache: "What's the matter, Moises? Don't you love me anymore? Don't I excite you anymore? Tell me what to do to make you happy, Moises? Please, Moises . . ."

Lupe   How did you do it, Moises?

Moe   I left. I just left. I never said goodbye . . . I snuck away . . . like a . . . like a . . .

Lupe   Coward.

The phone rings. **Moe** *begins to scream.*

Moe   Oh, my God! It's her! It's her! (**Eddie**, **Alice**, **Martin**, *and* **Tamara** *enter.*) I don't want to face her. Promise me, Eddie. Don't leave me alone with her! Check her purse. Pat her down. Put her through the metal detector. (*He screams up to God.*) Damn you! Why did you make her love me so muuuuuuuuuch?!

The music plays. Lights come up.

Lupe (*sings*)

> Yo siento en el alma
> Tener que decirte
> Que mi amor se extingue
> Como una pabesa
> Y que poco a poco
> Se queda sin luz

Moe *sings with* **Lupe**.

Lupe/Moe

> Yo sé que te mueres
> Cual pálido lirio
> Y sé que me quieres
> Que soy tu delirio
> Y que en esta vida
> Yo he sido tu cruz

Moe *jumps out of bed and everyone joins in on the song and they perform a big dance number.*

All

> Ay amor ya no me quieras tanto
> Ay amor no sufras más por mi
> Si nomas puedo causarte llanto
> Ay amor olvídate de mi
> Si la pena que sigas sufriendo
> Tu amor desesperado
> Yo quisiera que tú te encontraras
> De nuevo otro querer
> Otro ser que te brinde la dicha
> Que yo no te he brindado
> Pa' poder alejarme de ti
> Para nunca más volver

Dance break!

> Ay amor ya no me quieras tanto
> Ay amor olvídate de mi
> De mí!

End of Act One.

Act Two

Scene One

Eddie *is reading to* **Moe** *who is in bed with his eyes closed. Lights up on* **Lupe**.

Lupe (*sings*)

Igual que en un escenario
Finges tu dolor barato
Drama no es necesario
Ya conozco ese teatro
Mintiendo
Que bien te queda el papel
Después de todo parece
Que ese es tu forma de ser
Yo confiaba ciegamente
En la fiebre de tus besos
Mentiste serenamente
Y el telón callo por eso teatro
Lo tuyo es puro teatro
Falsedad bien ensayada
Estudiado simulacro
Fue tu mejor actuación
Destrozar mi corazón
Y hoy que me lloras deberás
Recuerdo tu simulacro
Perdona que no te crea
Me parece que es teatro

(*Spoken.*)

Y acuérdate que según tu punto
de vista Yo soy la mala—Ay!

Lights come up on **Moe**. *He is standing center stage in his black, silk underwear.* **Lupe** *holds up the dress.*

I still think you should wear the dress. You are letting this woman control your life! What happened to your revolutionary spirit, Moises? What happened to self-determination?

Moe   What happened to the left? It left. Along with my courage. Don't you understand, Lupe? The last time she saw me I was . . . her husband. If she saw me in a dress, I'd be . . . embarrassed.

Lupe   Que, que?

Moe   I come from a generation when being called a "Puto" was an insult not a compliment. I come from when being gay meant . . . I don't know. Not being a real man. We were so scared people would "know." All we could wish for was to be "normal." To "feel" like a man, love a woman and have kids like a man. Do you know how many of us got married, had kids and did what we were "supposed" to do? Do you know how many of us are still pretending? Still stuck, still trapped. Still wanting? Fathers, grandfathers, brothers who have lived their lives for everyone except for themselves? Still dying of "cancer" or "pneumonia" because their families are still ashamed to say they died of Aids. I loved Rachel and I wanted to be her husband and be the father of her children. But it's so hard to pretend. So hard to pretend . . .

Lupe   So, stop pretending! Moises, por favor! Show me one act of courage while you're still alive!

Scene Two

Moe *speaks to* **Lupe**.

Moe   So what if I'm a coward! I've never been courageous. I'm not that kind of person. There is no greatness in me. Who the hell wants to be great, anyway? Heroes are honest and don't care about the consequences. I'm no fucking hero. I'm a coward and I like it that way.

Eddie *appears*.

Eddie   Moe? Moises? Moe? Compadre? (*He sits on the bed where* **Moe** *lies still.*) Moe?

Moe *opens his eyes.*

Moe   Eh . . .

Eddie   You scared the shit out of me.

Moe   Is she here?

Eddie   No, she's on her way.

Moe   Tell me the truth, compadre; do you think we pay for our sins when we die?

Eddie   Nah. I think God is all forgiving. He made us imperfect—therefore we are. And when we die he takes us in his arms and fills ours souls with unconditional love.

Silence.

Moe   God, that's corny. But, I guess corny's better than cynical right now. (*Pause.*) I sure hope you're right. Cuz if you're not—I'm fucked. (*Silence.*) (*Pause.*) What should I do, Eddie?

Eddie   Huh?

Moe   About Rachel? Should I tell her?

Eddie   About Elias? (**Moe** *nods.*) I don't know. Do you want to?

Moe   Nah.

Eddie   Then don't. What Rachel doesn't know . . .

Moe   Maybe she already knows and that's why she's coming.

Eddie   And maybe she doesn't. If she doesn't . . .

Moe   But what about coming clean? I mean, don't you think I should before I, you know, take the trip?

Eddie   Hey, some things are between you and God.

Moe   "Some things are between you and God?" What kind of bullshit is that, Eddie? Don't tell me what you think I wanna hear. It's the story of our friendship. You always let me off easy. I mean, I love you for it, but damn, just once I wish you would tell me I'm a fuck-up. I know I'm a fuck-up and you know I'm a fuck-up so why haven't you ever told me I'm a fuck-up?

Eddie   Why haven't you ever told me I'm a fuck-up?

Moe   Because I'm a fuck-up, too.

Eddie   Exactly.

Moe   I'm a fuck-up, you're a fuck-up. Somos una bola de fuck-ups.

Eddie   It's called being human.

Moe   No, it's called being hypocrites.

Eddie   Whatever you say, Moe.

Moe (*mocking* **Eddie**)   "Whatever you say, Moe." Can I be perfectly honest with you, Eddie?

Eddie *thinks for a second.*

Eddie   Now? Why would you wanna do that now?

Moe   Because I'm dying.

Silence.

Eddie   Okay, go ahead.

Moe   I think you're an insincere motherfucker. Don't get me wrong. I love you for it, I do. It's just that we were a team and a hypocrite and a coward don't make a good team. We were supposed to be great. Create a great theater; be innovative, ingenious, and original. What are you gonna do without me, Eddie? Now, you'll never be a great writer. You're too dishonest to be a great writer. You'll never be a great writer, Eddie! Never! (*Tears come to* **Eddie**'s *eyes.* **Moe** *reaches for his hand.*) The truth hurts, Eddie.

Eddie   I know . . . I know . . .

Moe   Promise me something?

Eddie   What?

Moe   Don't steal this scene after I die for one of your plays.

Eddie   I'm not promising, you shit, you monster!

Moe (*à la-Frankenstein*)   "He's alive! He's alive!"

Scene Three

The Commodores "Brick House" plays and **Moe** *dances while* **Alice, Eddie, Martin,** *and* **Tamara** *look on in awe of the Feliniesque scene they are witnessing.*

Moe   Come on, guys! Let's party! (*One by one they cannot resist the energy of* **Moe**'s *spirit. One by one they begin to dance, party, laugh, enjoy the moment.* **Moe** *is in the center of the circle dancing, while they all cheer him on with: "Go Moe," " Orale, Moe," etc.*) Soultrain line! (*Everybody gets in a Soultrain line and one by one they go down the aisle and* **Moe** *yells out:*) Skate! (*Everyone does the Skate.*) Football! (*Everybody does the Football.*) Penguin! (*Everybody does the Penguin.*) Bump! (*Everybody does the Bump.* **Moe** *begins to gasp for air. They lay him down on his bed.* **Martin** *puts his oxygen mask on him.* **Moe** *sighs.*) Ay . . .

Silence.

Martin   Moe! Moe! Are you okay? (**Moe** *smiles and nods. Everyone laughs.*) God, I haven't danced that much since we were kids. (**Moe** *nods and smiles some more.* **Martin** *begin to cry.*) Remember all the stupid things we did when we were kids?

Moe (*sighs*)   Ay . . . Martin . . .

Martin   Like the time we got busted for shoplifting. Remember they caught me and you ran away?

Moe   Uh huh.

Martin   Then you came back and turned yourself in.

Moe *and* **Martin** *laugh.*

Moe   Que pendejo . . .

Martin   No, it was sweet. After all, it was your idea.

Moe   Yeah.

Martin   Our mom's had to come and pick us up.

Moe   Yeah. They were pissed, huh?

Martin (*laughs*)   Yeah. Remember that ugly girl you took to the prom?

Moe   Mary Rodriguez? Ugh! Well, your date was no prize. That ugly white girl with the zits, Amanda Smith.

Martin   Who put my hand on her tits!

Moe   Ugh!

Martin   She gave me my first blow job.

Moe   Ugh!

Martin   I just closed my eyes and used my imagination.

They crack up.

Moe   Remember when you lived with Virginia?

Martin   And you lived with Rachel.

Moe   What were we thinking?

Martin   That we were straight.

Moe   Ugh!

They all laugh. The doorbell rings. They all look at each other. **Tamara** *leaves to answer the door. The only sound we hear is* **Moe***'s breathing.*

Scene Four

Raquel *appears in the doorway. She wears sunglasses and a black dress, and her black hair is pulled back tight.*

Raquel   Hi, Moises.

Moe   Hi, Raquel. It's good to see you. You look fa . . .

Raquel   Fat? Go ahead, say it.

Moe   I was going to say . . . fabulous.

Raquel   Oh . . . Thanks.

Silence.

Moe   And then there was a terrible silence.

Alice   Listen, we'll wait outside . . .

Moe *gives them a "don't go" look.* **Eddie** *goes to* **Moe**.

Eddie   Are you gonna be okay?

Moe (*whispers*)   No!

Martin   Moe, cut it out! (**Moe** *stops.*) Come on, Eddie.

Eddie *slowly follows* **Martin***,* **Alice***, and* **Tamara** *out.* **Moe** *turns to* **Raquel** *with the sweetest smile he can muster up.*

Moe   Hi, Rach.

Raquel   Hi, Moe.

He extends his hand. She looks at it for a second, then she takes it. He pulls her close. She sits on the bed.

Moe   Take down your hair, Rach. I like down. (*She pulls the pins out of her hair and lets it fall. It is long and thick and black. He runs his fingers through her hair.*) I always loved your hair, Raquel.

Raquel   I know.

She puts her head on his chest and an old familiarity returns. She cries and **Moe** *strokes her head.*

Moe   Shhh . . . Shhh . . . Don't cry . . . (*She begins to laugh.*) What?

Raquel   You still smell like you.

He smiles.

Moe   So do you. You're lucky, Rach. Most of the time, I smell like shit.

Raquel   Moe, you're dying . . .

Moe   I know I must look horrible. But guess what? We're just days away from a cure.

Raquel   I wished this on you . . .

Moe   I thought so . . .

Raquel   I wished it on you and it happened.

Moe   Can you take it back?

Raquel   We were supposed to grow old together.

Moe   Well, Rachel, you better catch up quick.

Raquel   Moe, I came here because . . .

Moe   Yeah?

Raquel   You know how they say that time heals all? Well, it doesn't. I tried. I swear I tried to "let it go." People would say "Forget him, Rachel. He's not worth it. You're better off without Moe," and I knew they were right. But, I thought you were confused and searching. I was sure you would miss me and come back. But, you didn't and I realized that you didn't love me . . .

Moe   No, Raquel, I . . .

She stops him.

Raquel   Shut up! Let me finish. You didn't love me the way I wanted you to love me and I began to hate you because it was the only thing I could do, Moises. Do you understand? I turned my love into hate and when that subsided what was left was a nagging resentment that became a part of me like an . . . incurable illness that one learns to live with. And it wasn't until the other day that I realized that I could get rid of it. And that's why I'm here. I came here to say . . .

Moe (*he hums Beethoven's Fifth*)   Tan, tan, tan, tan. Tan, tan, tan, tan. (*Lights change and* **Moe**'s *mind takes off.*) A suspended second as she takes a breath, a pause. I look at her as she brushes her hair back from her face before she continues to speak and a faded memory comes back to me. I remember her tender touch. How she used to comfort me with those loving hands. How she used to kiss my face and I realize that I haven't been loved so much since. And in this millisecond all the possibilities go through my mind. Will she be forgiving, will she be cruel? (*He sings.*) "Here's what she said to me."

Lupe (*sings*)   Que sera, sera.

Moe (*sings*)   Whatever will be, will be. The future's not ours to see. Que sera, sera.

Lupe (*sings*)

>When I was just a little . . . boy.
>I asked my mother, what will I be?
>Will I be pretty, will I be rich,
>Here's what she said to me . . .

Moe & Lupe (*sing*)

>Que será, será
>Whatever will be, will be
>The future's not ours to see,
>Que sera, sera

Lights change back to reality.

Raquel   Moises?

Moe (*singing*)   Que será, será . . . Whatever will be, will be. (*He comes to.*) What . . . What were you saying?

Raquel *looks confused.*

Raquel   Are you okay? Moises, I want you to know that . . . I . . . I forgive you . . .

Silence.

Moe   What did you say, Rach?

Raquel   I said I forgive you.

Moe   You forgive me? You forgive me? (*Lights change and* **Moe**'s *mind takes off.*) Did you hear that everybody? She forgives me!

Scene Five

Lupe *appears and* **Moe** *jumps out of bed.*

Moe   Lupe, she forgave me!

Lupe   What are ju so heppy about? She let you off easy. She forgave you, but for what? For breaking her heart? She still doesn't know the truth.

Moe   What she doesn't know won't kill her . . .

Lupe   But, you can't die until she does.

Moe   Yes I can!

Lupe   Try it!

Pause.

Moe   You mean I can't?

Lupe   No.

Moe   Listen, this is my death and I'm gonna die the way I want. Not the way anybody else wants me to. Not Martin, not Alice, not Eddie and not you! (**Lupe** *laughs.*) (**Moe** *begins to cruise.*) I'm gonna cruise right out of here. I'm gonna go the way I came. Head first and calling the shots.

Scene Six

Raquel *is calling out.*

Raquel   Eddie, Alice! (**Alice**, **Eddie**, **Tamara**, *and* **Martin** *enter.*) We were talking one minute and then . . .

Alice   It's dementia . . .

Raquel   I . . . told him . . . I came to forgive him . . . I . . . didn't want him to die without knowing that.

She sobs. **Moe** *suddenly stops. He looks around at his friends. He smiles.*

Moe   I'm baaaack!

Tamara   You went off!

Moe   Sorry.

Raquel *goes to him.*

Raquel   Moises, do you remember what I said?

Moe   About forgiving me? Yes, I do, baby! And I am so glad! (*Sings.*) "Heaven must've sent you from above, Oh . . ." (**Raquel** *smiles.*) (**Moe** *sighs.*) Ay. (*Everyone laughs.*) Hey, put on the music. What do you wanna hear, Rach? Some Aretha? You want a drink?

Raquel   Okay.

Moe   Eddie give Rachel a drink. A shot of tequila?

Raquel   Sure.

Lupe *watches from the side.*

Lupe   Hmmm. . . . She's a husband again . . .

Moe (*to* **Lupe**)   Cállate!

Raquel   What?

Moe   No, not you. I guess you noticed I'm losing it. I can't help it. It's part of this damn illness. "La Sida."

Eddie *hands* **Raquel** *a shot.*

Raquel   Thanks, Eddie.

Moe   Y yo, ¿qué? (**Eddie** *serves* **Moe** *a shot.* **Moe** *toasts.*) To my friends, my family and my ex. I'm glad you're all here tonight before I take flight, I know I'm a fright, but hey that's alright, cuz it's outta sight! Salud.

They drink their shots. **Tamara** *puts on some music:* **Lupe** *sings Aretha's "Ain't No Way."*

Lupe (*sings*)

> Ain't no way for me to love you,
> if you won't let me
> It ain't no way for me to give you all you need
> If you won't let me give all of me
> Ooh, ooh, ooh, ooh, ooh, ooh . . .

Moe (*to* **Raquel**)   Remember that, Rach?

Raquel   Yeah. (*They all listen to the song for a second.*) God, it's been so long since we've all been together.

Nobody speaks. Nobody knows what to say or where to begin.

Lupe   And then there was a terrible silence . . .

Finally, **Moe** *speaks.*

Moe   We have a lot of catching up to do. Well, Martin is still a hairdresser . . . I mean, hair designer.

Raquel   Really?

Martin   Yes and working on myself, my spirit, my inner purpose . . .

Moe   Keeping up the facade, you know. Still working on the West Side trying to hide, living the lie . . .

Martin (*to* **Raquel**)   Moe's still mad because I didn't stay on the East Side, bleaching hair and doing chola perms all day.

Moe (*à la seventies*)   "You've got to see the beauty of your peepo! Brown is beautiful! Don't let the man make you ashamed of who you are."

Martin   It's not the man who's making me ashamed, Moe.

Moe   What is making you ashamed?

Martin *looks at* **Moe**.

Martin   What is your point?

Moe   My point? My point is that you left the East Side, moved to the West Side and became a big puto.

Martin   No, Moe, I was a big puto before I left.

Moe   Not in public you weren't.

Martin   Oh, come on, Moe. (*Laughs.*) We were two little queers growing up on the East Side. That's why we got our asses kicked by those cholos. They were so mean, so hateful. They beat us up, Moe. Because we were different. They called us names. They kicked us. That was the day I said to myself "If that's who I have to be to be a man, then I don't want to be a man." That was the day I turned and walked away. I'm not saying I'm better because I left, Moe. All I know is that I had to leave. I was such a disappointment to everyone. My mother, my father, my sisters, my brothers. I had to leave, Moe. You went away to college and I had no one. So, I moved away. I had to. I had to leave and just be me.

No one speaks. **Moe** *reaches for* **Martin**'s *hand. They embrace.*

Tamara   Wow, that's heavy.

Raquel *goes for a drink.*

Raquel   We were all so naive, weren't we? (*She pours another shot of tequila.*) Remember, Eddie? You and Moe were gonna change the world . . . What happened?

Eddie   What do you mean? I'm still writing.

Raquel   Are you?

Eddie   Yes, I'm working on a new play now.

Moe *is surprised, amused, and hurt, all at once.*

Moe   Really? You hadn't told me, Eddie. What's it about?

Eddie   It's about . . . truth and honesty.

Moe   What about truth and honesty?

Eddie   I question whether being truthful and honest is all it's cracked up to be. I think people use truth and honesty as an excuse to absolve themselves of their guilt.

Moe   Okay, those are the themes. What is the story?

Eddie   Well, I just started writing it, but it's about a couple . . .

Martin   A gay couple?

Eddie   No, a straight couple.

Moe   Y? Keep going . . .

Eddie   A couple that's been married for many years and . . . (**Eddie** *can't continue.*) It's complicated . . .

Moe   Oh, come on, Eddie. (*Getting ugly.*) A playwright should be able to tell what the play is about in one sentence. Now, go on . . . A couple's been married for many years and what?

Eddie   And maybe I'm not able to explain it in once sentence . . .

Moe   Alas, he confesses his mediocrity. But, we're all so painfully aware of it, Eddie. I was always the talent, you were merely the brawn. Give us the premise, at least. Let us help you. A couple has been married for many years and what?

Silence.

Alice   . . . And the woman has an affair with a twenty-five-year-old man.

Moe   Uh oh.

Martin   Oh, it should've been a gay couple. You have no imagination.

Moe   Shut up. Go on, Eddie.

Eddie   That's it. That's what it's about.

Moe   That's it?

Alice   And the man can't get over it.

Martin   You mean they stay together?

Alice   Yes.

Martin   Well, that's not believable.

Moe   Martin, please! (*To* **Eddie**.) That's not believable.

Alice   Why not?

Moe   Oh, come on. Any man who finds out his wife is having an affair and stays with her has got to be an idiot!

Martin   Make it a gay couple!

Moe   There has to be a reason for her to go out and sleep with the young man. Maybe he was a virgin and she was doing him the favor. Maybe her husband is impotent or just never satisfied her or maybe he's just confused . . . and so she seeks out this young stud . . .

Eddie   Sometimes people have affairs for no reason at all and don't care about the consequences!

Raquel   I don't believe that.

Moe   Neither do I!

Tamara (*to* **Eddie**)   You gotta tell why she would do it . . .

Eddie   Great, now everyone's a playwright!

Moe   There had to be reasons!

Eddie   There were no reasons!

Martin   How does he find out about the affair?

Alice   She tells him.

Tamara   Stupid!

Moe   Nobody's gonna believe that!

Alice   She tells him because she wants to be honest! What's so fucking unbelievable about that?

Everyone is surprised by **Alice**'s *outburst.*

Tamara (*shaking her head*)   Nah. I don't buy it.

Martin   She liked the guy and she wanted to screw him that's all. I know what that's like.

Moe   I'll say.

Alice   That's not true, there are reasons!

Moe   Really? What are they Alice?

Alice   She feels lonely, excluded from his life, she feels . . . unfulfilled . . . She feels taken for granted. She feels that her husband isn't interested in her or what she does. It's always about him and his work. His next project. His next idea . . . His new play . . . She just wants to feel . . . wanted.

Everyone, except **Tamara** *realizes that* **Alice** *is talking about herself.*

Tamara   Does she fall in love with the young guy?

Alice   No, it only happened once. Just once and it never happened again.

Tamara   Once? Her husband better get over it! Her big mistake was telling him. What you don't know won't hurt you.

Alice   But what you don't tell will. It's hard to live with.

Moe   It eats you up inside. It gnaws at your soul. It strangles your heart. It unravels your brain.

Raquel (*to* **Alice**)   I think telling him was a big mistake. I believe in weighing the consequences and if your world is gonna crash down on you, keep it to yourself.

Moe   You do?

Raquel   Yes. I mean, look at what happened to us, Moe. You left me because you realized you didn't like women. But I wish you'd never told me. I do. Because I held on to this bad, foul feeling toward you and I wished all those bad things on you, you know . . .

Tamara   You wished this on him? You wished this on my uncle? That's fucked up.

Raquel   I know.

Tamara   Why, though? Why did you want this to happen to him? (**Raquel** *doesn't know what to say.*) Is it because of . . . what's his name?

Pause.

Raquel   Who?

Tamara   You know that guy? The guy he fell in love with. (*To* **Martin**.) What's his name? The one he always talks about. (**Martin** *doesn't answer.*) He has a weird name. Shit, what is it?

Martin   He met a lot of guys . . .

Eddie   Yeah and his mind . . .

Tamara   No, no, he talked about him even before he started losing it . . . You know, the one he said was "fine as wine and all mine." (*She looks to* **Alice** *and* **Eddie** *for an answer, but they don't speak. Then it comes to her.*) (*English pronunciation.*) Elias! That's it. Elias.

Raquel   Elias?

Silence.

Eddie   I don't think it was Elias . . .

Raquel   My brother?

Martin   No, it was another Elias. (*To* **Tamara**.) Are you sure that was the name?

Tamara   Yeah. The one that ran away with a cult.

There is an uncomfortable silence. **Raquel** *looks at everyone. She looks at* **Moe**.

Raquel   Moe?

Moe *can't answer. He goes off.*

Moe   Pull the plug! Pull the plug! Martin, I put you in charge. Now pull the plug! This story is getting old. It's playing over and over and over and over in my brain. My record's skipping because it's scratched, damaged, cracked in half. Somebody pull the fucking plug.

Scene Seven

Lupe   You're not a TV, remember?

Moe   I don't want to hurt her. She herself said she'd rather not know. I don't wanna come clean. I wanna go dirty. I don't want to look at her face. She'll be so hurt, so pitiful, so broken . . .

Lupe   Try again.

Scene Eight

Raquel is in a rage. She grabs **Moe** *by the neck.* **Eddie**, **Alice**, *and* **Tamara** *try to pull her off.*

Raquel   You motherfucker! How could you? That's why you left me? That's why you didn't want me to have the child.

Moe   No, that's not why I didn't want you to have the child!

Raquel (*cries*)   Oh, Moe . . . Moe, how could you? My brother? Not my brother? That's why he ran away with that cult.

Moe   I'm sorry, Rach. I didn't mean to. I tried not to. Honest, I did. But he was so . . . (*He looks up and sees* **Elias** *in his room.*) . . . beautiful. I knew it was wrong. But I couldn't help myself. The more I tried to stop the urge, the more I craved, longed for, desired him. You know . . . the forbidden . . . fruit? And then after we gave in to our illicit lust we fell in love and if he hadn't been your brother we would have run away together . . .

Raquel   Stop it!

Moe   Forgive me?

Raquel   I'll never forgive you, Moe. Not a night goes by that I don't think of you before I go to sleep. I loved you. I really loved you.

Raquel *exits.*

Scene Nine

Nobody moves. Finally **Alice** *speaks.*

Alice   Oh, Moises, how could you do that to her? Why didn't you tell her the truth?

Moe (*à la Jack Nicholson*)   "Because she couldn't handle the truth!" I only keep secrets because I don't want to cause people pain.

Alice   That's a cop-out!

Moe (*pissed*)   No, you're a cop-out, Alice! You're a fucking cop-out. It takes a lot of balls to keep a secret, you know that? It's easy to be whiny and honest! (*Mocking* **Alice**.) "Eddie, I have something to tell you . . . You see, it's like this. I fucked a young man the other day . . ."

Eddie   Cut it out, Moe!

Moe   She wants the truth, Eddie. Well, let me give it her. Did you know that Martin is really Mexican? Oh, and by the way after Elias dumped me, Eddie and I . . .

Eddie   Shut up, Moe . . .

Silence.

Alice   Eddie and you what?

Eddie   He doesn't know what he's saying, Alice.

Alice   You and Eddie what?

Moe   Well, you see Alice, it was like this . . .

Eddie   Moe, stop!

Moe   We were young, drunk and horny . . .

Eddie   Moe.

Moe (*getting ugly*)   Oh, come on it's the climax of your play, Eddie. The husband has been making the wife's life miserable over a stupid one-night stand with a twenty-five-year-old boy, but then she finds out that he had a sexual encounter with his best friend and never told her! You see it's not about truths at all it's about lies and hypocrisy! Damn! Why do I always have to give you my ideas? Don't you have any of your own?!

Eddie   Shut up! You fucking idiot!

Moe *stops. He can barely breathe.* **Alice** *looks at* **Eddie**. *She exits. He looks at his horrified friends.*

Moe   Oops . . . (**Eddie** *looks at* **Moe** *helplessly.* **Moe** *begins to cry.*) I'm sorry, Eddie. I don't know what's wrong with me.

Martin (*scared*)   I think you're possessed.

Moe *covers his own mouth.*

Tamara   This is fucking weird.

She runs out.

Scene Ten

Eddie *comes out on the porch where* **Alice** *is.*

Eddie   Alice . . .

Alice   You've made my life miserable. You've taken advantage of my guilt. You used it to manipulate me, my feelings. You've played the victim and allowed me to feel like the immoral wife, the cheating wife, the loose woman! I can't even look at a young man without feeling like a slut. You've done this to me. Well, it's over, Eddie. I did it! I had an affair with a young man . . . who had just lost his little brother . . .

Eddie   I don't want to know.

Alice   . . . and you know what? It was a beautiful, intimate, pure experience and I refuse to feel guilty about it anymore! And if you can't get over it, that's too fucking bad! How could you put me through that when you had done the same with Moe?

Eddie   It wasn't the same.

Alice   No?

Eddie   Moe wasn't a stranger. Moe was . . . (*Silence.* **Alice** *waits for him to continue.*) Moe is my . . . my partner, Alice. My soulmate, my companion for life . . . I love him . . .

Alice   Oh, God . . .

Eddie   No, not like that. I mean, yes like that . . . I love him the same way I love you . . . but, without the sex, you know. (*Pause.*) We were drunk and having such a great time, a great talk . . . the kind of talk I can only have with Moe . . . about life and love and art and theater, our future and it's like we wanted to share so much with each other and then he started talking about how lonely he was, Alice. About how he wished that he had someone to hold . . . And I held him . . . I caressed him . . . He began to cry and I kissed him . . . and we made love. The next morning we looked at each other and felt really stupid, you know. We never talked about it after that. I'm sorry, Alice.

Alice   For not telling me or for making love to Moe?

Eddie *thinks for a second.*

Eddie   For not telling you.

He exits.

Raquel *comes out onto the porch.*

Raquel   You all knew, didn't you? You all knew and not one of you told me. What did you all do? Laugh? Make jokes about it?

Alice   No. (*Pause.*) He didn't want to hurt you, Rachel.

Raquel   He didn't want to hurt me? He left me for my brother!

Alice   I know, it's awful . . . I didn't think it was my place.

Raquel   We were friends. (**Alice** *looks away.*) Weren't we friends, Alice?

Alice   It was just one of those horrible things that no one wants to repeat. Moe was my friend, too.

Raquel   You should have told me, Alice.

Alice   I couldn't. Don't you see? I knew Moe was wrong, but I could never go against him.

Raquel   Why? (**Alice** *doesn't answer.*) Why, Alice?

Alice   Because I was afraid to lose Eddie.

Tamara *comes outside, overwhelmed.*

Tamara   You guys are scaring me and I think you're scaring my baby and I'd get the hell out of here if I had some place to go. I feel like I'm in some weird horror movie.

(*The women don't answer.*) (*To* **Raquel**.) I'm sorry. I didn't know you didn't know and I didn't know he was your brother. (*To* **Alice**.) And I didn't know . . . well, you know. (*The women don't answer.*) Life's fucked, huh?

Raquel   Well, it's ironic.

Tamara   Ironic?

Raquel   Well, yes. You see, Tamara, I fell in love with a man who couldn't love me, left me for my brother, I'm childless and I wonder why in the hell God would do this to me!

Tamara   I know why. Because you're a self-centered, selfish bitch. All you think of is yourself and your tough breaks. Shit! You think you're the only one with problems? You think it's terrible being old and childless? Try being single and pregnant! (**Tamara** *begins to cry.*) You know, I used to think that older people were . . . I don't know . . . smart. I always thought that when I got older I would be able to make sense out of everything, you know, and make wise decisions and do good things. Now, I'm really scared because I realize you don't get smarter you just get older. I thought my generation was bad, but you guys . . . You're really fucked-up. (**Alice** *goes to her and embraces her.* **Tamara** *sobs on* **Alice**'s *shoulder.*) You know, sometimes I feel sorry for my uncle. Yeah, he loves men. But, you know what? He loves women, too. You know how I know that? Because I'm a woman and he loves me. He is so full of love and I would do anything for my man to love me with just a tiny bit of the love my uncle has for me and for you and for you and for everyone. And for your brother. He just can't help it. All I can say is . . . he loves you and you gotta forgive him. You got to . . . (*Silence.*) (*She touches her stomach*) Poor kid. It's kicking like crazy. Watch. Feel that? (*She puts* **Alice**'s *hand on her stomach.*) I'm naming her Paloma for my Uncle Moe.

Raquel   Moe asked you to name her Paloma?

Tamara   Yeah. He said he had a little bird once that he let fly away. He said he always wanted to have a little girl named Paloma.

Raquel   He did?

Tamara   Yeah. (*She touches her stomach again.*) There she goes again. Watch. Feel it. (**Alice** *puts her hand on* **Tamara**'s *stomach.* **Tamara** *looks at* **Raquel**.) You wanna feel?

Raquel *touches* **Tamara**'s *stomach and she feels the baby move.*

Scene Twelve

Moe *lies in bed, alone. He calls out.*

Moe   Lupe! Lupe!

Lupe *appears in a white sequined gown. She is beautiful. The music plays and she sings.*

Lupe (*sings*)

> There was a boy
> A very strange enchanted boy
> They say he wandered very far,
> very far, over land and sea.
> A little shy and sad of eye,
> but very wise was he.
> And then one day,
> a magic day he passed my way
> And while we spoke of many things,
> Fools and queens,
> this he said to me:
> The greatest thing you'll ever learn,
> is just to love and be loved in return . . .

Moe *rises from the bed and he begins to dance, slowly, gracefully, then passionately.*

Lupe (*sings.*)

> The greatest thing you'll ever learn,
> is just to love and be loved in return . . .

Moe *lies in bed.*

Scene Thirteen

Raquel *enters* **Moe***'s room and picks up her purse. She looks down at* **Moe** *as he sleeps, then she turns to leave.*

Moe   Are you leaving?

Raquel   Yes.

Moe   Without saying goodbye?

Raquel   I don't belong here . . .

Moe (*looks at* **Raquel**)   I did love you, Rachel. I loved you the only way I could.

Raquel   I know that, Moises.

Moe   You know what my only regret is, Rach? Not having the child.

Raquel   I know . . .

Moe (*sings*)   "Paloma negra, donde, donde andarás . . ." (**Moe** *breathes harder.*) Forgive me, Raquel?

She turns to look at **Moe.**

Raquel   I can't.

She exits.

Scene Fourteen

Lupe *enters* **Moe***'s room. She sings as* **Martin, Eddie, Alice,** *and* **Tamara** *enter.*

Lupe (*sings*)

> Once we loved
> And love was my purpose
> Through the pain of life
> I found myself now
> To be safe in the shade of your love
> Was all I lived for
> Love was good
> Love was pure . . .

Lupe   Are you ready?

Moe   Just about. (*To his friends.*) I'm sorry about the end. I wanted it to be different . . . It just didn't work out, you know. All my life I tried to find myself and in the end I find out I'm just me. Moises, Moe . . . whatever. But there is something I want you to know . . . Everyone said, "Be careful, Moe." I knew better, I knew better. I did, I did. I knew he was sick. I knew he was so sick. (**Moe** *looks over and sees a young man with a kind face.*) But, I looked into his eyes, those eyes . . . reminded me of Elias. And I thought I saw a glimpse. A glimpse of the possibility that he might love me. He might, I thought he might. He needed to be loved. To beloved. To be. And I didn't care. I didn't care. You see, you're right, Eddie. Sometimes people do something and don't think about the consequences. I just want to say I'm sorry. I'm so sorry. I know how hard this has been for all of you. I'm sorry Martin, Eddie, Alice . . . (**Martin** *sobs.* **Alice** *and* **Eddie** *comfort him.* **Moe** *gasps for air.* **Martin** *tries to put his mask back on.*) No, I don't want it. (**Moe** *looks at* **Martin** *and* **Martin** *turns away. Then he looks at* **Tamara**.) Mija, come here.

Tamara *goes to him. He whispers something in her ear.*

Lupe (*whispers*)   Exit plan B.

Tamara *looks at the others.*

Tamara   You guys need to leave the room. I need to change him.

Moe (*cries like a baby*)   Wah! Wah!

They all leave the room as **Tamara** *begins to change* **Moe**.

Lupe (*sings*)

> Se acabó
> lo nuestro está muerto

Se acabó
te juro que es cierto
Si hay un poco de fe
en nuestro amor
Todavía me quedaba
ya no existe
Ya no hay nada
Se acabó

(*Spoken*:)

Se acabó en English means it's over, baby! All over!

(*Sings*:)

Se acabó!

Scene Fifteen

Tamara *injects a syringe of drugs into his IV tube. His breath becomes shallow.*

Moe   You know what you have, mija?

Tamara   What?

Moe   Huevos.

Tamara   Thanks.

Moe *lies back.*

Moe   I wanna cruise where there's no dark, just light. Where spirits enter each other and fill each other with puro amor. Amor puro . . . I wanna cruise . . . (*He closes his eyes.*) Elias . . .

Moe *stops breathing.*

Tamara   Uncle Moe? Uncle Moe? (*She takes* **Moe** *in her arms. She holds him. She rocks him.*) I love you, Uncle Moe.

The music plays. **Lupe** *appears. She sings.*

Lupe (*sings*)

This is my life
Today, tomorrow for love will come and
find me for that's the way
I was born to be
This is me
This is me
This is my life
And I don't give a damn for lost emotion

There's such a lot of love
I've got to give
Let me live Please,
let me live!
This is my life!
This is my life!
This is my life!

Moe *appears nude. He bows.*

Moe   Thank you. Thank you very much. Gracias . . .

Blackout.

End of Play.

Las Mariposas Saltan al Vacío

José Milián

Compañía Nacional de las Artes—Bogotá, Colombia

2 *Las Mariposas Saltan al Vacio*, Compañía Nacional de las Artes, Bogotá, Colombia, 2017. Photo courtesy of Compañía Nacional de las Artes.

Snapshot

Patricia Herrera

When death inevitably knocks on your door the pursuit of answers to the meaning of life becomes eminent. This is the quest that *Las Mariposas Saltan al Vacío* undertakes. This contemplative offering by renowned Cuban writer José Milián, which first premiered in 1994 at Café Teatro Brecht, dives deep into the existential abyss of who am I, why do I have to die now, and what am I doing here amidst those living with HIV or Aids. Caught between reality and fantasy and mixing genres from farce to tragedy, realism to melodrama, *Las Mariposas Saltan* journeys into an HIV-positive sanatorium world of heterosexuals, homosexual, and transsexual patients—Fermín, Arsenio, whose transvestite stage name is Lavania la Salvaje, the director of a play they act in, their friend La Gorda, her ex-lover Gresil, and el payaso (the clown). Directed by Jorge Cao, Bogotá's Compañía Nacional de las Artes performance of *Las Mariposas Saltan*, in Spanish with English supertitles, was in honor of Cao's artistic life of fifty years. The play spotlights the debilitating containment imposed onto people living with HIV and Aids, not far from Cuba's response of secluding people infected with HIV in the 1980s. While the characters convey an overwhelming sense of entrapment, the set reminds audiences that there is life beyond the sanatorium. The luminous bright white full moon nestled between cotton fluff clouds with its white tail extends onto the multi-leveled scaffolds on the stage while Arsenio/Lavania la Salvaje frequently asks if there is a full moon. The character of el payaso (clown), played by two red-winged clowns striding their topless chests with red suspenders securing their black leather pants, adds a poignantly humorous flair to a taboo subject, Aids, the global epidemic that would forever alter the way we think about and talk about sex and sexuality. The less than angelic clowns serve as the inner consciousness of Fermín, Arsenio, and La Gorda, probing into their ugly past and relishing in their fears, passions, and desires. All along they are in the backstage dressing room preparing for their performance as the audience "listens in" to a series of conversations and internal dialogues addressing the beauty and complexity of human relations, friendship, love, and most importantly betrayal. Betrayed by Gresil, her much younger boyfriend, La Gorda is trying to get over him. While she mentally knows that their relationship is over her heart pulls her back into the romance, lust, and sex as Gresil appears lashing his whip, wearing black leather fitted pants gesticulating his hips back and forth stimulating copulation as he pleads La Gorda to take him back. Even though she wants to be with him, she resists and rejects him. We learn that Fermín also betrayed his partner but now yearns to be loved and Lavania avenged his partner for betraying her. Everyone is healing from various acts of infidelity. It is in the act of reflecting that these characters move toward transformation and renewal. Even as the body is diseased, we learn that we must take a leap of faith and jump into the abyss of the unknown as life unfolds.

Quemar las naves. El viaje de Emma

Rocío Carrillo Reyes and Organización Secreta Teatro

Mexico City, Mexico

3 *Quemar las naves. El viaje de Emma*, Organización Secreta Teatro, Ciudad de México, 2017.
Photo: Luis Quiroz.

Profile

Teresa Marrero

Within the framework of the Encuentro festival, the aesthetic choices of Mexico City's Organización Secreta Teatro, headed by writer-director Rocío Carrillo, could not be more different than the others. Their interdisciplinary, collectively created piece *Quemar las naves. El viaje de Emma* (*Burning the Ships. Emma's Voyage*) offered a lush visual feast orchestrated to the ambient sounds generated by the actors (voice coach Margie Bermejo), a live percussionist (actor Tabris Berges), and an enigmatic musical score (Betsy Pecanins) matched by an epic, larger than life scenic, visual, and costume design (Érika Gómez), with video design by Mayeli Torres and Chantal Vidal, and live singing by Óscar Acevedo.

Without a doubt the visual, musical, and sound score are cast on equal footing with the actors. This is a carefully orchestrated, complex staging that weighs in numerous variables. While the play's guiding mastermind, Carrillo, asserts that this is theater and not dance, personally it took me back to Pina Bausch's memorable performance in *Bluebeard's Castle* by Béla Bartók. The resonance relates to Bausch's iconic daring and the commitment to deliver a bare-all performance, authentic and true down to the bone. This is a memorable visual/sound feast that indelibly finds its way etched in our collective unconsciousness, to resurface now and again as if enticing us to look again, think again, there are more layers to unfold here.

One of the unique features of this full-length piece is that there are no speaking parts, except for a sentence or two in the closing scene. Thus, the entire weight of the production falls upon the physicality of the actors. Loosely based on the archetypical, mythical structure of the Greek classic *The Odyssey*, it is described as "a feminist adaptation of Homer's epic poem . . . [Emma] and her ragtag crew of sailors, pirates, past loves and Greek gods face trials and challenges of mythical proportions as she sets on a journey after her husband's untimely passing." This piece took a year of collective creation to portray a rite of passage that is infrequently mythologized: that of an adult woman once liberated (be it by widowhood or divorce) from the societal restraints of marriage. It is a story of loss, of beyond-the-imagination adventure, of sexual awakenings, and ultimately of the freedom to choose one's own path and steer one's own metaphoric ship. It is a woman-centered story that calls upon the awakening of her own inner strength in a veritable rite of passage. Unlike the male-dominant penchant to create archetypical voyage-of-the-hero narratives (which are often seen not only in the theater but also in films), this one is signified physically and symbolically articulated through the body of a mature female.

Georgina Rábago plays the title role of Emma, displaying a tremendous vocal and emotional range. Her expressions of bewilderment, loss, vulnerability, and her ultimate joy and exuberant liberation are truly captivating. Except for the title role, all other actors match each other's outstanding commitment to the performance by morphing into numerous and divergent roles. Tabris Berges plays Hermes, Cyclops, Calipso, and voyager, Ernesto Lecuona the Capitan y Poseidon, Alejandro Joan Camarena plays a Cyclops, Orpheus, and voyager, Beatriz Cabrera portrays an amazingly powerful Circe, mermaid, Baubo, Nausica, and voyager, Jonathan Ramos tackled the roles of Circe, Medusa, Penelope, and voyager, and Margarita Higuera the Mermaid, Baubo, Calipso, Penelope, and voyager.

The penchant for framing theatrical work intellectually as well as creatively is a characteristic of Latin American theater as a whole. Looking towards European rather than American theatrical models also marks a difference in aesthetics choices. The US educational system tends to focus their programs in the preparation of actors not as a co-creative agents but rather as adept servers of the director's proposed vision. The dream of working for a LORT (League of Resident Theatres) theater and membership to the Actors' Equity Association drives US university theater programs. This paradigm prioritizes pragmatic aspects of professional theater work, rather than fomenting time-consuming innovation, such as this one.

Formal experimentation falls in line with Carrillo Reyes's and the company's aesthetics since its inception in 1991. A guiding principle for this production is based on the notion of the stage as a space of unconscious creation. Carrillo clarifies her notion of unconscious creation in her 2009 thesis *El espacio inconsciente como poética de la puesta en escena* (The unconscious space as a poetics of the *mise en scène*). It is anchored on the Jungian principle of the collective unconscious evidenced by archetypes that prevail universally. Adding to the mix is the specificity of the theatrical space as an autonomous universe that is constantly transformable, always looking for its own ways of narrating.

She clarifies that her use of the concept of poetics corresponds with that of Italian novelist, theorist, and semiotician Umberto Eco in his seminal *Obra Abierta* (*The Open Work*): "the operative program that the artist proposes to him or herself over and over again, the emergence of the work, as it understood explicitly or implicitly by the artist." This dynamic perspective stands as a differentiating factor from Aristotle's dramatic norm proposed in his classic *Ars Poetica.* Eco's and Carrillo's notion embraces rupture and chaos as an integral part of the creative process. Thus, the Jungian archetypal finds an organic theatrical process through collectively devised work, one which requires—in any given project—a long-term commitment by the actors, designers, and the director herself. The personal experiences of the company members are folded into the process, each coming to the table with not only a particular intellectual and emotional understanding of the subject at hand, but also one articulated through their bodies without the spoken word. Obviously, this time-intensive process requires a safe space in which to be vulnerable, to dig deep into one's own psyche. This is a trademark of the Organización Secreta Teatro's work in experimental and in more traditional dramatic forms.

In terms of typical US tastes for dramatic realism, *El viaje de Emma's* post-dramatic structure confounded even the sophisticated audiences at the Encuentro. Latin American theater-goers are steeped in traditions that stem from the post-World War II European avant-garde, to the more politically engaged influence of German Bertolt Brecht, to Brazilians Augusto Boal and Paulo Freire's *Pedagogy of the Oppressed* (1968), and to the seminal work of Eugenio Barba's Odin Teatret (Denmark) in Mexico, Peru, and Cuba. In broad strokes, Latin American theater, while sharing common ground with the more political branch of Chicanx and Latinx works, hails from a broader anchoring in aesthetic experimentation. Seeing Latin American theatre involves either extensive travel to various countries, or attending international festivals. As such, the Encuentro de las Américas filled a gap in our knowledge and understanding of Latin American theater. It also provided fertile ground for conversations.

At the Encuentro, the audience reception to this rich and complex piece varied widely. Some deemed it ambiguous and confusing, while others were awestruck by its deep symbolism and artistry. Some objected to the nudity of the female body, calling it a further objectification of women, while others saw the nudity as a symbolic rite of passage, one in which the old is stripped away and the metaphorically reborn is bathed in the purifying waters of self-discovery. In any case, no one walked away from *Quemar las naves. El viaje de Emma* without an opinion.

Interview with Rocío Carrillo Reyes
Teresa Marrero

Teresa Marrero   I posed a few open-ended questions to Rocío Carrillo Reyes, director of *Quemar las naves. El viaje de Emma*, as a starting point for our interview. I wanted her to feel free to address any aspect to which she felt drawn without the hindrance of being tied down. This is the framework of the questions I presented to her: Can you identify common grounds within the Encuentro de las Américas? Were there points of positive or negative encounters between the Latin American and the Latinx works that problematized the notion of sharing some sort of common ground? In what ways did your piece challenge or reinforce the idea of what we share in common, within our particular historical, chronological, and geographic specificities? What kind of themes and aesthetics did you perceive in the works presented in the festival, and how did your work fit or not within what you saw? What kinds of conversations between artists, critics, scholars, or the general community did your work particularly generate?

Rocío Carrillo Reyes   The Encuentro de las Américas has been one of the most important international experiences for my company. It offered us the opportunity to know the current interests of theater practitioners from Latin America and the Chicano artists of North América.

I suppose that the mestizo origins that we all share explains the need for Latin Americans to consolidate an identity within our contemporary context of post-revolutionary, post-dictatorships, insurgencies, and counter-insurgencies witnessed during the twentieth century. For the Chicanos, it seems that the concern focuses on strengthening the stronghold that they already occupy within their own transcultural spaces within the US.

Several of the companies, ours included, have the common need to deepen the understanding of the issues related to the individual characters, be they post-revolutionary Cubans who witnessed the split of their families in Argos Teatro's *10 Millones*, that of the experience of a homosexual approaching death from HIV who confronts his personal ghosts in *Dementia* by the Latino Theater Company, or, in our case, Emma's transformational voyage, one that signals her approaching middle age.

As I commented to the Cuban director Carlos Celdrán, I was very surprised with how "the personal" can be subversive within contemporary discourses. On the other hand, in the case of the Chicano companies, the definition of an intercultural identity seems to stem from the sociological to confront the particular conflicts of one or more characters.

To summarize, it seems to me that we all share the common need to reassert the collectivity of our peoples, our communities, in order to combat racism, gender-based discrimination, the abuse of immigrants, etc., and also to reflect upon our own artistic endeavors. The aesthetic expressions seen within the Encuentro shaped an enriching fan made of a multiplicity of *mise en scène*. However, I would identify the use of live music as a common denominator among the works presented. We tell stories from the starting point of our music, a common language that celebrates life and honors death. This aspect for me was very moving.

I believe that our work *Quemar las naves. El viaje de Emma* directed the gaze towards the importance of rethinking of the feminine from newer, more complex and inclusive perspectives. Several colleagues from the Encuentro were surprised by a story told without words which appeals to the depth and universality of myths in order to communicate meaning, and is successful at it.

Myth and Sonority in *Quemar las naves. El viaje de Emma*
A Very Surreal Way to Create
Rocío Carrillo Reyes

Poetic Staging

For more than twenty years I have worked with my company Organización Secreta Teatro (Mexico City, Mexico) on staging the potential of myths and their impact on our contemporary culture. My interest has centered on the way we translate the typical symbols of myths into theatrical language and from the stage we reboot them to communicate to the audience what makes us universal as human beings. The myth, according to the theories about the collective unconscious developed by Freud, Jung, Eliade, etc., is expressed through archetypes that persist inside human consciousness. Perhaps, for people of the modern world, myths no longer represent a guide for going through the stages and key events of life as they would have worked for people in antiquity, but they still evoke aspects of our inner world, hence they are repeated again and again in literature, film, and other artistic expressions.

The staging of *Quemar las naves. El viaje de Emma* narrates the path of the hero in Homer's classical Greek text *The Odyssey*. However, now this journey is made by a woman. In this version, there is no Troy, no Ulysses, nor the Achaeans who seek to return to Ithaca. The heroine is Emma, a mature woman who, in the wake of her husband's death, begins a journey to face her own fears and discover the meaning of life.

To talk about *Quemar las naves. El viaje de Emma*, a *mise en scène* without words, it may be appropriate to refer to Umberto Eco's version of the poetic concept. We understand the concept of "poetic" in the definition that Eco gives in *Open Work:* "as the operational program that the artist proposes over and over again, the project of the work to be carried out as understood explicitly or implicitly by the artist." In short, we employ the notion of the poetic not only as the material that makes up the *mise en scène,* but as a means of arranging or structuring the work.

The experimentation of Organización Secreta Teatro, in staging *Quemar las naves. El viaje de Emma*, focused on exploring the unconscious as a space with evocative and poetic possibilities, and as a form of representation where the construction of symbolic images takes place. In other words, the unconscious as the main poetics of the *mise en scène* through myth. The unconscious is meant in two senses. The first refers directly to the territory of the psyche that Carl G. Jung defined as the realm of the Unknown, the reality where forgotten memories, dreams, and symbolic images take place and which is beyond the control of consciousness. Secondly, it is also the space of representation, of the *mise en scène*; it is the stage that houses this autonomous universe and transforms it, looking for its own narrative form.

Dramaturgy presents itself as another element of experimentation within the unconscious space. This *mise en scène* is an example of a form of writing images and emotions within a collective project and how it is articulated in a stage language which seeks to evoke the symbols and archetypes of myth.

Robert Wilson's theater has been an inspiration to me. In 1999 I saw the staging of *Persephone* that was presented in Mexico at the Cervantino International Festival. One of the most striking scenes of the piece was an ancient Greek dialogue—from the Homeric Hymns—between Demeter and Persephone. The text combined the meaning of the words with their evocative potential manifested in the sound—amplified by microphones worn by the actresses—of the ancient Greek language and its dramatic recitation. The text was more than its meaning; it brought us near the language of the gods.

My conception of the *mise en scène* coincides with Hans-Thies Lehmann's version in his book *Postdramatic Theatre* about Wilson as the creator *of a neo-mythical theater* in which the narrative does not conform to the formal, logical, canonical ordering. However, Organización Secreta Teatro does not work with historical figures as Wilson does in some pieces, but rather with myths and plastic representations of our pre-Hispanic and mestizo past that interact with Greek cosmogony.

We seek that the myth depicted in Emma's journey, the female version of Ulysses, through interdisciplinary stage discourse, one without words, translates into a scenic reality susceptible to multiple readings. We have explored the myth as a poetic that encompasses the content of the *mise en scène,* as well as what organizes it and shapes it in way of image creation, video art, sound design and aesthetic construction. It has evolved in our search for ways to express its intangible reality, particularly that which is common to all of us, where the myth is still reflected in people's internal imagination. It is a perspective that proposes new conundrums around the function of myths today and the creation of a discourse that aspires to evoke them as a way of glimpsing our long-lost inner spaces.

Mythical time is qualitatively different from historical time. People of archaic cultures or tribal societies still governed by their mythology live within cycles of sacred time through the rituals that commemorate their myths. To evoke that time in the performance it was necessary to build a sound dramaturgy.

Staging Sound

In *Quemar las naves. El viaje de Emma*, we decided not to use words, but to highlight the interaction between the actor's expressiveness, the sound design made by Betsy Pecanins, the sound dramaturgy that the musician Óscar Acevedo creates in the moment, and the training and vocal exploration that Margie Bermejo has carried out with the company to generate the atmospheres, such as the wind, the waves of the sea, the sirens, etc.

The creation of the scenes took place through improvisations with the actors and the musician. From the beginning we aimed for the sound to endow the actions with a rhythmic temporality. The participation of the musician on stage takes on a profound meaning in the plot: it can be said that the actors draw their physical interpretation on space, subject to certain rhythms. If we think of rhythm as a temporary organization of sound, we can imagine that by amplifying into the actor's body and interacting with the visual elements of the *mise en scène*, the music becomes a dramaturgy parallel to the myth.

Each sound, each movement of the light, and each video projection corresponds to a very precise dramatic body score that is articulated in space that generates an integrated whole. Even when recorded music acts as a background, live music emphasizes the recording and the physical actions affect the evolution of the bodies in space, creating a dramatic score by accelerating, sustaining or slowing down the actor's movement. This adds a layer to the video and lighting designs.

The live sounds are transformed into signs because they make sense within the poetics of the unconscious, which has its own coherence. They do not propose a unilateral meaning that we can rationally identify, but an experience of the senses and spirit. Circe's actions on Emma's body have sound. The sorceress is, in this version, Emma's ally; she clears her melancholy by stirring the air with her fans and with bouquets of aromatic herbs as Mexican healers do. She gives her two spheres of light to illuminate Emma's path and teaches her to spit out sadness, as well as rings her rattles to scare away the ghosts of death.

Each action *sounds*: the spheres of light are placed in Emma's hands and that action is enhanced by the sound of subtle bells that the musician generates live on his percussion set; Circe's breath over Emma's head to clear her mind is the pulse of a violin bow on the edge of a chime cymbal. This particular scene is created as an evocation of the sacred. The reality of Greek myth merges with the pre-Hispanic tradition of *cleaning the bad humors* that Mexican healers execute. If, according to James Hillman in *Re-visioning Psychology*, the myth makes us imagine, we freely imagine characters from other myths invited to accompany Emma's journey. Thus, in our version of this female *Odyssey*, Orpheus materializes with his singing to save Emma from the mermaids. Orpheus's chant mutes the mermaids as in the story of Jason and the Argonauts. Orpheus sings in the *mise en scène* with the voice of Alejandro Joan Camarena, actor and bass-baritone.

In the play, the voice of the actor does not express words, it builds a language through sound: the actors create a vocal atmosphere to evoke the waves of the sea moved by the wind; Cyclops create a grave and continuous sound that hypnotizes sailors and pushes them to destruction; Circe's groans and cries heal Emma's soul as the unintelligible prayers of the other actors live, amplified with microphones, sound like a litany; Orpheus's singing scares away the sirens and celebrates a party with the sailors; Emma manages to escape the marine underworld through a deep and long cry which expresses the pain of the burning ships next to Nausicaa and accepts taking on the risks of a new life. Betsy Pecanins' sound atmospheres are textures created on a synthesizer and/or a cello. For the siren's scene, the voices of two singers were recorded. Some percussion tracks were tapped with electric sounds that gave a contemporary tone to the sound.

Some of the material that makes up the *mise en scène* comes from the dreams of the actors and mine, from the drawings, from the embroidery on fabric, from the *exquisite corpses* we create. Exquisite corpse was a game invented by writer Andre Breton, leader of Surrealism. Breton called for art that engaged the unconscious by using dreams and automatic drawings as creative fodder. The way the game is played is that players write in turn on a sheet of paper, fold it to hide part of the writing, and then pass it to the next player for their contribution. All of this is integrated as a collage. It is a very surreal way to create. As Lehmann expresses, "dreamlike thoughts form a structure which resembles collage, assembly and fragment and not to the development of logically structured events." A few years ago, I earned a degree in Deep Psychology with Dr. Sven Dohener, a specialist in the research of the sounds of dreams. Somehow, the sound design, created for *Quemar las naves. El viaje de Emma* and for other pieces built on myths, seek this dreamlike quality. I believe that if we can get the audience to evoke their own dreams through image and sound, we will have achieved deep and empathetic communication.

Section Two

Staging Transnational Realities of Race, Ethnicity, and Class

Ropa Íntima

Lynn Nottage

Ébano Teatro—Lima, Peru

4 Lynn Nottage's *Intimate Apparel/Ropa Íntima*, adapted by Ébano Teatro, ICPNA Miraflores, Lima, Peru 2016. Photo: Morfi Jiménez.

Profile
Gina Sandí-Díaz

Lynn Nottage's *Intimate Apparel* premiered at South Coast Repertory in Costa Mesa, California and Centerstage in Baltimore, Maryland in 2003. American audiences and critics widely celebrated it for its commentary on race and gender bias against African-American women, in the early 1900s.

The story follows Esther, an illiterate black seamstress living in a Lower Manhattan hostel. Her excellent skills and discretion have gained her a good reputation, granting her access to clients of different cultural backgrounds and wealth. Although her popularity as a seamstress enables her to make a decent living, she is a lonely woman with no marriage prospect and all the other young women in the hostel where she lives have married or are soon to be married, causing her landlord, Mrs. Dickson, to continually pressure her to find a husband. One day she receives an unexpected letter from a gentleman working the Panama Canal, Mr. George Armstrong. Although

Esther has been saving money for years with the goal of opening a beauty salon for black women, her heart's desire is to be loved, appreciated, and respected by a man. When the letter arrives, she is immediately swept off her feet by the elegant handwriting and the gentle, musical words printed on paper by the hand of a man she has never met.

The cultural impositions of the time push Esther to believe marrying the unknown Mr. Armstrong is the only possibility for her future, and so, with the help of her clients and friends, she corresponds Mr. Armstrong's letters. The central conflict of the play erupts when George arrives in New York to marry Esther and turns out to be completely different than the man on paper. On their wedding night, Esther does everything possible to delay the consummation of their marriage. To break the ice, Esther stuns George with her family's tragic story, revealing in the process that she is saving money to open a beauty salon and prompting George into taking advantage of the situation. When she encourages him to get a job in town, he sees an opportunity to belittle her and take over her life's earnings.

The play also highlights Esther's relationship with women of different social classes and status, unveiling the complexities of women's relationships at the time where they must put their loyalties to the test to survive in a man's world. Esther's relationship with Mrs. Dickson, her African-American landlord, is maternal, but her attention is shared by the many other young single women who work and live under her roof, making Esther jealous. Then there is Mrs. Van Buren, an affluent client of Esther's. She attempts to erase the social divide between the two of them, treating Esther as an equal, and then snapping at her when she expresses her opinions. Esther, however, is acutely aware of her status in society and finds it impossible to reciprocate Mrs. Van Buren's insensitivity. Then, there's Mayme, a town prostitute who Esther sees as an equal and trusts as her friend.

Through the relationship of these women, Nottage explores the limited access to the world black women, in particular, had at the time. Mrs. Van Buren complains she is criticized by society for not "giving" children to her husband and Mayme, although an educated musician, must work as a courtesan due to the color of her skin. One of my favorite scenes in the play is when Esther and Mayme fantasize they are wealthy and prestigious. Mayme becomes a famous piano player, and Esther a wealthy businesswoman, the life both women could have had if allowed to employ their talents. In their fantasy, they meet for tea and indulge in their expensive possessions and furniture.

There is one more character in the play, Mr. Marks, a Romanian Orthodox Jewish man, owner of the fabric store where Esther shops for her creations. He sees Esther for who she is. They respect each other and enjoy productive conversations. There is undeniable chemistry between them, but the racial divide of the time is an invisible barrier between them. He is in love with the way she admires the fabrics, and he notices the way in which she touches each piece of fabric. He even has a story for each piece she purchases, because he knows how much she appreciates the very existence of the material.

Ébano Teatro offered a beautiful, sober rendering of Nottage's piece, topped with honest performances and a clean, efficient *mise en scène*. I was delighted to learn the editors paired me up with Alicia Olivares, founder of Ébano Teatro, to interview her regarding her experience at the Encuentro 2017 because I was much impressed by her words during a session on "Aesthetics in the Americas," where she was one of the panelists. It had been a long, exciting day in which I had already attended several working sessions and performances. I was sitting in the audience, feeling tired and thinking I should go out and get a coffee when she suddenly grabbed the microphone and immediately denounced the lack of black bodies and their stories in stages all over the Americas. Well, I thought to myself, coffee is going to have to wait. "Yo creía que era sólo en mi país," she said, referring to the void in the representation of black culture in Peruvian theater, "porque el pretexto de los directores y los productores es que no hay actores negros," she explained, and then let out a short sarcastic sigh at the irony just spoken.

Her statement shook me and forced me to take a look at my surroundings. Most importantly, her choice of words—"yo creía que era sólo en mi país"—kept resonating in my head, unveiling she had noticed the obvious, that the same void existed in the room we were in. Up to this point, the conversation had stayed confined to the conceptualization each artist had of aesthetics and how it played methodologically in their work, but Olivares's words immediately placed us back in the physical, material reality of the room we were in, demanding we address the lack of Afro-Latinx bodies in our gathering. Her words acknowledged the void.

After college, Alicia Olivares served as executive producer for the play *Al otro lado de la cerca*, a translation of August Wilson's *Fences*, by Marianella Pantoja. The production opened in July of 2014, becoming "the first production in Lima to showcase an all-black cast." The production was a box-office success and motivated Alicia to create her own company.

Ropa Íntima, the production showcased at Encuentro 2017, premiered in 2016 and was the company's first production under the name Ébano Teatro. I would like to close this introduction with Alicia's own description of her work. Upon Encuentro's invitation to perform in Los Angeles, the group set up a website to promote the event. On it, Olivares describes the group's mission with the following words:

> Como artista y gestora cultural siento la profunda necesidad de romper con la desigualdad de oportunidades que existe en las artes escénicas para actores y actrices afro-descendientes a pesar de tener la misma preparación y el mismo talento. Necesitamos abrir el camino para que nuevas generaciones de actores afro-descendientes tengan la oportunidad de ejercer su arte sin distinción de raza, ni condición social. Nuestra misión es visibilizar uno de los más silenciosos, pero latentes males de nuestra sociedad: la discriminación y el racismo en todas sus formas.

> [As an artist and cultural worker, I feel a deep need to break with the lack and unequal opportunities present in the scenic arts for Afro-descendant actors, even though these actors possess comparable training and talent. We need to open pathways of opportunities for younger generations of Afro-descendant actors so they can exercise their art without distinctions based on race or social conditions. Our mission is to provide visibility to one of the most silenced, yet latent ills of our society: discrimination and racism in all its manifestations.]

Interview with Alicia Olivares
Gina Sandí-Díaz

Gina Sandí-Díaz   One of the Latinx Theatre Commons' primary objectives during Encuentro 2017 was to create a space for artists from all over the Americas that identify as Latinx, to meet, discuss, and straighten "the common ground" we share as artists, but also to unpack and problematize such common ground. Based on your experience at Encuentro, how would you describe this "common ground"?

Alicia Olivares   I think the theater is compelling because it allows for a constant migration process. What I mean by this is that theater artists translate individual stories of struggle in a particular context into universal stories, and it is through the experiences of characters trapped in their world that we confront our society and our dramas, our dreams, and hopes. To me, "the common ground" is that we are all people, equals, with no borders. We might have different cultures, but our humanity is the same.

Sandí-Díaz   In thinking about the repertoire of shows participating at Encuentro, what aesthetic forms and social themes did you notice seemed to belong to that "common ground" discussed above?

Olivares   Most of the performances, regardless of their companies' place of origin, explored common themes such as racial discrimination, gender bias, sexism, and the mistreatment of immigrants. Concerning aesthetic expressions, my takeaway is that is made up of a very diverse and enriching range of scenic devices in each of the shows. A common thread I noticed is for companies to create their own dramaturgy, usually based on their life experiences, or on the need to tell a story that could transport the audience to a better world. And, with regards to the shows I attended, what I can say is that they all offered us unique voices, strong audiovisual presence, live music, and contemporary dance.

Sandí-Díaz   One of Ébano Teatro's main objectives is to exalt Afro-Latinx culture on the Peruvian stages, which, as in most of the Americas, continues to be excluded and reduced to simplistic stereotypes. How is Ébano Teatro challenging these old notions?

Olivares   I am quite aware of the racism and sexism that exist in my country, and even more so of the discrimination people suffer because of it. The visibility of Afro-descendant actors in the performing arts only became a reality a few years ago, and still, there are very scarce opportunities for black actors to perform in Lima, and that is not even mentioning the TV and film industries, where chances are even rarer. Peru needs to break away from the harming stereotype that black culture is only about singing and dancing, because it is so much more than that, and our stories matter. Based on this need, I created Ébano Teatro, right out of college. My purpose at the time was to produce shows that made it possible for black artists to work professionally, but also for the audience to start seeing and recognizing black actors in Peru. On the same note, I must mention that there are little, if any, materials [texts] about Afro-Latinx culture in Peru, so we had to start with big names in the Western canon such as August Wilson and Lynn Nottage, and the truth is that both productions achieved great acceptance from the public and the local critics. Without a doubt, this is a vast and complex challenge, but we believe as theater artists we have the responsibility to build the world we want to live in.

Sandí-Díaz   In *Ropa Íntima*, you played Esther, the leading role. How did you navigate the creative process for the part?

Olivares   Yes, I played Esther, a beautiful character with a heavy dramatic load, both physically and emotionally. This character demanded a lot of me as an actor and as a woman, but the show was an experience I will cherish close to my heart because it taught me so much. Giving life to Esther forced me to confront some of my own life experiences, times when I was discriminated against or limited because of my gender, or for the color of my skin. The more I explored inside of me, the more links I found to connect with Esther.

When on stage, I am devoted to my scene partner. Trust and active listening I believe are the pillars of my acting technique and what allows me to create truthful performances. That's how I work. I devote all of my attention to my scene partner, to being present in the moment with all my body, mind, and soul.

Sandí-Díaz   *Intimate Apparel*, one of Lynn Nottage's most important texts, premiered in 2003 with real positives reviews by critics and audiences alike. Ébano Teatro used a translation by Marianella Pantoja that was then adapted and directed by Miguel Pastor. How did the Los Angeles audience react to Ébano's production, considering it was performed entirely in Spanish?

Olivares   Nottage's play—as any great play—transcends history with the clear intention to denounce racial discrimination against African Americans then and now. The audience responded positively to our show. We performed without supertitles and were nervous that audience members might not understand, but based on the responses we received we conclude people stayed engaged throughout the show. Some of the recurrent topics of conversation with audience members had to do with aesthetic, highlighting the practical use of space, along with the versatility of the scenic pieces to convey a period piece traditionally performed on full set proscenium stages. Other comments focused on acting, praising the honesty of the performances.

Miss Julia

J.Ed Araiza

Vueltas Bravas—Bogotá, Colombia

5 *Miss Julia*, Vueltas Bravas Producciones, Bogotá, Colombia, 2014. Photo: Federico Rios.

Critical Introduction
Carla Della Gatta

Entering the LATC's blackbox theatre, audience members walked onto a runway stage, with a window set toward the small back wall and rows of seats on each side. A live band played a cumbia, and although it was only 10:30 a.m., shots of rum were handed to us so that we could drink and dance our way to our seats. The rhythms of the acoustic band carried the festivity of the Encuentro de las Américas into the fiesta atmosphere of *Miss Julia*. People clapped and danced, and eventually sat down, only to realize that we occupied the position of the partygoers just outside where the dramatic action takes place.

J.Ed Araiza's *Miss Julia* is a compressed tale of power dynamics between servant and master, confounded by gender, cultural, and linguistic differentiation. The gravity of the themes and the realistic premise of the struggles between dominance and submission are set in the kitchen of a mansion during La Noche de San Juan, the eve of the feast day for Saint John the Baptist, and the contrast between the indoor (and inner) conflict and the celebration outside elevates the stakes to high theatricality.

An adaptation of August Strindberg's 1898 play *Miss Julie*, *Miss Julia* retains the terse dialogue, naturalistic set, pantomimed choreography, and class dynamics of the original. Strindberg dramatizes the disastrous results of competing psychoses and ideas of free will and natural selection through a story of class disparity. Miss Julie entices her male servant, who is already married to fellow servant Cristina, to have sex with her, but gender and class dynamics intersect to result in her downfall.

Strindberg's play was written in Swedish, set in Scandinavia, and first performed in Copenhagen. While Latinx adaptations and appropriations of European classics have increased in quantity and complexity over the last decade, the strategies of adaptation vary widely. Araiza abbreviates the already tense one-act Strindberg play into a three-person play with an optional Greek chorus who appeared once in performance. The transposition is clear: Strindberg's setting of Midsummer's Eve becomes La Noche de San Juan and the characters' names and some of the dialogue are translated into Spanish. Complicating class difference by adding on ethnic and linguistic difference, *Miss Julia* brings forth a more contemporary inter-ethnic dynamic. In so doing, Araiza puts a white Western standard-bearer such as Strindberg in direct conversation with Latinx culture and the Spanish language.

Here the servants, Juan and Cristina, are Colombian and Miss Julia is of "Anglo European heritage." While Miss Julia can speak Spanish, albeit with an unpractised accent, and both servants can understand and speak English, language and ethnicity amplify the class distinctions. The clear divide between the Colombian servants and the Anglo Miss Julia is evident in every moment. From Miss Julia's attempts to speak Spanish, her attire, movements, and sometimes confusion at what the peasants are singing, she is distinct from Juan and Cristina. But the dialogue does not include one line explicitly acknowledging ethnic difference. Ethnicity is understood as an implicit foundation for Miss Julia's entitlement of superiority rather than made a priori.

Questions of translation arose throughout the Encuentro and became an ongoing discussion point. Productions at the 2017 Encuentro de las Américas were in English or Spanish, and some were bilingual. When Culture Clash's predominantly English production employed some Spanish, translations in English were projected onto the wall. *El Apagón* switched back and forth between languages, with translations in both languages projected on the wall throughout. Other productions such as *La razón blindada* were entirely in Spanish with no translations into English. But *Miss Julia*, twice translated from Swedish to English, then from English to partly in Spanish, required its audiences to be fully bilingual to understand the action of the play.[1] The play begins in an exchange between Juan and Cristina, entirely in Spanish. Like bilingual speakers, they begin to slip between languages, by the ninth line of the play, with Juan saying, "En serio. I saw everything!" and Cristina replying, "¡What??? ¿Qué pasó?"[2] When Juan reports to Cristina on Miss Julia's behavior, he does so in Spanish, so that the Spanish-speaking audience knows what has happened before the monolingual English-speaking audience does.

In Strindberg's play, Miss Julie is first heard speaking to someone outside, then she speaks to Christine about the abortion elixir she is making for the pregnant dog, and only after Jean interrupts the women does she ask/command him to dance. In Araiza's play, she enters "with a strong intent" and speaks Spanish, "Juan, come—baila con migo."[3] Her Spanish is (mostly) grammatically correct, punctuated by a forced accent,[4] and simplistic in sentence structure. She begins the play with a command and addresses

Juan in the familiar, "¿No me prestas Juan?"[5] as Juan continues to address her formally. She finishes the scene stating, "Tonight we are all the same, no ranks, no orders."[6] When Juan maintains the class distinction and linguistic formal tense, she responds, "'Gracias'. Y usted, won't you have some too?"[7] Miss Julia's desire to be linguistically equal while simultaneously reinforcing the class hierarchy later becomes defunct when the misogynistic structures in the culture betray her ability to either be master or equal.

The Spanish language forces the clear distinction between the formal and familiar tenses of direct address, and a bilingual Spanish–English play therefore amplifies this difference. In the original, Miss Julie throws out some phrases in French and is surprised that Jean responds in French. This provides a moment of intimacy and elevates his perceived class mobility. Jean has worked in Switzerland and shows his aptitude and interest in acquiring a speaking command of another language. Jean responds that he worked at the "biggest hotel in Lucerne"[8] and when he serves her a drink says, "Mademoiselle!"[9] French comes up between them again, as flirtation, command, but always a sign of shared experience/status and in short form. Whereas Strindberg uses language to denote experience, education, and travel, Araiza plays with language intimacy and exclusion. At the end of the first act, Miss Julia cannot understand the vulgarity of the campesino song in Spanish, and Juan serves as her translator to information about the people she supposedly outranks and employs.

Reviewing the Encuentro de las Américas in its entirety, Marci R. McMahon and I wrote, "language differences will not inhibit us from communicating with each other across regions and countries."[10] The sessions at the Encuentro were simultaneously translated in English and Spanish. The dominant languages of the US and Latin American theater were a process point (translators sat in the back of all large sessions), a debate (how should we communicate across communities), and a dramaturgical theme. When Juan tells Miss Julia that he wants to start a hotel, she asks about capital. He responds, "I've got my expertise, my professional experiencia, my knowledge of English, I think that's a lot of capital" (20).

Along with this realistic comment about the benefits of bilingualism and multilingualism, physical language figured prominently as a means of expression and communication. The playwright and the actors met at a SITI Summer Intensive in Saratoga Springs, and *Miss Julia* grew out of this experience. Movement, physicality, and international collaboration inform the SITI experience, and *Miss Julia* bridges any confusion resulting from language shifts with choreography, no-dialogue scenes set to instrumental music, and physical gesture. Strindberg's play incorporated pantomime as to not interrupt the naturalistic dialogue and scene with set changes and cumbersome actor entrances and exits. Araiza, by contrast, made these pantomimes "somehow ritualistic and out of time."[11] Regarding the Encuentro conversations, Olga Sanchez Saltveit wrote, "Language is an essential element of theatre, and mixing languages can affect audiences differently with their different tempos, cadences, implications."[12] This includes non-verbal languages, and in the case of *Miss Julia*, the mixture of Spanish, English, music, and physicality worked together affectively to reach a culturally and linguistically diverse audience.

Strindberg ends with the sounds of outside authority. "*Two loud rings on the bell.*"[13] Jean says, "It's horrible. But it's the only possible ending. Go!" And Miss Julie "*walks firmly and through the door.*"[14] Araiza ends his play with Miss Julia asking a question, "What would you do if you were me?"[15] and Julia and Juan fight in silence, with perhaps

Julia prevailing as stronger.[16] Miss Julia remains onstage to fight, stopping and starting, but still engaged in the action. Ultimately, many of the conversation topics at the Encuentro—languages, adaptation, the stories that we tell, and the fiesta outside the theater door—cohered in this adaptation of a familiar tale. And *Miss Julia* theatricalized the interplay between them.

Notes

1. The Encuentro program said that subtitles would be included, but I sat through a performance where there were none. Moreover, *Quemar de las naves. El Viaje de Emma* was another adaptation of a Western classic, Homer's *The Odyssey*. It was a movement and visual piece performed with no spoken text.
2. J.Ed Araiza. *Miss Julia* (unpublished script, 2018), 2.
3. Araiza, 4.
4. In performance, Miss Julia was played by Australian actress Tina Thurman, who spoke English with a flat, American accent.
5. Araiza, 4.
6. Araiza, 5.
7. Araiza, 8.
8. August Strindberg. *Miss Julie*. Translated by Michael Meyer. Ed. David Thomas and Jo Taylor. (London: Bloomsbury, 2016), 9.
9. Strindberg, 10.
10. Carla Della Gatta and Marci R. McMahon, "Coming Full Circle: the 2017 LTC International Convening." HowlRound. December 21, 2017. Accessed March 1, 2018.
11. Araiza, no page number
12. Olga Sanchez Saltveit. "Estamos Juntos / We are Together: Report-Outs from the Latinx Theatre Commons International Convening." HowlRound. 20 Nov 2017. Accessed March 1, 2018.
13. Strindberg, 46.
14. Strindberg, 46.
15. Araiza, 34.
16. Araiza, 34.

Miss Julia

An adaptation by
J.Ed Araiza

based on *Miss Julie* by August Strindberg

Additional text/edits by
Jhon Alex Toro
Gina Jaimes
Tina Mitchell Thurman
Lorenzo Montanini

A bilingual adaptation by J.Ed Araiza

Based on *Miss Julie* by August Strindberg

Production History

Miss Julia premiered in September 2013 at the Casa Ensamble in Bogotá, Colombia with an international company from Colombia, Australia, and Italy. In 2014, it was presented at the XIV Festival Iberoamericano de Teatro in Bogotá, Colombia; the XXXVI Festival Internacional de Teatro in Manizales, Colombia; the Décima Fiesta de las Artes Escénicas in Medellin, Colombia; and the XXIX Festival Iberoamericano de Teatro de Cádiz, Spain. In 2015 productions included the Teatro Estudio Julio Mario Santo Domingo in Bogotá, Colombia; and the Napoli Teatro Festival in Naples, Italy. In 2017 a United States tour presented at the historic La Mama ETC in New York in June; the Latin American Theater Festival Destinos in Chicago in October; and in November *Miss Julia* was presented as part of the Los Encuentros de las Américas Theatre Festival at Los Angeles Theatre Center in California.

Note: The actions listed as "pantomimes" are just that, something more than naturalistic staging. They can be stately or crude but somehow ritualistic and out of time.
There is perhaps something of a Greek chorus about them or at least an exploration of such. The action of the play takes place on the Noche de San Juan (summer solstice), in the kitchen of the Señor's, Miss Julia's father's, estate.

Characters

Miss Julia, *Anglo-European heritage, aged twenty-five.*
Juan, *a Colombian/Latino servant, aged thirty.*
Cristina, *a Colombian/Latina cook, aged thirty-five.*

Act One

Scene One (Español—Mostly Spanish)

A pantomime: as the audience enters perhaps **Juan** *offers them a shot of Aguardiente. A lively sensual cumbia is playing and he dances with* **Cristina** *playfully and at times suggestively. It is an athletic, exuberant dance; the audience may clap or even dance. As the houselights fade* **Juan** *guides the audience back to their seats, takes one last shot and crosses to the exterior entrance as* **Cristina** *turns to the stove. He turns/ enters and speaks.*

Or:

Simply, **Cristina** *stands cooking something on the stove. She wears a kitchen apron. There is a lively rural cumbia playing in the distance.* **Juan** *comes in through the door. He is wearing his uniform.*

Juan   Esta noche la señorita Julia está loca, ¡¡completamente loca!!

Cristina   ¡SHHH cállate que te puede escuchar el Sr.!

Juan   Llevé al señor a la estación, y de regreso pasé por el granero, porqué quería echar un baile. En ese momento Miss Julia estaba bailando con el guardia. Cuando me vio, se dirigió a mí y me invitó bailar con ella, y desde ese momento se puso a bailar de una manera como nunca he visto antes. Está completamente loca.

The music fades.

Cristina   Sí, siempre ha estado así, pero nunca tanto como estas últimas dos semanas, desde que la dejó el novio.

Juan   ¿Y que pasó en ese asunto? El novio es un buen muchacho, aunque sin mucha plata. Sin duda, los señores tienen sus caprichos y fantasías. En cualquier caso, es extraño que la señorita Julia prefiera quedarse en casa con nosotros en lugar de acompañar a su padre a visitar a sus familiares. ¿No?

Cristina   Sí. Pero después de todo lo que pasó con su novio está como avergonzada.

Juan   ¿Sabes, lo que pasó Cristina? ¡Yo lo vi todo!

Cristina   ¿En serio?

Juan   En serio. I saw everything!

Cristina   What??? ¿Qué pasó?

Juan   Fue una noche allí en el establo, y "Miss Julia" estaba "entrenando" al novio, según decía ella. ¿Qué crees que hacía? Lo hacía saltar sobre el látigo como un perro entrenado. Ella decía "Hop!" y él saltaba, "Hop!" Y él saltaba, "Hop!" . . . ¡No! ¡La tercera vez no saltó! ¡Le arrebató el látigo, la rompió en dos y se largó!

Cristina   ¿Eso es lo que pasó? . . . ¡No lo puedo creer!

Juan   Sí, eso fue lo que pasó. Oye, Cristina, no me vas a dar algo rico de comer, porque tengo hambre . . .

Cristina   Bueno, aquí tengo unos riñoncitos que acabo de cortar del asado de la ternera.

She serves **Juan** *a plate of food.*

Juan   Pero has debido calentarme el plato, porque lo siento como frío . . .

Cristina   ¡Hey! Su mercé es más sexy que el señor . . .

She ruffles his hair affectionately.

Juan   ¡Ay, suave Cristina, suave! Ya sabes que soy muy delicado.

Cristina   Pero si fue solo un cariñito porque lo amo. ¿Juan, pero tu piensas bailar conmigo esta noche?

Juan   "But of course my Horse."

Cristina   ¿Me lo prometes?

Juan   Yo no prometo nada. Yo siempre hago lo que digo.

He stands to leave but hears someone outside. He quickly hides the bottle he was about to open and stands respectfully.

Scene Two (English)

Julia *enters quickly with a strong intent.*

Julia   Juan, come—baila conmigo.

Juan (*hesitating*)   I don't mean to be rude, señorita, but I already promised this dance to Cristina.

Julia   Well, she can have another. Isn't that right? What do you say, Cristina? ¿No me prestas Juan?

Cristina   Is not my job. If the Señorita is nice to ask him pues he must say yes. Vé y agradece el honor a Miss Julia.

Juan   Without meaning any offense, do you think it's wise, Miss Julia, to dance twice in a row with the same man, especially when la gente de esta casa are always ready to jump to conclusions.

Julia (*explodes*)   What do you mean? What conclusions?

Juan   If you don't understand me, I must speak honestly. It doesn't look well to prefer one of your servants when others are hoping for the same honor.

Julia   Prefer? What ideas are in your head? I am absolutely astonished. I, the lady of this house, honor my servants' fiesta with my presence, and if I want to dance I'll do it with a man who has manners, so that I won't be laughed at.

Juan   As you command, Miss Julia. Estoy a sus ordenes.

Julia (*softly*)   Now don't talk of orders; this evening we're simply men and women at a fiesta. Tonight we are all the same, no ranks, no orders. Give me your arm. Tranquila Cristina, I'm not going to steal your tesoro.

A pantomime: **Juan** *offers her his arm and leads her away.* **Cristina** *sits alone, then faint music at some distance, a sensual bolero.* **Cristina** *keeps time with the music as she stands and dancing sensually clears the table where* **Juan** *had been eating, washes the plates, and puts them away. She sensually takes off her kitchen apron, takes a small mirror out and looks at herself. She goes to the door, looks out, comes back to the table, finds the handkerchief. She puts the mirror down on the table and picks up the handkerchief, smells it, pensively spreads it out, and slowly folds it.* **Juan** *comes back alone through the door. A pause as they look at each other.*

Scene Three (Spanish and Bilingual)

Juan   ¡LOCA pero completamente loca! ¡Todo el mundo burlándose de ella en todos los rincones ¿Qué piensas, Cristina?

Cristina   ¡Que debe tener la regla! Siempre se pone así en estos días. ¡Oye! ¿Vas a bailar conmigo o no?

Juan   ¿Ya estás enojada por haberte dejado plantada antes? ¿Estás enojada porque fui a bailar con Miss Julia?

Cristina   ¿Por esa cosita? Nah . . . además yo conozco mi lugar.

Juan (*crosses behind Christina and embraces her*)   Eres una buena muchacha y serás una excelente ama de casa.

Julia (*enters*)   A fine gentleman you are, abandoning your lady like that. Charmant!

Juan   Al contrario, Miss Julia, I hurried home to find the girl I left behind.

Julia   You know, I'm sure you're the best dancer there. But why are you wearing your uniform to a party? Go on, take it off at once.

Juan (*long beat*)   Alright, Miss Julia, but I must ask you to leave for a moment, because my Sunday jacket is hanging right here.

Julia   Were you born here?

Juan   My father was a campesino en la hacienda next to yours, but I saw you, Miss Julia, when you were a child, aunque usted nunca se dio cuenta.

Julia   No . . . ¿en serio?

Juan   En serio, and I remember one time in particular. But we don't talk about that.

Julia   Oh, yes now you must tell me. What? Go on, please, for me.

Juan   No, really I can't now. Maybe en otro tiempo.

Julia   Another time usually means never. Why? Is now too dangerous?

Juan   It's not "dangerous" but it's probably better to leave it alone. Cristina . . .

He points to **Cristina***, who has fallen asleep in a chair.*

Julia   She'll make a cheerful wife. She probably snores as well.

Juan   No ella no ronca . . . pero habla dormida.

Julia   How do you know that she speaks in her sleep?

Juan (*pause*)   Because I've heard her.

Julia (*pause*)   ¿Siéntate?

Juan   I shouldn't really sit in your presence.

Julia   Y si te ordeno.

Juan   Obedezco.

Julia   Sit por favor; but, wait a moment, get me something to drink first.

Juan   I don't know what's in the icebox. Probably just cerveza.

Julia   Cerveza is fine. Personally I've simple tastes, I prefer it to wine.

Juan   ¡A su servicio!

He takes a bottle out of the refrigerator and a glass and plate, on which he serves the beer.

Julia   "Gracias." Y usted, won't you have some too?

Juan   I'm not what you might call an aficionado de la cerveza, pero si me ordena.

Julia   ¿Ordena? It seems to me that a courteous caballero might accompany his lady.

Juan   Quite right, my lady.

He takes a glass and pours for himself.

Julia   Now drink to my health! (**Juan** *hesitates.*) I do believe the big boy is blushing.

Juan (*kneels and lifts up his glass*)   ¡A la salud de mi señora!

Julia   Bravo! Now, as a finishing touch, you can kiss my shoe. (**Juan** *hesitates, then grabs hold of her foot confidently, pauses, and then kisses it lightly.*) Bravo! You should have gone on the stage.

Juan (*gets up*)   OK, Miss Julia, that's enough. Somebody might come in and see us.

Julia   So what?

Juan   People would talk, that's what, and make no mistake, la gente ya está hablando mucho.

Julia   And what do they say? "Dime," but sit down first.

Juan (*sits down*)   I don't want to hurt your feelings but they used . . . crude expressions . . . innuendoes—you can guess for yourself. You're not a child anymore, and, if a lady is seen drinking alone at night, with a man, even if it's only her "criado" then . . .

Julia   Then, then what? And, besides, we're not alone: Cristina is here.

Juan   Sí, dormida.

Julia   Then I'll wake her up. (*She gets up.*) ¿Cristina, estás dormida?

Cristina (*in her sleep*)   voy voy voy voy voy . . .

Julia   ¡Cristina! ¡Levántate! Boy, the woman can sleep!

Cristina (*in her sleep*)   Las botas del Conde ya están . . . pongo el café a la vez, ya voy, ya voy voy voy ahíííí.

Julia (*takes hold of her by the nose*)   Wake up!

Juan   ¡Déjala! Let the poor woman sleep!

Julia   How dare you!

Juan   Una persona que ha estado trabajando día y noche en la cocina tiene derecho a estar cansada por la noche y su sueño debe ser respetado.

Julia (*in another tone*)   That's very well said and does you credit. "Gracias" . . . now come out and pick some flores conmigo.

She holds her hand out to **Juan**. *During this* **Cristina** *stands, and exits in a daze.*

Juan   With you, miss?

Julia   With me . . .

Juan   Impossible, absolutamente imposible.

Julia   I don't understand. What can you possibly be imagining?

Juan   Not me, pero la gente sí.

Julia   ¿Qué? ¿Estoy enamorada de mi sirviente?

Juan   I know I'm not an educated man, pero se sabe que las cosas pasan, y no hay nada más sagrado para la gente que el chisme.

Julia   I do believe the man is an aristocrat.

Juan   Yes; yes I am.

Julia   And I'm stepping down.

Juan   Oh, no señorita, no descienda. Nadie creerá que ha descendido. People will always say you fell.

Julia   I have a better opinion of people than you do. Come and try. Venga.

Juan   Usted es muy extraña.

Julia   Perhaps I am strange, "pero tú también." Besides, everything is strange. Life, men, everything is like an iceberg which drifts, it drifts across the water until it melts and sinks. I have a reoccurring dream that haunts me. I am sitting on the top of a high pillar and can't see any possible way of getting down; when I look down I get dizzy but I know I have to get down, I must. I haven't got the courage to just jump. I can't stay where I am, I want to just fall, but I can't. And I know I won't get any peace, no rest until I've fallen and yet I know that when I get to the ground I'll want to be swallowed by the earth. Have you ever felt anything like that?

Juan   No; I usually dream I'm lying under a big tree in a dark forest. Quiero subir hasta la copa de este árbol y observar el paisaje resplandeciente donde brilla el sol, and plunder the birds' nest where the golden egg lies, así que subo y subo, but the trunk is so thick and so smooth, y es un viaje tan largo hasta esa primera rama; but I know, si solamente llego a esa primera rama, just that first branch, I can make it to the top, como si fuera una escalera. I haven't got there yet, but I'll make it, aunque solo sea un sueño.

Julia   And here I am now sharing dreams with you. Vamos, just out into the park.

She offers him her arm; he takes it slowly.

Juan   Hoy es noche de San Juan, Miss Julia, deberíamos dormir under nine Midsummer Night herbs, cacao, manzanilla, laurel, yerba buena . . . then our dreams will come true. (*They turn to go but* **Juan** *stops and covers one of his eyes.*) ¡Ay!

Julia   Something in your eye? Let me see.

Juan   Polvo. Just a bit of dust, I'll be fine.

Julia   My sleeve must have grazed your eye. Sit down and let me see. (*She takes his arm and sits him down on the table. She then takes his head in her hands, looks and blows in his eye.*) Don't move, be still! (*She strikes his hand.*) "¡TRANQUILO!" Will you obey me now? Uh . . . I do believe the big big boy is trembling. "¡Y tú tan macho!" With your big strong arms.

Juan   Miss Julia . . .

Julia   Oui, Monsieur Jean.

Juan   ¡Cuidado! Sólo soy un hombre.

Julia   Quieto hombre. There! All gone! Now kiss my hand and tell me "gracias."

Juan (*stands up*)   Miss Julia, listen to me. Cristina has left and gone to bed. Escúchame.

Julia   Kiss my hand first.

Juan   Escúchame.

Julia   Bésame la mano.

Juan   Muy bien, pero usted será responsable de las consecuencias.

Julia   What consequences?

Juan   You're not a child anymore. Don't you know it's dangerous to play with fire?

Julia   Not for me. I'm insured!

Juan   ¡¡Lo dudo!! And even if you are there's other explosive material very close.

Julia   Oh, and is that you?

Juan   ¡Un hombre es un hombre!

Julia   A man with big strong arms and incredible vanity! On my honor, Juan, I do believe you are a Don Juan!

Juan   Do you really believe that?

Julia   I almost fear it. (**Juan** *goes to embrace her.* **Julia** *slaps him.*) DOWN, BOY!

Juan   Are you serious or joking?

Julia   Seria.

Juan   En ese caso, todo lo que ha pasado es serio también, your game is serious, seriously dangerous. Yo ya me cansé, con su permiso—I have work to do.

Julia   You're so proud.

Juan   A veces sí . . . y a veces no.

Julia   Have you ever been in love?

Juan   Amor? What does that mean? Nosotros no usamos esa palabra. Querer . . . I've wanted many girls, and once I was sick not to be able to get the girl I wanted. Sick you know as those princes in *The Arabian Nights*, who couldn't eat or drink for being so sick with love.

Julia   Who was she? (*Silence.*) Dime?

Juan   Oh no. You can't make me.

Julia   If I ask you as a friend, as an equal? ¿Quién?

Juan   Tú!

Julia (*sits down*)   Now that's funny.

Juan   If you really want to know it wasn't funny—it was ridiculous. ¿Usted sabe cómo se ve el mundo desde abajo? No, por supuesto que no. Usted es como esas águilas o esos halcones, cuyas espaldas un hombre nunca puede ver porque están siempre en el aire. I grew up in a campesino's choza . . . Pero podía ver desde la ventana into the walls of your father's estate with manzanos growing overhung with fruit. Yo, y otros muchachos hambrientos, encontramos la forma de llegar a ese árbol de la vida y . . . do you despise me now?

Julia   What? For stealing apples? All boys do that.

Juan   Eso dice, but you despise me anyway. One day, with my mother I went inside of this garden of paradise, and saw a small room . . . gente entraba, gente salía, in and out all the time, the door stood open. So I sneaked in. Nunca había estado dentro de la casa de su padre y nunca había visto nada aparte de la capilla del pueblo, asi que entré, miré y . . . me senté . . . I sat on the throne like a gentleman . . . suddenly un ruido—alguien venía. Había por supuesto una salida, one door for the beautiful people, y otra para mí, and I had no choice, so I held my nose and took it . . . And then I ran and I pushed through a lilac bush, rushed through raspberry bushes and fresas and then I came out by a rose garden. There I saw a pink dress and a pair of white stockings . . . and that was you.

Julia   Don't you think that all poor boys must have the same thoughts?

Juan   That all poor boys . . . seguro.

Julia   Debe ser terrible ser pobre.

Juan (*intently*)   Ay, señorita . . . un perro puede dormir en el sofá del señor, a horse can have its muzzle petted by a lady's hand, pero un criado . . . Yes, once in a while a man has enough stuff in him to get to the top, but how often is that the case? Esperanzas? No había esperanzas de ganarla a usted. Pero usted era la prueba que no podía escapar de la clase social donde había nacido.

Julia   You know, you can tell a charming story, even that one. Did you go to school?

Juan   Escúchame, Miss Julia, please go up to your room and go to bed.

Julia   You want me to obey you?

Juan   Por primera vez, I beg you; Está cansada, está borracha. The moon is moving your blood and spinning your head. La gente viene a buscarme. Y si la encuentran aquí . . . you are lost!

Singing is heard in the distance and gets nearer.

Chorus *singing.*   *This should be a Colombian, or Spanish, suggestive, slightly raunchy carnival song, Perhaps "El Muchacho" or "Juepale" by Cumbia Soledena . . . but with lyrics. It should be a peasant/campesino song.*

Julia   I know these people, and I love them just the same that they love me. ¡QUE VENGAN! Then you'll see.

Juan   No, no no, Miss Julia. La gente no la quiere, comen su pan pero se ríen de usted! Listen to what they are singing!

Julia (*listens*)   Why? What are they singing?

Juan   ¡Chistes vulgares acerca de usted y de mí!

Julia   About us? How disgusting! They are, they're . . . CHUSMA!

Juan   Si chusma y cobardes pero no puede enfrentarles—solamente esconderse, correr.

Julia   Run? Where? We can't go out there, and we can't go to Cristina's room either.

Juan   Venga a mi habitación. La necesidad es la ley—you can trust me. I'm your true, loyal amigo de respeto.

Julia (*significantly*)   You promise me?

Juan   ¡Se lo juro!

A pause then **Julia** *runs out.* **Juan** *looks around the room; perhaps he takes a drink and then he follows her.*

The song gets louder, faster, and much raunchier. The campesinos enter. Pantomime of a mock wedding party: they drink, then make a ring and dance. Then they go out, singing again, through the door—or perhaps we just hear the song get louder and louder, faster, raunchier, and added noises of people, laughing, drinking, glasses breaking, and fighting . . . It should rise to a climax. If there is no chorus of peasants, then **Juan** *might stumble on his exit and knock over a chair, knock a bottle off the table, and make a mess.*

Act Two

Scene One

Pantomime: Dawn of the next morning. **Julia** *enters slowly and sees the mess in the kitchen. She picks up* **Cristina**'s *mirror—perhaps it is on the floor—and sees herself. Her makeup is smeared. She touches her hair or face . . . it is perhaps an understated version of "the walk of shame."* **Juan** *enters quickly.*

Juan Do you think it's possible to stay here now?

Julia No. But what can we do?

Juan Correr, lejos, far away from here.

Julia Lejos? Yes, but where?

Juan ¡Al norte! México, Miami, Nueva York . . . Panamá, have you ever been to Panamá?

Julia No; is it nice there?

Juan Oh! Panamá is beautiful! They have . . . a canal.

Julia But what would we do there?

Juan Panamá está lleno de turistas. Podríamos abrir un hotel allí, "first class services for first class tourists!"

Julia A hotel? That sounds fine, very nice, but first you must give me courage. Juan . . . Take me in your arms and tell me "Te amo."

Juan No puedo, no aquí, no en esta casa. I want to. No debe dudar esto, Miss Julia.

Julia Miss? There's no barriers between us now. Not "usted," but "Tú." Llámame: "Julietita."

Juan No puedo. En esta casa no somos iguales.

Julia I am leaving all that behind. Juan tell me "te amo" if you don't then—what am I?

Juan I'll say it a thousand times but not here, not now—después . . . But now, no scenes—no drama, or we will lose everything. We must quietly examine everything, quietly, like sensible people. You sit here, I'll sit there; tendremos una conversación como si nada hubiera pasado.

Julia O my God! Have you no heart?

Juan Ningún hombre siente más que yo, pero me controlo.

Julia But last night you kissed my shoe!

Juan Yes, that was then but this is now and we have other things to think about.

Julia   Don't speak so brutally to me.

Juan   I'm not brutal just "sensible." We made a foolish mistake once—pero no más. Besides, what do you think of my plans for the future? Do you agree?

Julia   They seem fine, but one question, for such big plans you need big capital. Have you got it?

Juan   Of course I got it! I've got my special expertise, my professional experiencia, my knowledge of English, I think that's a lot of capital.

Julia   But that won't pay for a single train ticket.

Juan   That's why I need somebody to finance the operation.

Julia   Where can you find someone and quickly?

Juan   Well, that will be your job if you want to be mi mujer.

Julia   Oh, no! I couldn't do that, and besides I have got nothing myself.

Juan   Entonces, ni modo.

Julia   And?

Juan   Everything stays the way it was, the way it is.

Julia   Do you think I'll stay under this roof as your—amante? Do you think I will let the people point their dirty fingers at me, that I could look my father in the face? No! Take me away from here, take me away from all this shame and dishonor! O my God! What have I done! O God! God!

Juan   "Oh my God what have I done! What have I done!" La misma cancioncita, as a thousand other girls.

Julia   And now you despise me? I'm falling, falling!

Juan   Caiga, caiga a mi nivel, y yo la levantaré.

Julia   What horrible power dragged me down to you, the attraction of the weak to the strong? Falling down to someone rising? Or was it love? Was that love! Do you even know what love is?

Juan   Me da lástima . . . but I admit once upon a time when I hid in onions and saw you in the rose garden, I had the same dirty thoughts as many other criados.

Julia   But you said you wanted to die for me!

Juan   O, esta historia era pura mierda.

Julia   You were lying?

Juan   ¿Qué querías? Women like romantic stories.

Julia   ¡Mentiroso!

Juan   ¡Mierda!

Julia   Was I only the first branch?

Juan   Yes, but the first branch is rotten!

Julia   Was I to be the advertising for the hotel?

Juan   Yo soy el hotel.

Julia   Sit in your office, smile for the tourists, fake your bills.

Juan   Yo hago eso.

Julia   How can a human soul be so filthy!

Juan   ¡Lávate la jeta primero! Your face is dirty.

Julia   Servant! Lackey! You stand up when I talk to you.

Juan   ¡Cállate el hocico hija de puta! ¡Quieres que sea grosero? ¡Crees que alguna criada haría lo que tú hiciste? Do you think that a nice girl, a lady, gets a man hot the way you do? Have you ever seen a servant offer herself the way you did. No solo los perros y las putas.

Julia   That's right, hit me, kick me when I'm down. I deserve it all. I'm a miserable wretch. But help me! Help me out of this if there's some, any, way.

Juan   It was an honor seducing you, I accept my share, pero usted piensa que una persona como yo se habría atrevido siquiera a mirar a una persona como usted if you hadn't invited me to?

Julia   You are so proud.

Juan   Run away with me.

Julia   Run away? Yes, of course run away. (*She looks at her dress.*) But I'm so tired. Give me a glass of wine. (**Juan** *pours a glass.* **Julia** *looks around the room.*) We'll run away, but we'll talk first, I mean, I will talk, because up till now you've done all the talking. You've told me all about your life, now I'll tell you about mine so we will know the truth about each other before we begin our journey. (**Julia** *drinks the wine and holds out the glass for more.*)

Juan   Perhaps you should reconsider revealing your secrets before you regret it.

Julia   ¿No eres mi amigo?

Juan   A veces sí . . . (*He fills her glass.*) but don't trust me too much.

Julia   I don't think you really mean that. Besides, everybody knows my secrets. My mother—was a commoner, with a distinct aversion to marriage. When my father proposed, she said that she would never be his wife but they could be lovers. And so they were cut off from his world and social circle. Then I came into the world against the wishes of my mother, so she brought me up to be a child of nature, and I had to learn everything a boy learns, so that I could be a living example that a woman is as good as a man. She taught me to mistrust and hate men, because she hated men, and I swore to her that I would never be a slave—to any man.

Juan   But you were engaged to that gentleman.

Julia   He was to be my slave.

Juan   Pero él no quería.

Julia   Oh he wanted it . . . . I didn't, I got sick of him.

Juan   I saw you two in the stable.

Julia   What did you see?

Juan   How he broke off the engagement.

Julia   ¡Mentira! I broke off the engagement. Did he say that? The little swine!

Juan   Do you really hate all men, Miss Julia?

Julia   Most of the time . . . but sometimes I get weak. (*She pours herself more wine.*)

Juan   So you hate me as well?

Julia   Infinitely. I'd like to have you slaughtered like a beast. (*She drinks.*)

Juan   I told you to stop drinking, it makes people talk too much and some people shouldn't talk.

Julia   I'm sorry, I'm sorry for it all, the drink, the talk . . . everything! If only you loved me!

Juan   What do you want me to do? Do you want me to cry, to jump over your whip; do you want me to kiss you, or seduce you for three weeks and then what? What? Eso ya me cansa, por eso es mejor no meterse con mujeres. Miss Julia, I know that you suffer, I know that you're unhappy, pero no la entiendo. Entre nosotros esto no pasa, nosotros no odiamos. We don't hate each other, el amor es un juego when work is done and we have a bit of free time but we don't spend día y noche talking about it, we don't have time for fairy tales, we have to work! Look at you, you're sick and your mother was mad.

Julia   I can't stay I can't go. ¡Ayúdame Juan! I am so tired, dead tired. Juan, ¡ordéname! Help me, make me move or . . . I can't think anymore, and I can't . . . anything.

Juan   Que criatura tan miserable. ¡Bueno te ordeno! You! Go, up to your room change your clothes, get some money for the travel and then come right back down here!

Julia (*gently*)   Come up with me.

Juan   ¡A su habitación? ¡Más que loca está demente, vaya!

Julia   Juan, speak kindly to me, por favor.

Juan   An order never sounds kind. Now you know how it feels. (**Julia** *exits.*) NOW YOU KNOW!

Scene Two (Spanish)

Cristina *enters dressed for church. She sees the chao in the kitchen and stops.*

Cristina   Pero dios mío ¿qué es todo este desorden? ¿Qué pasó aquí?

Juan   ¡Nada! La señorita invitó a la chusma a que entrara. ¿Pero como dormías, tú no te diste cuenta de nada, o sí?

Cristina   ¡Caí como una piedra!

Juan   Y ya lista para ir a la iglesia . . .

Cristina   ¡Pues ya me ves! ¡Prometiste venir conmigo, hay que comulgar hoy!

Juan   ¡Sí, es cierto . . . hay que comulgar hoy! ¿Qué evangélico toca hoy?

Cristina   Pues es el Día de San Juan . . . supongo que será el de la degollación de San Juan Bautista. (*She pulls his hair or perhaps yanks his collar.*)

Juan   ¡Ay, suave, Cristina! (*Pause.*) Estoy cansado, tengo sueño.

Cristina   Sí, ¿y qué has estado haciendo mi señor, despierto toda la noche? ¡Tienes una cara!

Juan   Nada, aquí, "talking with Miss Julia"!

Cristina   ¿Cómo que . . .talking? ¡Esa niñita no se sabe comportar!

Juan   Oye, Cristina . . .

Cristina   Dime.

Juan   Es todo bien raro, sabes . . .

Cristina   ¿Qué es lo que te parece tan raro?

Juan   ¡Todo! Ella, Si uno se para a pensar.

Cristina   ¿Pero no me digas que estabas bebiendo con la Señorita Julia anoche?

Juan   Eh . . .

Cristina   ¡Vergüenza! ¡Mírame a los ojos! (**Cristina** *sniffs him.*) ¿Es posible? ¿Es posible?

Juan   Pues sí!

Cristina   ¡Pufftt ¡Jamás lo hubiera creído! ¡Jamás! ¡Sin vergüenza! ¡Ayyy. ¡Qué asco!

Juan   ¿No me digas que estás celosa?

Cristina   ¿Celosa yo? ¿De ella? ¿NO! ¡Si hubiera sido Clara o Sofía hasta te saco los ojos! ¡Pero Miss Julia, me da asco!

Juan   Entonces . . . ¿estás enfadada con ella?

Cristina   ¡Con ella no, gran pendejo- contigo! ¡Esto fue mal hecho, muy mal hecho! ¡Ha sido una desgracia! ¡China pendeja! Y ¿sabes qué? ¡Yo no quiero seguir en esta casa, una casa donde no puedo respetar a mis padrones!

Juan   ¿Y por qué tenemos que respetarlos?

Cristina   ¿Y me lo preguntas tú que eres tan listo? ¿Es que puedes servir a señores que se conducen en esa forma? Nos desharíamos.

Juan   Sin embargo, es un gran consuelo el pensar que ellos no son mejores que nosotros. Now I know, "we are all the same"!

Cristina   ¡Pues no! ¿No estoy de acuerdo, porque si ellos no son mejores que nosotros qué sentido tiene trabajar toda una vida para ser gente decente? ¡Y además pobre el señor! ¡Con todo lo que ha tenido que vivir! No quiero quedarme en esta casa . . . ¡Y además con un hombre como tú! ¡Si al menos hubiera sido con su novio o alguien de su clase como Dios manda . . . pero tú!

Juan   I'm better than them! ¿Y a mí que me falta?

Cristina   Nada, tú estás bastante bien para lo que eres, pero recuerda que todavía hay diferencias entre unas gentes y otras. ¡No, yo nunca podré olvidar esto de la Señorita! Ella, tan orgullosa, tan maltratada de hombres . . . ¡y a un tipo como tú! ¿Sabes que? "I QUIT!" (*Pause.*) El mismo día veinticuatro de octubre me voy!

Juan   ¿Y entonces?

Cristina   Y entonces, ya que estamos en esto, va siendo hora de que busques un trabajo para que nos casemos.

Juan   De casado ya no podré trabajar en una casa como ésta.

Cristina   ¡Eso se sabe! Pero siempre podrías trabajar de portero o con el estado. Ya sabemos que no pagan bien, pero la viuda y los hijos, por lo menos, se quedan con una pensión.

Juan   Ándale, ve termina de arreglarte y nos vamos a la iglesia.

She looks at him and then exits back to her room.

Scene Three (Mostly English)

Julia *enters dressed and washed, carrying a small covered birdcage.*

Julia   I'm ready now.

Juan   Shhh! Cristina's awake.

Julia   Does she know anything?

Juan   No.

Julia   Juan, listen to me. Come with me, I've got the money now!

Juan   How much?

Julia   Enough to begin with. Come with me, I can't go alone, not today. I can't, I can't!

Juan   I'll come with you. But now before it's too late.

Julia   ¡Sí! You get ready. (*Picks up the birdcage.*)

Juan   No luggage. That would only give us away.

Julia   No luggage. Only what we can carry.

Juan   What do you have there?

Julia   Only my canary—my little pajarito. I couldn't bear to leave her behind.

Juan   ¡Por dios! A bird cage? ¡Más que loca! No, leave the pajarito.

Julia   Just one thing from home; the only living creature that loves me! Don't be so cruel! Let me take her!

Juan   Leave the cage.

Julia   I won't leave her with strangers . . . I'd rather you killed her!

Juan   Bueno. Dámela.

Julia   I . . . ayyyy . . . alright, but don't let her suffer. (*She hesitantly offers the cage but then grabs it back.*) No, I can't! I can't!

Juan   Pero I can!

Swiftly and dispassionately he chops the bird's neck.

Julia (*screams*)   Kill me too! Kill me! If you can slaughter an innocent creature without your hand shaking, kill me. Oh, I hate you. I loathe you! Maldito! There's blood between us now! I curse the moment I saw you, I curse the disgusting moment I was conceived in my mother's womb! ¡Maldito!

Juan   ¡Me importa un culo sus maldiciones! ¡Vámonos!

Julia   No, todavía no—no puedo—(*Approaches the chopping block, drawn against her will.*)

– quiero ver . . . (*Listens to the sounds outside while gazing at the block.*) Do you think I can't bear the sight of blood? Do you think I'm so weak? Oh, I'd like to see your blood, your brains, on this chopping block. I'd like to see your whole sex, swimming in a sea of blood, like this. I could drink from your skull, wash my feet in your open breast, I'd roast your heart and eat it. You think I'm weak; you think I love you, that my womb desired your evil seed; you think I want to carry your hijo beneath my heart, nourish it with my blood, bear your breed and take your name? Wait a minute, what is your name? Do you even have a real "nombre"? What is your surname? SIR? I've never heard it. You probably haven't got one. Would I become "Mrs. Gatekeeper" or "Señora Bootblack"? You perro, with my collar around your neck. Am I to share you with my cook? Compete with my maid? Oh! NO! You think I'm a coward who wants to run away? No, I'm staying now, let the storm come! My father will come home soon, find his desk broken open and his money gone. Then he'll ring that bell, twice for his "criado." Then he'll call the police and I'll tell them everything. All of it. Then he'll have a stroke and die, and that perhaps will finally end it. Quiet, peace, eternal rest. Our coat of arms will be buried in his coffin. El linage del señor will be extinguished and the hijo del criado will wind up in an orphanage, learning about life in the gutter and end up in jail.

Juan (*softly*)   Bravo, Miss Julia!

Cristina *enters, dressed for church, carrying a Bible.* **Julia** *staggers to her and falls into her arms.*

Scene Four (Bilingual)

Julia   Cristina! Help me! Ayúdame con ese hombre.

Cristina   ¡Qué locuras son éstas en el día de San Juan? (*She sees the blood.*) ¿Qué porquería han hecho ustedes aquí? ¿Por qué alborota—why you scream?

Julia   Cristina, tu eres mujer, mi amiga. Beware of this animal!

Juan (*quietly*)   While you ladies are talking, I'll go and shave. (*Exits.*)

Julia   You'll understand me; you must listen to me!

Cristina   No, yo no entiendo nada de estos subterfugios. (*She looks closely at* **Julia**.)
¿Qué hace usted vestida así? ¿Where you going?

Julia   Escúchame Cristina, listen to me and I'll tell you . . . todo!

Cristina   ¡NO! ¡Yo no quiero saber nada!

Julia   Escucha—por favor

Cristina   ¿Qué? ¿Sus tonterías con Juan? ¡No señorita ya lo ve usted que no me importa! Pero si usted intenta largarse, entonces yo les corto el camino.

Julia   Cálmete Cristina y escúchame. No puedo quedarme aquí, y Juan tampoco. I can't—¡Tengo una idea! Por qué no nos vamos, los tres . . . to Panamá! Podemos abrir un hotel. Tengo dinero. And Juan and I could run the hotel and you, well I thought you could be the cocinera! Wouldn't that be fun? Yes? Please say yes! Dime si, Cristina. You'll be . . .. ¡Cristina de la cocina! You won't have to slave over the hot stove yourself, no you'll be nicely dressed when you bring the food to the guests. And with your looks, no es burla, Cristina one day you'll catch a husband, a rich American—oh they're so easy to catch!—and we'll be rich and build ourselves a little villa on a mountain . . .

Cristina   Miss Julia, do you believe esta historia?

Julia (*long pause*)   Believe?

Cristina   ¿Sí, sí, usted cree esto?

Julia (*tired*)   No sé . . . I don't know what I believe anymore. (*She lowers her head to the table.*) Nothing! (*She bangs her head softly.*) Nada, nada, nada.

Cristina (**Juan** *has entered with an open razor and a towel around his neck.*)   ¿Así es que pensabas largarte desgraciado?

Juan (*carefully lays the straight razor on the table*)   Tanto como largarme no. ¿Pero escuchaste la propuesta de la Señorita Julia? Aunque la señorita esté muy cansada por . . . falta de sueño, el proyecto no es un sueño, es perfectamente realizable.

Cristina   ¿Así que es tuya la idea de que yo le siga cocinando a ésta?

Juan (*harshly*)   Debes emplear palabras más apropiadas cuando hables de tu señora.

Cristina   ¿Mi señora?

Juan   Tu señora.

Cristina   ¡Esto es lo último que me faltaba!

Juan   ¡Lo que te falta es esto! ¡Hablar menos y escuchar más! ¡La señorita Julia es todavía tu señora y si la desprecias a ella te desprecias a ti

Cristina   Yo siempre he tenido respeto por mí misma . . .

Juan   . . . ¡y siempre has podido despreciar a los demás!

Cristina   Nunca me he rebajado de mi condición. ¡Vienes ahora a la iglesia—o no? Porque después de lo que ha sucedido—(*She looks at* **Julia**.) last night! ¡Necesitas un sermón—bien grande!

Juan   No, hoy no voy a la iglesia: es mejor que vayas sola ha confesar todos tus pecados.

Cristina   You see it, Miss Julia? Now I go to the church—alone. Y al pasar ordenaré que no salga ningún caballo hasta que vuelva el señor, no horse, no travel, no way . . . Adiós.

She exits.

Juan   ¡Zapa! ¡Metida! Todo por un puto pájaro.

Julia   Leave the bird out of this. Well, do you see a way out of this? Any way to end it at all?

Juan   No.

Julia   What would you do if you were me?

Pantomime: **Juan** *looks at her and then slowly lowers his gaze.* **Julia** *follows his gaze, looks down at the razor on table between them. They both go to touch the razor—their hands meet. They look up at each other with mingled intentions. They both push the table towards each other* hard *and it flows into a battle of wills, a dance/movement sequence. A stylized series of actions and images drawn from the previous staging and scored to a hard passionate, dissonant version of the chorus song at the end of Act One.*

These sequences should be both fast and slow, with strong stops full of intent and subtext; it should be more expressionistic than naturalistic. It grows in tempo and intensity, it is very violent but they rarely and barely touch each other. **Julia** *and* **Juan** *are equal partners in this dance and in the end perhaps* **Julia** *is the stronger.*

Fin—End.

El Apagón (The Blackout)

Adapted by Rosalba Rolón, Jorge Merced, and Alvan Colón Lespier

Pregones Theater—the Bronx, New York City, New York

6 Pregones/PRTT's *El Apagón/The Blackout* at Puerto Rican Traveling Theater, 304 West 47th Street, New York, NY, 2014. Photo: Marisol Díaz.

Snapshot
Chantal Rodriguez

Pregones/Puerto Rican Traveling Theater (Pregones/PRTT) is a pillar of US Latinx theater. Stewarding two bilingual arts facilities in the Bronx and Manhattan, the historic company is not only a multigenerational ensemble but also a multidisciplinary arts presenter. PRTT was founded in 1967 by the legendary Miriam Colón, as one of the first bilingual theater companies in the United States. PRTT had a profound influence on the training of generations of Latinx theater artists, and developed innovative community engagement and touring models. Pregones Theater was founded in 1979 by a group of artists led by Rosalba Rolón, committed to creating new work in the style of Latin American ensembles, or "colectivos." While based in the Bronx, Pregones has performed in over 400 cities and thirteen countries. The two powerhouse, award-winning companies merged in 2014 and, under the leadership of Rolón, Pregones/ PRTT continues to honor the mission of championing Puerto Rican and Latinx cultural legacies through the performance of original plays and musicals, exchange and partnership with other artists, and engagement of diverse audiences.[1]

Lovingly referred to as "the quintessential Boricua play." *El Apagón* (*The Blackout*) is one of Pregones' most beloved and critically acclaimed plays. *El Apagón* premiered at Pregones in the spring of 1992 and has since been performed throughout the United States and internationally.[2] *El Apagón* is an award-winning adaptation of the short story "La noche que volvimos a ser gente" (The night we became people again) by José Luis González. Performed bilingually in Spanish and English, with accompanying supertitles, the play includes popular Spanish songs from the 1950s and 1960s played live by a band on stage, combining theater, music, movement, and oral storytelling tradition in Pregones' hallmark style.

The Encuentro de las Américas production featured veteran actor and original cast member Jorge B. Merced, alongside singer, poet, and actor Flaco Navaja, and an ensemble of talented musicians including Hammadi Bayard, Waldo Chávez, Desmar Guevara, and Nicky Laboy. Beautifully adapted by Alvan Colón-Lespier, Jorge B. Merced, and Rosabla Rolón, the play features two characters, a Puerto Rican factory worker and his best friend Trompoloco, as they navigate the Great Northeastern Blackout of 1965.[3]

As the lights come up, the image of a simple bar and the sound of a saxophone welcomes the audience. Under Rolón's deft direction, Merced and Navaja seamlessly switch roles throughout the storytelling and they begin by simultaneously declaring "¿Que si me acuerdo?!" (Do I remember?!) answering an implied question about the blackout from the audience. The hilarious and heartwarming story that follows recounts the factory worker's experience of needing to leave work early after being alerted to his wife's going into labor by his best friend Trompoloco. While riding the subway uptown from Brooklyn to El Barrio, the pair are caught in the blackout. Through language, humor, and music, the factory worker weaves social and cultural commentary into the story, highlighting the monotony of assembly-line work, the fear and absurdity of being trapped in the subway, the relief of finally arriving home, and the awe of witnessing the miracle of new life.

Basking in the joy of meeting his first-born son, the factory worker is suddenly drawn to the rooftop of his building by the sounds of an impromptu party. While the blackout caused New York to come to a halt, the darkness allowed the stars to shine as brightly as they do in Puerto Rico on any night of the year, prompting a celestial celebration in El Barrio. "After so many years of not seeing stars, we forgot they existed . . . that was the night that we became people again," he joyfully exclaims.

El Apagón was one of the biggest hits of the Encuentro de las Américas. Despite the joyful tone of the piece, playing during the aftermath of Hurricane Maria the image of a blackout affecting thousands of Puerto Ricans was sobering. A special benefit performance of *El Apagón* was presented as part of the festival on November 10, 2017 in association with the Latino Theater Company, Hero Theatre, Taller Kurubina, and Cunyá. All proceeds for the event benefited Pregones/PRTT's Hurricane Maria Relief Drive for Artists and the Pa'Arriba Puerto Rico Hurricane Relief Fund. Ultimately, *El Apagón* reminded the festival artists and audiences about the courage, strength, humor, and resilience of diasporic communities as it invited us to tell our stories, and embrace our beautiful, fragile humanity.

Notes

1 For a detailed history of both the Puerto Rican Traveling Theater and Pregones, visit:
   https://pregonesprtt.org/about/
2 *El Apagón* was revived in 2007 to celebrate its fifteenth anniversary. An archival recording
   of that performance is available through the Hemispheric Institute Digital Video library:
   https://hemi.nyu.edu/hemi/en/hidvl-profiles/item/1820-pregones-apagon
3 The biggest power failure in US history, the Great Northeastern Blackout, impacted all of
   New York State, parts of seven neighboring states, and parts of eastern Canada. All together
   30 million people were affected and power was gradually restored after twelve hours.

Sensory Strategies

A Panel from the Encuentro de las Américas

7 Panel: Sensory Strategies at the 2017 Latinx Theatre Commons International Convening at Encuentro de las Américas. Photo by Bracero L.A.

Sensory Strategies

Artist Panel from the Encuentro de las Américas with Carmen Aguirre, Jorge Cao, Carlos Celdrán, David Lozano, Alicia Olivares, Brian Quirt, Roció Carrillo Reyes, Rosalba Rolón, Nicolás Valdez, and José Luis Valenzuela (Introduced and Moderated by Chantal Rodriguez)

The following discussion took place on November 11, 2017 at the Los Angeles Theatre Center, as part of the Latinx Theatre Commons International Convening at the Encuentro de las Américas festival, produced by the Latino Theater Company. This panel discussion was one of four large group sessions that all convening participants attended together, and sought to engage festival artists in conversation about their relationship to their aesthetics, process, and how their local communities influence their work. The panelists represent the following festival companies and productions: *Dementia* (the Latino Theater Company, Los Angeles); *Quemar las naves. El viaje de Emma* (Organización Secreta Teatro, Mexico); *El Apagón* (Pregones Theatre, New York); *Conjunto Blues* (Guadalupe Cultural Arts Center, Texas); *Broken Tailbone* (Nightswimming, Canada); *10 Millones* (Argos Teatro, Cuba); *Deferred Action* (Cara Mía Theatre Co., Texas); *Las Mariposas Saltan al Vacío* (Compañía Nacional de las Artes, Colombia). The event was presented in English and Spanish with live simultaneous interpretation via headphones. This transcription is presented in English with Spanish translations by Amauta Marston-Firmino.

Chantal Rodriguez   First I'd like to ask José Luis, Rocio, and Alicia: Does your company have a specific aesthetic, or does it change with each show?

José Luis Valenzuela (*translated from Spanish*)   I think so. In the last fifteen years, we've been on an [artistic] search. We make very specific theater especially for the Chicano middle class. And maybe it comes from there, this idea that we're never represented. I'm Mexican, almost Chicano, but we never see the Chicano or Mexican community represented in a way that's inclusive of who we really are. I'm a professor, and the people in the [Latino Theater] Company are all professionals, so our conversations around aesthetics always carry that idea. For example, with our production of *Solitude*, we adapted Octavio Paz's *The Labyrinth of Solitude*; and with *Premeditation*, we called it "Chicano Noir."

The Latino Theater Company has been together as a company in Los Angeles for thirty-two years, with the same members. Two members died, and one left the company. We have the actors [Sal Lopez, Geoffrey Rivas, Lucy Rodriguez] and Evelina Fernández, the playwright. Although we began as a collective devising ensemble, we later developed our roles so that she was writing the scripts and I was directing.

Rocío Carrillo Reyes (*translated from Spanish*)   Perhaps our aesthetic has changed with time. Our company was formed over twenty years ago, and some of our members have been with us for that long. The cast you saw are the youngest and most recent members, who I've been working with for around seven or eight years.

If I could speak about an aesthetic that defines our group, it would have to be something that was not, at first, an artistic intention, but rather a result of experimentation. *Quemar las naves* is the second piece we've made without words. We've had other processes in which there is a hybrid product—there are words, but words are not always what gives the piece form. We don't always stick to a particular dramatic structure, or a genre, or a style. So, there is hybridity in our *mise en scène*. Everything is present—words, images, sound—as a soundtrack but also as live music—forming a type of dramaturgy that conjoins physical actions, marks movement and contains it, as if it were a scenic score.

Perhaps what's been a constant is our work with images, which occurs over a long process. We look for images that are inhabited by emotions—the actors, with their gestures, their movements. But I don't want to define the theater that we make as a theater of images. I don't want to define it in any way. At this point, when we talk about drama, we're talking about an enormous amount of possibilities and a growing diversification of scenic languages.

Alicia Olivares (*translated from Spanish*)   Well, Ébano Teatro's first production just two years ago was *Fences* by August Wilson. It was the first theatrical production with a full cast of black actors in Peru. There had never been an all-black production before—because of all manner of excuses. Always, the directors and producers would say: "There are no black actors." So, as an actress—as I graduated from theater school—I saw this gap that exists in my country. Even now that I'm at the Encuentro, I see that it exists all over the world. There is a need for Afro-Latino actors to find a space, a voice within the artistic medium. I think that's important. And that motivates me, because I thought this gap was something that was only existed in my country. But when you face other realities, you identify yourself more, and you think to yourself: "We're going down the right path."

After *Fences* we had this platform for black actors and voices. In October of 2017, we produced *Ropa Íntima*. In terms of the aesthetic of our theater, I'm drawn to text-based work, work that transmits, that has something important to say, that transcends, and that touches the heart. Work that speaks about love, about identity. When the audience goes to see the work, I want them to leave heartbroken.

Rodriguez   Nicolás, who are your artistic ancestors and how do they influence your approach to your work?

Nicolás Valdez   In San Antonio and in Texas, we have a long history of *teatro* that goes back to the *Carpas*, which were started in the latter part of the eighteenth century, and proliferated probably around the nineteenth century up to the 1920s and 1930s. For those of you who aren't familiar with the *Carpas*, these were traveling tent shows, performed mostly in Spanish. They traveled freely across the border, and were based loosely on *commedia dell'arte*. There were acrobatics involved, there was music. Often times they would take the lyrics of popular songs and change them, typically to provide comedy but also social commentary. There were *comicos* (comics)—they didn't like to be called *payasos* (clowns)—as well as *actos*. There was a big fire in one of the major circus acts, and several hundred people died in this accident, so new regulations were enforced on the *Carpas* and the materials that they used, and companies couldn't afford to produce them anymore. So that *Carpa* tradition began to die out.

The *Carpas* were replaced by these basically vaudeville acts in houses that did a lot of the same work. They called them *Teatro Variedades*. There were several in San Antonio that existed for a long time: this was the Teatro Nacional, Teatro Zaragoza, as well as The Alameda. Those were extremely popular. They were based on one side of town, and the other *teatros* on the other side of town were for the Americans, the English-speaking audiences. Of course, we were always marginalized historically. Then, when film came out, those houses became movie houses.

There was a lull in the production of that kind of work until of course El Teatro Campesino reinvigorated the Chicano community to start doing *actos*. The Guadalupe was founded by a group of actors who came out of that same school and started producing work at the Guadalupe Cultural Arts Center in the early 1980s. And so that same aesthetic tradition was continued.

Our aesthetic continues to be defined by the resources available to us—really, the lack of resources. The *Teatro Rasquache* happened because they had to make their own props and costumes. In the *Carpa* tradition, they did it all—they sewed the tents themselves, they made all the props and costumes, and they would set it up themselves. They would often sleep on the stage, because they had nowhere else to go. That tradition continues at the Guadalupe in the kind of work that we continue to do.

The Guadalupe is a cultural arts center. We're not just a *teatro*. We have a music program, a literary program, a dance program, a film program. It's a big monster. Of course, the work has had its lulls over the years, and several people have commented on that. But there's a resurgence that's happening in San Antonio and the Guadalupe Cultural Arts Center, and I'm really happy to be part of this *nuevo movimiento de teatro* [new movement in theater].

I am a product of the Guadalupe's programming. I started taking accordion classes there when I was eight years old, and I was a member of the resident youth theater company. To have that experience of being empowered and encouraged to speak in our own voice has informed the way that I continue to work—combining elements of music, poetry, and, of course, the *teatro*, in a way that continues to provide some historical contexts for us as *Tejanos*. We've been stripped of our history through the political and the educational systems, and so the work that we do is important. It's based on historical figures and historical moments, because a lot of that has been taken away from us. And so, my show *Conjunto Blues* really aims to bring attention back to an art form that was so important in the development of the Mexican American community here in the United States.

Rodriguez   Rosalba, Carlos, and David: What is your process in creating a show? Do you begin with a text, an idea, a song, maybe a historical document, or a political issue?

Rosalba Rolón   We start from all of the above in many ways. We began our work in the 1970s with *teatro popular* as an inspiration. It was just *teatro de la calle* (street theater)—going to places, performing everywhere we could find a space. I always like to remind us that our first staged reading took place in a friend's apartment that accommodated just eleven people. Ten were seated, and one was standing, so I always say we had standing room only for our first reading, which was true.

Because it is ensemble-based and we approached the process as *creacion colectiva* [collective devising/creation] from the beginning, there have always been multiple voices in how we shape a project. That's more and more the case as we are joined by new generations of ensemble members. Right now, for example, I am artistic director, but we also have Jorge Merced as associate artistic director, Alvan [Colón-Lespier] as associate artistic director, and each one of us brings ideas and projects to the table.

For example, *El Apagón* (*The Blackout*), which we'll be performing at the Encuentro, originated when Alvan came one day and said, "I'm in love with this short story," Why? Basically, because most of our repertoire is based on non-dramatic texts that have been adapted to the theater. We just get such an urge whenever we see something—whether it's a grandmother's recipe turned into a song, it doesn't matter—if it's not theater, we want to turn it into theater and create something new out of it. That's why we have so many historical pieces. But we make a large variety of work.

When we begin the process we immediately involve our main composer and musical director, Desmar Guevara. He comes in with his own vision of the project and challenges the idea. We have always used live music, and we strive to strike a balance between form and content. Our work is very rooted in the Puerto Rican experience, in the United States or in Puerto Rico. But we don't approach ethnic identity or identity politics as our main subject. We want to have the freedom to approach as many themes as possible. We do share a common aesthetic core, and that helps us launch the idea and begin to knead all that information into what will become a dramatic text, what will become lyrics, what will become music and imagery.

Carlos Celdrán (*translated from Spanish*)   Argos Teatro always begins with something from our lived reality in Cuba: something that interests us, that is close to us, and interesting to present and to touch upon. It comes from a meditation on reality with the group. We are always looking for topics that are interesting to us and to our audiences, because those are the experiences that create a living theater. If it's not alive, we're only representing something. We are always on the edge of representation, or transgressing representation, looking for themes that are deeply part of our biographies, not just as actors or theater artists, but as people who live in this society and share an urgent and permanent dialogue with it.

That's the first step. And we always argue. There's always a struggle to find the text, because we always find a text or depart from a text to arrive at the problem—we either adapt it or transform it, or it's already been written. There are many sources that help us arrive at the theme of our projects.

David Lozano   At Cara Mía Theatre Company, we have a different process for each project. For example, *To die:go in Leaves by Frida Kahlo* was a devised piece. We actually began with Kahlo's paintings. We created movement sequences based on the paintings and we read as many books as possible. We were also drawn to images in the biographies. So, for example, there's a story of when Frida Kahlo was bedridden as a child with polio, and she would draw a door on her misty window, and imagine walking through that door into the dream world of a ballerina. That was a very vivid image. Then, of course, the image of the trolley accident.

While we're looking through all of this biographical information, we're looking at the paintings. I remember looking at a painting called *Moses*, which is phantasmagoric, with all of these historical figures. I just happened to be at the bookstore—when we still had bookstores in Dallas—and I walked down the aisle and I saw that the painting was inspired by a book by Sigmund Freud. I happened to be walking through the bookstore, not looking for it, and I just saw the book, and I started reading it. And the thesis of the book is that our mythical heroes are usually injured at a young age, and then they gain powers that allow them to transcend their circumstances. So the trolley accident became a phantasmagoria in the play, that became one of her injuries through which she was able to gain strength. In the play, we broke up the sequence of the trolley accident and interspersed historical scenes between different segments. While the accident took place she had this dreamlike experience that recalled her fantasies from while she was bedridden. All of this was brought together by the ensemble. Everyone was reading different books, and we were all looking at different paintings. None of us had full-time jobs at this point so we were working about eight hours a day for about eight weeks, and we were able to put that together.

For *Deferred Action* [2016], we took this process into the studio as a co-production with the Dallas Theater Center, the LORT theater in Dallas. We started working on our feet in similar ways, because we're always looking for that impulse that comes from the performer, that heartbeat, and how we can bring that to the stage—rather than just a calculated, technical process. We started by creating improvisations of movements with five company members from both companies. And we started discovering characters; for example, the character of Darrel Jenkins was developed by the impulses of an actor in a split-second, and is one of the main characters in our current production. But since Dallas Theater Center is a union house, we weren't actually able to spend that many hours working on that kind of devising process and really delving into that. So, we only had about two weeks of that kind of process, because we couldn't afford it.

After that, the director of new play development from Dallas Theater Center, Lee Trull, and I went off to write the play. At that point I was reading the newspaper religiously, multiple newspapers every day. I started seeing dynamics play out as we headed into the primaries. For example, Hillary Clinton would be protested by DACAmented adults during her rallies, saying that she wasn't speaking up on immigration reform. And then two weeks later she would hire a DACAmented youth to become the director of Latino outreach. So, we're looking at these kinds of patterns, and then soon we saw Jeb Bush announce in his campaign that he wanted to deliver a path for full citizenship for all eleven million undocumented immigrants. So, we found our play in the newspapers. And that became the problem of the play. That's what we carried through. After that, it became a process of dramaturgy with text.

Rodriguez   I have a two-part question for Jorge, Carmen, and Brian. How do your collaborators influence the aesthetics of your work, and how does your artistic practice intersect with your community?

Jorge Cao (*translated from Spanish*)   I come from a long tradition of Cuban theater that evidently has a European influence. The great artists of the last sixty or seventy years in Cuba started translating all of that influence and transforming it into a totally national theater. When I arrived in Colombia, having done my training in Moscow, I was received as a Russian actor from the way I translated that training to our mannerisms. I began directing work wherever I could, going from *novela* to *novela* [soap opera to soap opera]—in other words, I made money in television and spent it on the theater. That way of working has been a constant for twenty-five years.

Four years ago, I found a group of young theater artists coming out of training with the Teatro Libre de Bogotá, who wanted to become independent and make their own work. They wanted to find their own methods, to make work that is representative of what they think, and with the world in which they live. For me, that was very revitalizing, because they were very young, they're almost my children, my grandchildren even. This company became Compañía Nacional de Los Artes.

When they asked that I direct something, I really didn't know what to do. I proposed several titles, and then we decided on *Las Mariposas Saltan al Vacio* by a Cuban playwright, José Milián. I took away Milian's structure, I took away the particularities or specific details about Cuba from the last fifty years, and what remained was the human aspect, the universal, and the transcendental. I tried not to limit us to a dramatic genre. We played with everything, from tragic farce to musical comedy, and we kept testing throughout that process to see how capable the actors were of expressing themselves in a variety of ways.

Right now, in addition to all the work and training we do for future generations in children's theater and theater for young audiences, the company are deeply absorbed in the work that I've been leading: an investigation into family, beginning with the great classic texts of the nineteenth century, but adapted by two young playwrights in our company. We have two playwrights and two directors. One of the greatest shortcomings that I feel in Latin American theater today is the lack of a substantial body of playwriting [literally: substantial dramaturgy] that can compete on a global level with work that is being done in other parts of the world. A body of work that is intimately ours—that's the battle we're fighting now. Last year we premiered a version of *The Pelican* by Strindberg, and that was part of a trilogy. In Strindberg we covered the theme of family from the viewpoint of the mother. Now we're going to be looking at family from the viewpoint of the children, with a text by Pepe [José] Triana, titled *La Noche De Los Asesinos* (*Night of the Assassins*), with an adaptation by Alejandro Gómez. Later, we'll come back to Strindberg with *The Father*, which Nelson [Celís] will be directing. That's how we work, by changing roles. It's a very young company, and we're finding our footing, people are defining us, they're following our work and we're still in development.

Brian Quirt   I'll speak to collaboration within Nightswimming. Because we're a dramaturgical company and our key collaboration is between the company and the commissioned artist; for example, Carmen Aguirre in the case of *Broken Tailbone*. We have another show that's running in Canada right now that we made with Anita Majumdar, a South Asian artist. Our relationship with those artists developed over many years, more than a decade in both cases. The nature of the process that we designed in collaboration with them is different, unique and special in relation to the commissioned project. *Broken Tailbone* is our second show with Carmen; the process in both has been related, but again it differs because of the subject matter, the aesthetic interest that we had, because of the content, because where we are in time, in our lives, and in our careers. And that's true of all the projects at Nightswimming. Everything is designed in collaboration with the central artists that we commission, so that the process that we use to enact their desires, their dreams, the shows they want to make, arises out of their specific needs.

We often invite designers into the process. Designers are part of workshops from as near the beginning of the process as possible. We do a lot of workshops, from first drafts or pre-first drafts, and we bring actors in early to read all the works. The information that all of those artists bring to the growing knowledge about the world of the piece that we're making, whether its theater-, dance-, or music-related, is fed back in and filtered between myself as dramaturg and the central artist, and then redesigned and reshaped to continue the process as we move forward.

I know Carmen will talk about community, but I wanted to mention that, because we're not a producing company, even though we're producing this tour, the company doesn't have a community in a traditional theater sense. I like to think that we have a community of audiences, and one of them is online. We create websites for all of our shows. For brokentailbone.ca, we commissioned a theater artist to create a site for this show. So, if you're seeing the show this weekend, I invite you to go to brokentailbone. ca. If you're not able to see the show for any reason, I still invite you to go to brokentailbone.ca because you can dance with and hear some of the stories that Carmen is telling.

Carmen Aguirre   I'll talk about the community part, not about *Broken Tailbone*, but just about my work in general. I'm a Chilean refugee. I arrived in Canada in 1974 as a child with my parents who were fleeing the Pinochet dictatorship and had suffered extreme violence. Everything I do in my artistic practice is in relation to that experience and to that community, which is, as you can imagine, a very marginalized community in Canada.

All of my work is unabashedly left wing, unabashedly political, and it speaks to the refugee experience in opposition to the immigrant experience. The refugee experience is one of the triumphant return to the homeland—that's the state of mind of the refugee—while the immigrant experience is about re-inventing yourself in a new land. These experiences are in opposition to each other. I was raised with the belief that I need to put my skill set in service to the community. And the community that I put my skill set in service to is not only the Chilean refugee community, but the Latinx refugee community and refugee communities in general in Canada.

For example, the first one-person show that I wrote in 1995 was called *Chile con Carne*, and it was the first time in the history of Canadian theater that a play had been written by a refugee about the refugee experience from the point of view of a child. The main character is an eight-year-old refugee. I knew that that subject matter and that play would speak to the Chilean refugee community in Vancouver, and that they would come to the show and that they would identify with it. I never foresaw that it would tour for years and years and years, that it would receive many different productions, and that refugee communities from all over the world, living in Canada, would identify with it.

Those are the communities that I feel a responsibility towards, those are the communities that I'm writing about and that I'm writing for, and constantly fighting for in Canada—against complete erasure, against invisibility. We only have one Latinx theater company in the entire country of Canada. I could really relate to what Alicia was saying: we are constantly being told by the theater community at large that we don't exist, that there are no Latinx actors, no Latinx designers, writers, directors. It's a constant struggle.

Rodriguez   I'd like to open it up to questions from the audience.

Audience Member   I was very excited to see Alicia's work, as an Ecuadorian who knows about Afro-Ecuadorian culture. From the beginning, the way that you possessed the words in *Ropa Íntima* was phenomenal. I could hear the text—which is a beautiful text. Did you do the translation?

Olivares (*translated from Spanish*)   No, the translation is by Maria Elena Pantojas.

Audience Member   In the translation, I could hear Memphis, I could hear New York. It was amazing. Are you making original work with the company, work that deals with the themes of Afro-Peruvian marginalization, in a culture that sometimes also marginalizes indigenous Peruvian people?

Olivares (*translated from Spanish*)   I have had varying opinions on that. Last night a playwright approached me and asked if I had considered an adaptation of the piece to our Afro-Peruvian culture that would represent us. And I responded that in Lima we don't have any plays that address black themes. We have a group called Kimbafá, that works a lot with Afro-Peruvian music and dance, but in text-based work, we don't have anything. That's why I see a need to look for other authors to begin working with. But this is a seed that is being planted now, in the schools, in playwriting workshops, now that there is an inclusion, a certain visibility that black actors now have in the scenic arts. Now I find it necessary that we write our own stories—those of our ancestors, of our identity as Peruvians.

I would like to come to the global Encuentro with a story of our own, written especially for us. I would also like, at some point, to do productions with black actors that aren't necessarily about black themes—black actors playing white characters. For me, an actor isn't defined by their skin color. An actor is a human being that is representing emotions. In this situation, we have to begin somewhere. Later on, I'd like to produce a Shakespeare play with an all-black cast representing the white characters. That's my dream, but it's one step at a time.

Audience Member (*translated from Spanish*)   I just wanted to reflect and give a bit of context on Ébano's productions in Peru. For me, by doing this production of Lynn Nottage's play without changing its name—because seeing it, I thought we were in Lima. I knew we weren't in Lima, but in my head we were in Lima. And it didn't matter to me that it mentioned places in English, because to me, you were narrating that separation of castes, the segregation of skin colors. I didn't feel like you had to speak specifically about your own history.

In the Peruvian context—where almost all black theater is based on tap dancing or on the "Son de Los Diablos," ["Songs of the Devils"] and body-percussion—it's refreshing to see this work. You don't have to sing, you don't have to sell fruit, you don't have to put on a mask. In other words, this is dramatic theater. And it appears to be, for me, within a kind of renaissance that I support, because I've brought the Teatro Milenio [an Afro-Peruvian dance/music ensemble] to Seattle for ten years. I love it, it has a place, but this work has a place too. It narrates by superimposing one reality over another, and it gives us a new perspective.

Audience Member   When you're doing these plays or ensemble pieces, how many compromises did you have to make when you're thinking about touring? Did you envision touring before putting these plays up?

Rolón   Pregones began as a touring company. Before we had a roof over our heads, we had been traveling for seven or eight years. Everything that we did was designed to be light on its feet and to travel. But we also appreciate design, and today we have the luxury of permanent theater spaces. We have deep roots and very broad wings. So, if we want to feel that whatever we do should be able to go places, we have that option—we can produce an international project with partners, because we can travel to each other's homes. Now, with *El Apagón,* for example, when we are at home, we have an actual bar, and walls and objects. But here we share a wall with our "roommates" in Theatre Three—Cara Mía—and that's how we did it here. You sit down and you re-design, and you re-envision. But I think it's all good. Your piece is your piece, you create it with what you really must have and want to have, and it will happen. There is an understanding that our field is very complex. Some of us are presenters, and there's a whole complicated presenting field. Presenters have very specific things that they require from guest artists—these are the things that you can do in my venue, and these are the things that you cannot do in my venue. And those are the conversations that will happen, one knows that. I would encourage artists to just fly with your imagination and do what you must do to make your work happen. And you'll see that those other things are things that can be dealt with.

Lozano   I wanted to talk a little about the economics of it. If you're responsible as a producer of a tour, you have to assume responsibility for the budget. And if you overspend on your tour, it may come out of your organization later. So, I think touring is something that one should be very frugal and careful about—financially speaking, not artistically—because someone somewhere will have to pay for it. And hopefully it won't be your non-profit organization or your own personal account.

Cao (*translated from Spanish*)   I think it's very difficult, in our countries, to create a show, bring an audience to the venue, and to make it happen with a small budget—this all has repercussions on the funds of a small theater company. When you begin to think about touring—I realized that I had never really thought about that. I'm a creator, and someone else takes care of the budget, right? And that's where I ran into a big problem. How did we get here, for example, on this tour? Well, because of José Luis's invitation and with great effort by the company.

We managed to put on many productions in many situations. We, for example, put on a production of *Mariposas* as a fundraiser and sold tickets. And all of our friends filled up the theater and supported us. That's how we make it work. But that shouldn't be the way. I'm seeing some new methods here that look very good to me, in the sense that I see a phenomenon here, and that is the opportunity to build relationships here between us . . . I would love to come here and direct something, or bring someone over [to Colombia] and have them direct over there, or to exchange actors, or to make international projects. We should begin thinking in that way.

Olivares (*translated from Spanish*)   I love it. I second your proposal. I'll tell you my experience of getting here. This is the first time that Ébano has left Peru. It took us six months to raise the funds just for the airfare. We got many "no's," thousands of "no's" everywhere we looked. I had to speak to the Minister of Culture on her personal phone. I had to do everything I could, because I think that each of us represent our countries, and your country has a responsibility, an obligation to support you. We artists are not beggars. And I should publicly acknowledge that we are here thanks to the support of the Peruvian Ministry of External Affairs and the Ministry of Culture.

I also want to talk about an experience from five years ago with our production *Los Cachorros* (*The Puppies*). I don't know if you've ever heard of Mario Vargas-Llosa. This piece was directed by the same director as *Ropa Íntima*, Miguel Pastor. He had a dream that the piece would tour all over the country—I mean the coast, the mountains and the jungle, everywhere. I told him: fine, find the funding and we'll make it happen so that it's free for the public. We took that production of *Los Cachorros* to all regions of the country. We took it to places where people had never had access to theater. And all the shows were funded by a large university.

I think it's possible to have a tour like that here. I was surprised by the amount of Latinos here, and they tell me there are many Latinos in many states in the United States. I think the goal is to find the funding, so that these pieces can tour, and be funded, and we can go to where the public doesn't have the economic conditions to see this work. There's much work to be done, as César Vallejo once said: "hermanos, hay mucho por hacer" ["Brothers, there's much to do"].

Valenzuela (*translated from Spanish*)   Mexico has one national theater company, just one. It's very difficult to tour in the United States—not only because of the technical aspects, but because, for example, our company operates under a union. The actors cannot work unless they're paid the union rate. If they go on tour, the salary doubles. You need to pay them double, and you need to give them benefits, and you need to give them airfare and food. For any production, a tour means that you will certainly lose money, even if you're being funded—because, in reality, they're not funding your rehearsals, they're funding your shows. It's interesting because I don't have a Ministry of Culture in the United States where I can say: I want to go to Bogotá, can you help me with the airfare, or can someone help my company tour to another country? We don't have that. In this city, I have this theater, and they [the City of Los Angeles] give me $7,500 a year. Which is not enough to pay even a month of electricity. It's a lot harder in the US.

When I was young, I made $250 a month, and we would tour all over the world. We would go, make the set, and load everything in, and put on the show, and we wouldn't charge for tickets. But what happens when you grow? I can't just tell my actors: Hey, let's go. I have to pay them and the designers, the technical staff, everyone. That's very important to discuss. Because, for example, you all have Iberescena [aid fund for the Ibero-American Performing Arts], right? But they don't consider us part of Ibero-America, because we're Latinos in the United States. So, we can never apply to Iberescena. I've had many discussions with them, because we're Latino. How are we not eligible? We should have a discussion about funding in the theater.

Rolón   I want to speak about the potential for collaborations. In the case of Pregones, we've collaborated with Roadside Theater from the Appalachian region for twenty-three years now. We visit each other, we go to their space and they come to ours, collaborating, fundraising together. The collaboration that we're just starting with Paul Flores is another example. Jorge is involved with groups from Alaska and Hawaii. What I mean is that there is a potential—not only because we've been doing it for so many years. Maybe it isn't being done enough. I think it's worth bringing this into the conversation, the potential that does exist, the possibility that together we can make these kinds of exchanges viable. Pregones has been to five hundred cities, thirty-seven states, eighteen countries, and the majority of that travel has been through connections—universities at first, but now it's lately just been through collaborations.

Valdez   There's also places like National New Play Network (NNPN) that provide those opportunities to create those collaborations and tour, so let's not forget about other organizations and resources that are available out there as well.

Section Three

The State, Politics, and Lived Experience

Deferred Action

David Lozano and Lee Trull

Cara Mía Theater Company—Dallas, Texas

8 Cara Mía Theatre's *Deferred Action*, Dallas, Texas, 2017. Photo: Karen Almond.

Snapshot

Teresa Marrero

In the tradition of political engagement from the legacy of El Teatro Campesino onward, Chicanx Theater has addressed the pressing issues of its time. It is no different with Dallas's Cara Mía Theater Company. Founded in 1996, Cara Mía's stated mission is to create theater that "inspires and engages people to uplift their communities through transformative Latinx theatre, multicultural youth arts experiences and community action" (from their webpage, caramia.org). Their work is both engaging and engaged; consider for instance the world premiere of a fascinating and experimental indigenous futurist play, *Where Earth Meets the Sky*, collectively devised by three women of color: company member Ariana Cook and Vanessa Mercado Taylor with Edyka Chilomé. With Dallas Children's Theater they co-produced Roxanne Schroeder-Arce's *Yana Wana's Legend of the Bluebonnet*, a theater for young audiences piece based on a Texas Coahuiltecan indigenous story. They have also included the works of contemporary

Latinx playwrights such as Virginia Grise (*blu*), Caridad Svich (*De Troya*), Octavio Solis (*Lydia*), Quiara Alegría Hudes (*Yemaya's Belly*), and Luis Valdez (*Zoot Suit*). The company's devised plays in which creative artistic director David Lozano has had a hand include *Crystal City 1969*, a historically accurate piece based on the high school student walkout in the South Texas town, *Dreamers, a Bloodline*, and *Deferred Action*.

Deferred Action is the second of a planned trilogy on the topic of immigration directed by Lozano.[1] The journey began with *Dreamers, a Bloodline* where the story of Javi, the protagonist of *Deferred Action*, begins. It is a harrowing story of a Central American woman and her baby (Javi) who flee a violent and futureless environment to risk all in the undocumented crossing from Guatemala, through Mexico and into the United States. Whereas *Dreamers* ends with Javi surviving the ordeal (but not his mother) by being adopted by an older woman he would call Abuela for the rest of his life, *Deferred Action* picks up the storyline when Javi is already a grown, undocumented youth, a recipient of the Executive Action that the DREAMers won in 2012 under President Barack Obama, called Deferred Action for Childhood Arrivals, or DACA. DACA only granted a two-year work permit and social security number. Javi's work permit is about to expire and he and his generation want action now. Will the Democratic Party deliver this time, or will Javi turn to a charismatic Republican politician for a platform on immigration reform? A political thriller, this play has muscle.

Deferred Action was developed at the Dallas Theater Center through an initiative entitled the Elevator Project, whose goal was to bring in local theater makers from smaller organizations by artists of color into the world of professional, regional theater. It worked. The end product is a tightly organized play that, even at two hours, flows quickly and irrevocably towards an unexpected, and to some undesired, ending. As a resident critic in Dallas for the online arts magazine *Theater Jones* (theaterjones.com), I have witnessed three productions of *Deferred Action*: its Dallas Theatre Center premiere, a production at the University of North Texas, and the one at the 2017 Encuentro de las Américas in Los Angeles. A mark of professionalism is that the quality of the performance rang true and crisp each and every time. The professional set design by Timothy R. Mackabee addresses both the epic quality of the issue as well as the very intimate nature of much of the conflict. Huge wooden panels encompass all three walls, accompanied by numerous huge upstage doors. The set has an Orwellian quality reminiscent of the 1941 film *Citizen Kane*. Clifton Taylor's lighting design nicely complements the set design to evoke a wide emotional canvas. The Encuentro audience's reaction to the play's ending was palpable. In a largely liberal, Democratic California, the resolution that Javi chose for his dilemma felt like a huge letdown. Its open ending leaves the door for the last play of the trilogy. Written during the Obama years, *Deferred Action* turns out to be strangely prophetic in the current anti-immigration politics spewed by the Trump Administration. The final play, like history itself, has yet to be written.

Notes

1   *Deferred Action* was co-produced in 2016 by the Dallas Theatre Center and developed as part of the DTC's Elevator Project. As such, Lee Trull, then director of new play development at the DTC, was involved in the co-writing of the play. Subsequently, in 2017, he was accused of misconduct. Since that time Cara Mía Theatre Company has distanced itself from Trull.

Culture Clash: An American Odyssey

Culture Clash (Richard Montoya, Ric Salinas, and Herbert Siguenza)—Los Angeles, California

9 Culture Clash portrait by Oscar Castillo, photo courtesy of Culture Clash.

Snapshot

Noe Montez

Latinx Theatre has held a long and intertwining relationship with politically irreverent humor and short performance pieces throughout the twentieth and twenty-first centuries. Fifty years after El Teatro Campesino began performing *actos* on the Delano Grape Strike picket lines, our communities continue to rely on comedians to provoke and discomfort audiences by telling the stories of the dispossessed, veterans, immigrants, and others whose stories could easily be erased. Few companies have engaged in this work as prolifically as Culture Clash. Core members Richard Montoya, Ric Salinas, and Herbert Siguenza brought some of their previous material to the Encuentro, drawing from previous productions including *Culture Clash in AmeriCCa* and *Radio Mambo*, along with new works created specifically for the occasion in *Culture Clash: An American Odyssey.* Directed by Robert Beltran, the audience enters a space in which a faded gray American flag serves as a vehicle for projections designer Yee Eun Nam to display still images and videos that connect to the scenes presented onstage.

In one of the production's opening moments, Ric Salinas eases the audience into the production through a lighthearted scene, playing Junior, a Nuyorican from "Loisaida" who tries to bridge his Spanish, Black, and Taíno identities through salsa. As the vignette continues Junior provides a lively interpretation of salsa styles as performed by people of Mexican, Dominican, Cuban, and Puerto Rican descent. For an audience of theater makers from Cuba, Mexico, Puerto Rico, Peru, and Colombia, the play provides a sense of the diasporic differences that encompass *Latinidad* in the United States.

From broad comedy inspired by stand-up to humor mined from ethnographic observation, Culture Clash shifts to two pieces that draw on the troupe's practice of recording interview subjects and then re-enacting and reinterpreting their subjects. In one instance, Herbert Siguenza plays a pre-operative transgender healthcare worker who vividly describes the process of sex reassignment surgery while drawing connections between Latinx homophobia and Aids rates. In this piece and in others, the company represented transgender individuals in ways that discomforted Encuentro spectators, leading to significant critique from members of the Latinx Theatre Commons community and causing some audience members to walk out of the performance in protest.

In other passages, however, the company's satire created more positively impactful political interventions, including when Siguenza and Salinas depict an interracial Florida couple who profit from obtaining government contracts to clean up after hurricanes despite their indifference to the communities that they're serving and the long-term effects that their labors have on the environment. In this documentary-inspired piece, Culture Clash mines merriment while revealing the ways that greed, entitlement, and ignorance bring harm to Latinx communities whether they're fostered by outsiders or those within.

Despite moments of pathos such as Richard Montoya's haunting portrayal of Arizona Sheriff Joe Arpaio reading from his memoirs and a tribute to the Puerto Rican activist and poet Pedro Pietri, the company chooses to enlighten its audience through laughter. At its core, the Encuentro de las Américas gave visibility to a wide swath of the Latinx diaspora and the journeys that we've made across time and geography. We share a common experience of displacement and marginalization, but rather than allow the legacies of colonialism and white supremacy to defeat us, *Culture Clash: An American Odyssey* suggests that we can laugh in its face and expose hegemony for its devastating callousness towards humanity.

Excerpt from Culture Clash: American Odyssey

Written by Culture Clash (Richard Montoya, Ric Salinas, and Herbert Siguenza)

The selected scene that follows premiered at the Encuentro de las Américas festival and was later re-written and appeared in Culture Clash's production of *Bordertown Now* at the Pasadena Playhouse directed by the late Diane Rodriguez. The role of Julie was performed by Sabina Zúñiga Varela.

Sisters of Mercy Safe House—Nogales, Mexico—Cartel Country

An American **Chronicler** *interviews* **Julie**, *a Mexican national, a safe house resident.*

Chronicler   Thank you for agreeing to speak to us.

Julie   Out *there*, you have to be esuper careful. The violence is random. Crazy. The Mexican men are the worst. You can be killed like this: (*Snap*). Or rape. The *coyotes*. They track us with the GPS burner phones they force us to buy when we leave Mexico. The gringo ranchers, the Minute Men on the other side the guys in the camo-gear . . . They carry the long rifles.

Chronicler   Like the movie *Cartel Land* . . .

Julie   I don't watch fake Hollywood movies, man. There are many guns at the border . . .

Chronicle   Yes I see . . .

Julie   Why you even come to Nogales?

Chronicle   To talk to you, to learn more about the border patrol . . .

Julie   You *choose* to be here?

Chronicler   Oh yeah. It's exciting. Like first responders!

Julie   *Idiota* . . . Who else you talk to?

Chronicler   We talked to a man with one of those long rifles.

Julie   And what he say?

Chronicler   That he's waiting for you.

Julie   Cabron . . .

Chronicler   Can I offer you some water or organic kombucha from Whole Foods?

Julie   I am good . . .

Chronicler   Tell me about the day you tried to cross . . .

Julie   That day, was so fucking hot, man. The sun eclipse that day, the birds go crazy and I thought I will die for sure because I feel it was like a sign. Like I have bad luck . . .

Chronicler   Yes . . .

Julie   But I never show fear. Even if I barely walk and my feets are bleeding.

Chronicler   What do you want?

Julie   What I want? Not to be capture . . .

Chronicler   Right . . .

Julie   Not to be capture again . . .

Chronicler   Right.

Julie   Sometimes you want to be capture because it suck so hard out there.

Chronicler   What else?

Julie   I want an EpiPen for my kid? I have a small boy he stay with my mother while his mother . . .

Emotion catching and stopping her.

Chronicler   Got it . . .

Julie   What else I want?

Chronicler   Yes . . .

Julie   Twenty-four-hour electronic dance music would be nice . . .

Chronicler   Why not? Hipsters at Burning Man shouldn't have all the fun . . .

Julie   What is Burning Mans?

Chronicler   A big party in the desert where people pay money to attend . . .

Julie   People *pay* to go to the desert?

Chronicler   A ton of it.

Julie   *Idiotas.* What you are writing now?

Chronicler   Just a note.

Julie   What it says?

Chronicler   "The Girl Who Kicked the Hornet's Nest at the Border."

Julie   Terrible title. I do not accept this gender-specific pronoun, dude . . .

Chronicler   Of course. What shall I say?

Julie   You can say: They. All. Ser. Joteria X.

Chronicler   What are you most afraid of, Julie?

Julie   To never see my baby boy again . . .

Chronicler   When will you see him?

Julie   When the Sister of Mercy say it is safe.

Chronicler   Where is your son?

Julie   Tejas . . .

Chronicler   Are you hopeful? Do you have faith?

Julie   A man say when I cross to the US . . . the Mormons will take us to the large white temple . . . (*Soft Mormon choir is heard.*) Where we cannot touch anything until we are baptized in the blood of lambs to be reborns. (*She holds her hands up in prayer. Choir stops abruptly.*) Fucking Mormons. They better come through for me, man . . .

Chronicler (*gently*)   When you meet the Ladder Day Saints, maybe *not* say *fucking* Mormons?

A far-off whistle.

Julie   I must go.

Chronicler   Is there anything you would say to Donald Trump?

Julie   He will never hear me.

Chronicler   He reads our tweets, sometimes. He's kind of petty that way . . .

Julie   What does petty mean?

Chronicler   Thinned skin?

Julie   I would say to your president, that I would like a job, I can help build his wall . . .

Chronicler   You would help build the wall?

Julie   Oh si! Woman can do the job better than man, we make it a real pretty wall, it gonna look real nice, with flowers and monarch butterflies . . . (*Projection of monarch butterflies.*) Is gonna be a very professional wall. Like Aztec engineers we build first class but we gonna know where the secret holes and tunnels are so we can sneak back in! *A toda madre!*

Chronicler   You will keep the civilian militias busy.

Julie   *En serio*, please tell them, when you think you will die in the desert, you get real cold, and what escare you the most is your own mind, your thoughts, you know? *Porque* out there is no safe space, no safe houses, no Jesuits, no Sisters of Mercy, no hippies from the sanctuary in Tucson, *nada*, and you are wondering, who hear you cry, who hear you prayer, who hear you die?

Chronicler   Must have been horrifying for you . . .

Julie   I have no privilege to be horrify.

Chronicler   Do you like America?

Julie   Oh yes I like. You can fix everything there! Fix your credit, fix your nose, fix your accent, is like a fix-it place to fix you. I cannot fix anything in the desert. Also I like very much the IKEA, you can "become" at IKEA? Become *Americano*!

Chronicler   IKEA is Swedish . . .

Julie   Why you have to ruin this for me, brother?

Chronicler   *Desculpa* . . .

Julie   *Si me permites?* . . .

Chronicler   Please . . .

Julie   Look, if there is no border, no wall, Trump he will lose control. If the drugs are legal and cheap in the US, the cartel lose control! They all lose control. The cartel guys want what Trump want, completely control *de todo*. What happen in the desert tonight affect so much the world. So. I am stuck in the shadow of all these big guys, so I do whatever my family need. Try to cross again? I will do it for sure.

Chronicler   You broke it down rather brilliantly . . .

Julie   They are all a part of *the same puteria* for sure. The border super suck, man. If everybody suck a little less it would help . . .

Chronicler   I will carry your important message north.

Julie   Gracias . . .

Chronicler   Maybe lose the sucking part?

Julie   No changing my words! *Pinche* LA writers . . .

Chronicler   OK. Will you ever stop trying to cross, Julie?

Julie   The fucking wall . . .

Sister of Mercy (*offstage*)   Watch the language in there!

Julie   Sorry, hermana . . .

Sister of Mercy   We must go soon, Julie.

Julie   *Aye voy, hermana!*

Sister of Mercy *Un minuto más.* . . .

Julie   You know the monarch butterfly?

Chronicler   Phenomenal . . .

Julie   The butterfly start not so beautiful, the larvae become the cocoon, then it be the moth, then the large monarch. I will be this, and fly right over the (fucking/silent) wall.

Chronicler   So you will never stop?

Julie   I will walk in the desert like Jesus . . .

Chronicler   Jesus? I studied Exodus 22:21—"Do not mistreat a stranger for ye were a stranger in Egypt once" . . .

Julie   Mexicans in Egypt? *Que desmadre* . . . I ask question now.

Chronicler   Go for it.

Julie   If Jesus, he is walking to you in the desert, he is coming, it is *him* for sure, he is the Way, the Light the Truth . . . (*Gregorian chants are heard.*) What America she will do? Arrest Jesus? Ask for his resident alien card? Give to him water as you would a dog?

Chronicler   You pose a moral imperative to America.

Julie   For me there is no moral question. For America, only moral ambiguity. When America fight with itself, it is good time for me to cross . . .

Far-off thunder is heard.

Chronicler   You are super-articulate, what did you do in Mexico, your occupation?

Julie   I was *maestra*, *profesor* at American University.

Chronicler   What did you teach?

Julie   Border Aesthetics . . .

Chronicler   You could get a gig at Cal Arts, *no*?

Julie   I send Occidental a text but I have no cellular coverage on this side of the line.

Chronicler   What mobile plan do you have?

Julie   Usually, Verizon . . .

Chronicler   Maybe try Metro PCS, you never know . . .

Julie   You are married?

Chronicler   Not yet but soon. We have a seven-year-old son.

Julie   Do you miss them?

Chronicler   Very much. I cannot imagine how you feel.

Julie   One day soon, I will be with him . . .

Chronicler   Can you see a legal path to US citizenship?

Julie   I can see yes, but the path is dark, lighted only by tiki torches . . . (*Wind chimes are heard . . .*) *Ah, esta brisa*, the breeze, the little wind, maybe it carry the names of all those who dead at the border . . .

Chronicler   What is your dream?

Julie   One day, and that day will be soon, I am with my little guy, and we are dressed in white, his little suit *con una corbata*, and his mama, me, in my beautiful wedding dress, with my veil, a dress that flow like river, *el agua* . . .

Chronicler   Where are you?

Julie   Friendship Park near the Pacific Ocean, and when they open the wall for only two minutes, then I will be married . . .

Chronicler   And where is the lucky groom?

Julie   There is no groom. I marry my wife . . .

Chronicler (*surprised*)   Two mommies? OK. I wasn't expecting that.

Julie   We can never be marry in Mexico . . . I finish my transition in the US. Then *mijo* have his mommy and daddy.

Chronicler   Yes . . . (*Thumbs-up.*)

Julie   I think maybe you are gay when I see you.

Chronicler   I was bi-cultural once but as long as I take bipolar meds I'm rendered straight . . . something like that.

This gets a smile from **Julie**.

Chronicler   Let me swap out the battery . . . (*He moves down to switch out the power, he looks up . . .*) Julie?

Julie *is gone like the desert wind . . . A sad Western guitar moves us along.*

10 Million

Carlos Celdrán

Argos Teatro—Havana, Cuba

10 Carlos Celdrán's *10 Million*, Argos Teatro, Havana, Cuba, 2017. Photo: Manolo Garriga.

Critical Introduction

Lillian Manzor

Theatre director Carlos Celdrán has played an important role in the transformation of Cuban theater since the 1980s.[1] He founded Argos Teatro in 1996 in search of a theater that presents a critical reflection of reality as opposed to reflecting reality. In order to achieve that critical reflection, he empties the stage of all superfluous elements and places the actor stage center in order to transform theater—the stage and its audience—into a space in which actors establish a dialogue with the audience and their present-day reality.[2] That pursuit has led Carlos Celdrán to theorize his theater as *la escena transparente* or the diaphanous stage.[3] The process is threefold. He works with actors to establish a relationship between their individual and collective biography and the character's that is (in)visible on stage through minimal gestures, controlled voice and emotion, and quasi-architecturally designed movement. The spectator can also relate to those biographical and contextual elements. Superfluous ornamentation disappears. Scenic and light designs along with original musical score are minimalist but beautifully create the physical space in which that documentation of reality unfolds. They also condition the visual and mnemonic spaces in which each spectator individually and the audience collectively partake of this witnessing of theatrical hyper-reality through the recognition of or connection with their/our own reality and context.

Given the Encuentro de las Américas' interests, it makes sense that *10 Millones* was the play selected to represent Cuba because it is Celdrán's best example of *la escena transparente*. The title refers to Fidel Castro's (in)famous failed plan of producing ten tons of sugar in 1970. The harvest, specific to a Cuban context, is the backdrop to a coming of age story and a *sui generis* coming out story through which we relive contemporary traumas and buried moments of revolutionary history: rejection of homosexuality, acts of repudiation surrounding the Mariel exodus, the role of familial and formal education in forging a disciplinary society, and political disillusionment.

In the performance at the Los Angeles Theatre Center (LATC), the only thing on stage is a two-level platform backed by a large dark gray parapet in which Waldo Franco playing Author writes throughout the play the "subtitles" of the various sections. This parapet, which functions most of the time as a blackboard, serves to underscore that this is a story about education—familial and formal. That the blackboard is gray and not black is telling for those who know revolutionary Cuban history. "Gray Quinquennium" is a misnomer given to the period between 1971 and 1976 in which ideological purity was at the center of Cuba's cultural and educational policies. As a result, homosexuals along with those who did not conform to the "parameters" of the revolution were persecuted and censored.

When the audience entered the LATC, it met the actor sitting or standing alone on stage next to a blue overnight case. The first movement the audience sees after the lights are dimmed is that of the same actor using a chalk to write "Dream" and turning to the audience to share the genesis of this play:

> No soy el autor. No escribo este texto. Lo digo en . . . nombre . . . del que escribe las palabras que digo ahora . . . Escribo para saber . . . Escribo: sueño. Lo primero es el sueño.

> [I am not the author. I didn't write this text. I'm speaking on . . . behalf of he who wrote the words I'm saying now . . . I write in order to know . . . I write: dream. The first thing is the dream.][4]

The opening suggests that this is a play that will take place in that liminal space between life and acting. As the performance unfolds, each character returns to the past to confront specters that haunt them. Their stories are made public and become interwoven with the private stories/memories of the spectator. The subtitles' place on the parapet/blackboard underscore the inward and outward movements of this retelling. On the two panels on the left, the words "Dream," "Journey," "Encounters" form a triptych and frame the stories of He (Daniel Romero), Mother (Maridelmis Marín), and Father (Caleb Casas): He loves to spend time in his father's home, away from Mother's disciplinary models for becoming a man: strong, courageous, unafraid, as opposed to weak and susceptible. "Therapies," written to the far left of the triptych, announces the psychological therapies He underwent in order to become a man—therapies representative of the ones used in Cuba as part of the revolution's medicalization of homosexuality.[5]

The familial and personal stories are given temporal and ideological markers in the performance through subtitles written to the right. "1980—Mass and Power," for example, frames the acts of repudiation that were inflicted upon those who, like father, left through the port of Mariel in 1980—another buried traumatic memory that *10 Millones* brings to the fore. Father narrates how his daughter shared the horrendous physical attacks father suffered before he was able to leave: "oyó historias de gente a la que al irse le pasó eso, pero que no lo relacionó." [He said he had heard stories of things that happened to people before they left, but he couldn't connect that with his father.][6] A leitmotif in *10 Millones* is a skillful questioning of understanding, knowing, seeing, and of the inability to relate what is going on at the macro-level with the characters' daily lives. However, in the present of the performance, the diaphanous stage allows the audience to recognize that that inability to relate is oftentimes present in their/ our daily lives in 2017 as it was then in 2012, the date of the Epilogue, written appropriately at the very center of the blackboard during the last four minutes of the performance.

The majority of the audience during the Encuentro were non-Cuban theater experts. As Luis Alfaro commented on a Facebook post, "it was the performance that varied the most in response. Folks either loved it or hated it. Some loved the language and emotion of the story. Others complained that it was too literary and static."[7] Indeed, there is very little action in this play, aside from the characters' retelling of stories that force the audience to relive those traumas without situating the characters or the spectator within the categories of "victim" or "perpetrator." The actors and characters dig up with the spectator painful memories. As Alfaro notes in his post, the actors "at various moments in the performance were overcome with erupting unplanned feelings." As a matter of fact, at the Encuentro one Cuban-American spectator seated next to me broke out in uncontrollable tears. The play has a cathartic effect for those who were directly impacted by those historical moments. And for the younger generations, the play helps to construct a historical past that is unknown to them. In other words, the play documents the past that official history has erased, the past that very few remember or want to remember.

The play forces us to revisit those moments where we acted in ways that we did not understand. Even if it is impossible for us to discover who we were because memory is personal and subjective, the diaphanous stage gives access to the past by conditioning the spectator to relate and connect who we are in the present to the actors' performance— in the present—of their characters' experiences in the past. But that reflection/ connection/relation is made possible through the act of writing. In the performance, the one action that we do see is the actor playing Author taking out the chalk and writing on the parapet/blackboard. Additionally, it is through writing that He and Author have been able to process their experiences—through his diary, first; through the play He (or Author?) wrote in New York—and through the performance on stage. The performance's last words voiced by Author are telling in this regard. "Escribir es más sencillo. Hablar es caro, imposible." [To write is simpler. To talk is expensive, impossible.][8] Indeed, writing offers the possibility of working through trauma in spite of the fact that it only offers an oblique and fragmentary access to facts and characters.

Talking is very difficult in these situations. But what is theater if not talking? Celdrán's diaphanous stage presents actors on stage telling a story that can open our minds in a non-threatening way. A story that we share with others in the audience, regardless of our background. Most importantly, we recognize that these stories are created and, as such, can be changed. They touch our sensibilities and intimate wounds, pushing us toward places that are hidden within us. This is what *10 Millones* brought to the Encuentro: in the present of the performance, the diaphanous stage created a space of shared experience through which Cubans and non-Cubans alike revisited the past and, through the performance of those inconsolable memories, opened the possibility to move forward.

Notes

1. For more information about Carlos Celdrán and his work, consult "Dossier," *Argos Teatro*, http://www.argosteatro.cult.cu/dossier.html and Lillian Manzor, "Carlos Celdrán," *Cuban Theater Digital Archive*. http://cubantheater.org/creator/336
2. For an outstanding analysis of Carlos Celdrán's use of space see Aimelys Díaz, "El actor y el espacio hacia una nueva documentación de la realidad en la escena de Carlos Celdrán y Argos Teatro. Entre Chamaco y Talco." *Tablas* Anuario (2011): 240–2, 247–8. http://cubantheater.org/media/publications/anuario-2011_1.pdf
3. See Carlos Celdrán, *La escena transparente* (La Habana: Ediciones Alarcos, 2006).
4. Carlos Celdrán, *Diez millones* (Matanzas: Ediciones Matanzas, 2017), 4.
5. As Abel Sierra Madero has studied, family, education, and political ideology were and oftentimes still are "at the service of producing machos." Abel Sierra Madero, "Academias para producir machos en Cuba." *Letras Libres*, January 21, 2016. https://www.letraslibres.com/espana-mexico/politica/academias-producir-machos-en-cuba
6. Celdrán, "Diez," 51.
7. Luis Alfaro, "Things that Only Happen at International Latino Theater Festivals." Facebook post, November 25, 2017. https://www.facebook.com/search/top/?q=luis%20alfaro%2010%20million
8. Celdrán, "Diez," 54.

10 Million

Carlos Celdrán

Translated from Spanish by Manolo Garriga

Production History

10 Million, directed by Carlos Celdrán, premiered on April 1, 2016 at Argos Teatro in Havana, Cuba. It's had more than 150 performances to date in Cuba, the United States (The Los Angeles Theater Center, Los Angeles, California, USA in November 2017; the Kennedy Center, Washington, DC, USA in May 2018); Mexico; and Spain. Select awards: Special Award from the Jury at the International Film Festival of Gibara in 2019 (Cuba); Literary Critics Award 2017 (Cuba); Critics' Award 2016 (Cuba); Cuban Union of Writers and Artists Award 2016 (Cuba). The Spanish version of the play (*10 Millones*) has been published in Cuba (Literary Critics Award 2017), the United States, Germany, and Mexico.

Characters

He
Mother
Father
Author

First Moment

Prologue

Author   Good evening. I am not the author. I didn't write this text. I'm speaking on behalf of the author who writes the words I'm saying now. These words. I say: I am the author. I am studying theater in New York, and I write. It's 2001. Summer. During rehearsals, a professor asks: *Who is she for you? Who is the mother for you in this scene?* I don't know. And I know. I write so that I know. There is also an absent father in the scene, annulled, removed. Then, I write. I answer the question. I write: *Dream.* The first thing is the dream, recurring even now.

Dream

He   It's the house. From the sidewalk, I can see the fluorescent lamp flashing. The dark garden, quiet, empty, full of earth and bushes. The door shut. The time? Any time. Night. It's night. Cold. Silence. The silence of late night in the town. Its humidity. The bag in my hand with the clothing of the allocated month. In the porch, alone, under the fluorescent lamp, I wait.

I get impatient. I knock on the door. Outside. Hard. I call out. I am afraid to be there, alone, with no answer. Afraid he will not open, he's not there. My father. It's my father's house. In that town. I finally hear the bolt sliding. He opens the door. It's me. There. At the door. Taller, thinner. Thirteen years old, maybe ten, eight. I don't know. Me. Cold. Late at night. The cold of the town. He smiles sleepily, strokes my head, and makes me enter the dark living room.

Father   *What happened? I thought you were not coming. I was waiting for you all day.*

He   I mention my mother. I justify her.
She couldn't send me earlier because of her job.
I lie, but it's OK with him, he knows her very well.

Father   *It's alright, it's alright.*

He   He kisses me.

Father   *It doesn't matter. You are here now. Have you eaten?*

He   I nod.

Father   *Come, the bed is ready.*

He   We walk to the bedroom in the dark. While walking next to him, I know my father doesn't live there anymore. He left "decades ago"? This is not the house. Not his house. I know, and yet I walk with him. I undress. In the dark, I search for the pillow next to him on the bed and hear him whisper: *Good night.* I'm still awake in the dark, quiet. It's not the house, there are other people living there. As I walk in I see a wall instead of a fence. The garden covered with cement and turned into a garage. The red flower tree is gone. I see signs, but I'm still in bed next to him. Pretending I am sleeping, under the mosquito net, distressed, not knowing how to say what I know, what I see, the signs, the changes.

I go to sleep wondering what would happen should I wake up.

Journey Towards Me

Mother   *Don't deny it.*

He   I deny and I deny, but she doesn't believe me. She will not. She insists, pushes, threatens, yells.

Father   It is the month allocated to be with me. At home. In the town. One month in the summer, during the summer holidays. Only one month. That's the agreement. Not even one day more. He spends the whole year waiting for this moment to come, at last, to come and do what he does here, what he can only do here. At home, during summertime. Once a year. During the agreed month of the year. Nowhere else. Before he leaves, you can see his mother's resistance to let him go. You can feel her annoyance when she orders the driver, upset, harsh:

Mother   *Take him to his father's house and come back to Havana quickly, I am very busy.*

Father   Always busy, in an endless job. Meetings, crisis, problems. The harvest and the ten million tons of sugar that will save us. Her deeds, her personal mission. Arranging the car and the driver, distracting her from her plans, creates a tension that falls on him—Why go to that house, to that town, with that man, that precise day which is full of last-minute emergencies—a displacement that makes the scheduled trip become an obstacle, into an imprudence, a thoughtlessness.

Mother   *This is completely inconsiderate.*

Father   She says without giving the order to go. He's been ready since early morning; bag in hand, waiting for the word. As a strategy, he pretends he's not interested in coming. But she knows he loves the holidays in that house. She knows. And his lie makes it worse at the last minute.

Therapies

Mother   *Don't deny it.*

He   I deny and I deny, but she doesn't believe me. She will not. She insists, pushes, threatens, yells.

Mother   *That's a lie!*

Look at me. Look at me! It's dangerous. You don't know how bad they are for you. For your future. You have no idea how dangerous it is for you, whenever you go there, to that house! I'm not letting you go until you tell me the truth. Everything they say. What they talk in front of you. I know they talk.

He   Then I talk. So that she will let me go. About the mockery, the criticism, about politics, everything they talk about and I hear. What I imagine they talk about. I talk and *exaggerate*.

She listens and nods.

Then, I notice as I speak she starts to relax, that something loosens in her. She sits next to me, smiles and looks at me differently. And instead of yelling *You won't go to that house anymore,* she sincerely counsels me to be firm, strong in my principles, and face them with courage, unafraid, by myself. Without her, with the help of no one. Myself, as a man. She says I have to understand, Because I am intelligent, that the enemy is within, not outside, in your head, in your heart, in one's weakness, in the apathetic and susceptible spirit, *your father's character*, she says, that could make me fail.

Her eyes on my eyes, mine on hers. For an instant, terrified.

To fail is the worst, to fail is everything. To fail is to fail. To them. To your image, her image. To the great image that floats on top of her, on top of me, on top of the world. I always tend to fail, I know, I know she knows that I see that in me, the one who fails, the one who will disappoint her and everybody, but her above all.

It is good to win her confidence, being with her for a moment. Sitting next to her. That's why I don't care about telling her what she wants to hear about my father, or anyone, but mostly about my father. About his influence on me, about me being like him, about the risk of turning into him being close to him and fail like a mistake, an inheritance, a disgrace. Sitting down talking about serious matters, about treason, about future. I fail, I fail, I betray and kill my father.

No one can stop me: I fail.

Mother   *Don't deny it.*

He   *They don't talk in front of me, I swear. Never. About politics, never.*

Mother   *That's a lie! It's dangerous. You don't know the evil they do to you. To your future. You have no idea how dangerous it is for you, whenever you go there, to that house! I'm not letting you go until you tell me the truth. What they talk about. Everything they talk about in front of you. I know they talk.*

He   Then I talk. I keep on talking about politics, everything they talk about, what I imagine they talk about. I exaggerate, I kill, I lie, just to go.

Mother   *Take him, drop him at his father's place and race back. I'm in a hurry.*

Journey Towards Me

Father   It's the farewell. He doesn't look back. He jumps into the jeep and runs away. He steals the threatened trip, guilty, inconsiderate. A journey to his father's house. A journey to me.

Open fields, sugar cane on both sides of the road. Smoke on the horizon. Heat. Heavy rain hitting the canvas of the jeep, and seeping in through holes and slits soaking the seats, the clothes, the faces. It blurs the windshield. The fields are blurred through the glass, by the lightning. The streets in the town are blurred. My house is blurred by the rain. I am standing soaking wet at the door. He comes to me, wet. Each trip is an obstacle, but it's worth it, I tell him later. A damned journey, dangerous, but it's worth it, I tell him again. And he, understanding what I say, complicit, nods.

Encounters

Father   *Hello . . .*

Mother   *What is this? Did you know about this?*

Father   *Can I come in?*

Mother   *I have asked you not to come here. To my house. This is my house. We can talk wherever you want, but not here.*

Father   We got divorced before he could see us together. That's the reason why having us both now, face to face in a room, looks weird, painful. Whenever we meet, I can see he feels her contempt for me making him feel ashamed and afraid. Ashamed of being responsible for making her endure me and talk to me. Whenever we meet, like now, it's because of something strange about him. And afraid because he fears to be hated or despised by her for that. Undoubtedly, it happens.

Mother   *I can't stand him coming here, tell him next time!*

Father   She yells at him when I leave. *I'm sorry . . . Can I come in or not?*

Mother   *Name the time and place and I'll be there, but please, I repeat, not here. Not now.*

Father   I could just walk away, leave all this, but I don't. I'm still there, intimidated, insecure, fragile, feeling apologetic for standing in front of her. Feeling ashamed in her presence.

Mother   *Didn't I tell you to tell him not to come here? He told you, didn't he? Isn't it clear enough?*

Father   Yes, there is always a lot of shame in these encounters, a lot of hidden contempt in her, and he cannot understand. I don't look at him, I avoid looking at him, but I know he's on my side, I feel it. He feels sympathy for me, unarmed as I am in front of her cold fury, her haughty looks, her impatience. She's always impatient to bring this to an end. In a hurry to stop the matter that's blocking her from doing more important things. She's a busy woman, important, with a real life and job.

Mother   *Something your father will never have.*

Father   She makes me see this during these encounters with all her heart. She never sits down when I'm in front of her nor invites me to sit. She stands there, like now, next to the door. She shoots blunt and precise short phrases that go to the core of the problem, his strange behavior. Sharp and precise. Monosyllables and interjections to close the matter quickly like when she's dealing with a subordinate worker. She's a specialist when dealing with subordinates, with inferior people under her command. Bothering her unnecessarily with imprudence.

Mother   *How imprudent!*

Father   In such cases, she's merciless and doesn't hesitate to put them in their place quickly and decisively.

Mother   *OK, what do you want? What do you need? Really, I have no time.*

Father   She's a woman who knows how to command and she doesn't bother to be considerate. So, I pretend not to be in a hurry, just when she is building her favorite strategy, my nerves, my pride or the unawareness of what she has become, make me want to have a more calm and respectful conversation.

Mother   *What?*

Father   *Listen.*

Mother   *No.*

Father   *Let's just sit down and talk.*

Mother   *We have nothing to talk about.*

Father   *Listen.*

Mother   *You are bothering me.*

Father   *Try to understand.*

Father   I can't avoid being polite, formal, and I appeal and appeal to sit down and talk like friends, like civilized people. That makes the situation more unbearable and ridiculous for him, knowing what will come next. Also knowing that I know that he's there watching this humiliation that I try to reverse, hide and overcome. There's no possibility of behaving normally with me, formally, respectfully. And it ends up in her kicking me out without even looking into my eyes or raising her voice or getting upset, like dismissing a driver or a servant.

Mother   *Go away, please, I am busy.*

Father   I leave him there, with her, with her contempt.

Mother   *What have we talked about? What have I said about him coming here? How many times do I have to tell you? Answer me!*

Father   She doesn't hate me or despise me for the past. It is clear for him that it is not that. It is clear for him, that she doesn't hold a grudge against me. A grudge after the divorce that ended the chapter of the love that once was. The classical hatred of parents' lost love. No. It's something else. He knows. I know he knows. It's pure and simple aversion. A visceral, cold, petrified and passionless aversion. The same aversion that falls on him. He should stay next to her. Hearing all the scolding for me getting close to her or visiting her.

Mother   *I don't want him here, ever.*

Father   It is a startling cold fear. He's afraid of her, very much afraid of that coldness. Afraid of the rejection of me. And him, for being the cause of that unpleasant and unbearable encounter due to his strange behavior. He's afraid of that coldness that is devoid of hatred, yelling, insult, beating, jealousy, contempt, claims, blackmail or hysteria, but something different that brings great fear and shame.

Father   *Easy, it's nothing, I'm OK. I'm leaving, it's late. I'll see you in the summer, OK? Call me. Give me a kiss.*

Father   I run away from there, from that. From that coldness. From me too, from him, from the two of us. It is beyond my strength. Something I leave behind as I save myself.

Therapies

He   *Fight!* I'm wearing the boxing gloves. I hear the command for the second time, stronger now. *Fight!* The other boy is waiting for my punch in a defensive stance with his hands up wearing enormous boxing gloves like me. I am the newcomer. He's an old timer here and feels superior. He's given beatings before. He's not being tested. I am. I have to pass the test of taking a punch to be approved by the doctors. The beating farce. He's still there, facing me. He waits. In spite of the smile he flaunts and the boxing moves he makes in front of me, he's afraid, he's terrified of being beaten. I see his eyes on mine and I know what's going on, I know what he feels, I know he feels what I feel. Fear. Shame. Inhibition. He hides all that better than me. He's learned how to act. He dances and moves like a real boxer, he smiles to provoke, he's showing off. At once, he realizes, in my hesitation, I am no danger, that I am ashamed of acting the way he does. Then he takes advantage to score more points. He shouts something. He flaunts. He exposes himself. He mocks me to my face. *Fight! On guard!* The doctor shouts, angry, upset, he pushes me from behind, I tumble on the other boy who pushes me strongly and smiles in victory. He's weak, skinny, ugly. I feel he's found his chance. He takes advantage of it. I'm ashamed of being like him, to act for the others, humiliate myself like that. I won't yield. I hate to be there. They all hate to be there, but they posture to get the prize, approval. I don't know how to do it. I prefer to cry. I cry. It's his chance to beat me. He punches me in the face. *Defend yourself! Don't be such a chicken!*

In spite of his weakness, the boy goes mad and gets all the applause from the onlookers, who stop making fun, get confused and start to celebrate him. They stand up from their chairs and carry him around the room on their shoulders. He keeps on acting, laughs and begets laughter. His lie is sad, his meanness, his triumph in the presence of the doctors. I am in the middle of the room, shattered.

To play out the game is enough for them. The show is enough for them and then they tell the parents outside in the waiting room. I cannot pretend. It's ridiculous. The therapy consists of duties. Boxing, undoing and redoing toy cars, hitting our heads with pillows, fighting hand to hand, catching another boy while the others watch from the tables. All the rest seem to be happy there. I am not. I know what they are plotting, what they are doing to us. I'm paralyzed. Knowing all that freezes me, it takes advantage from me. Nobody's happy here. It's a lie! It's always a lie. They mock, they act so that they will be left alone. For the parents outside to be happy, full of hope for the doctors' reports. I know that, and that affects me.

At the beginning, there's a murmur in the house, a growing menace around me. They look at me and mutter. They discuss what should be done with me. I hear them. I always hear everything, what is going on, what they see in me. They start to watch me, they ask bizarre questions. I know the answers for all those questions, but I don't answer. I confuse them instead. There is also scolding: *Put your hands down, don't talk like that, don't move your hands like that, don't play with that, go out and play.* I don't pay attention. I hate to obey those commands. I keep still and do nothing. I don't change a thing. I withdraw into myself. Against them. When they determine that I should be treated, my father opposes. My mother insists, but he opposes. Many of their meetings are about that, to decide what's to be done with me. My father wants me to live with him in his town. It's a solution, a real father, an example for a boy in trouble, I am in trouble. But my mother refuses flatly. And my father has to accept that I will be treated.

Take the chalk, go to the board and draw a man and a woman. They are all paying attention, curious, expectant of what I am going to do. I know what they are looking for. What they want to see in my drawing. I always know everything. That's my downfall, my intelligence. They felt it from the beginning and hated it. Another obstacle, intelligence. I walk to the board and draw a man and a woman. No hips, no shoulders, no boobs. *Is that a man? Is that a woman? Are you sure? I don't know how to draw.* He calls for a volunteer. Another boy goes to the board and draws a man and a woman. He knows how to do it without making them notice anything strange in the drawing. He's been there for a long time now, he's sold, he's on their side. Pale, with a girly face. He hates me. They are all like that there. They hate. They detest being friends. They are friends with the doctors who use them for buying snacks and be entertained while some beat the new one, any one.

These boys have given in. They submissively fight one another in front of the doctors in the room. They scratch one another, they bite and roll on the floor fighting while the others shout and bet for the winner. They try to kill time no matter what. Win no matter what. Not me. I am apathetic, passive, they don't like me. No one likes me. The doctors are young, a bit older than all of us. They get bored. They kill time in the morning or the afternoon with us. The parents wait confident, for the reports of the day, for the improvements of the day, outside. The success of the therapy. The doctors eat their snacks in front of us while they talk about women. They tell us what they do to women. The other boys laugh as if they were interested, as if they knew about that. The one who knows more wins, the one who tells something about that wins. The doctors tell us how they jerk off, they touch themselves and show us what it is, the way they do it. None of us knows anything about that yet, they say. But we have to know. We are men. Men stuff. It's not manly to tell our parents about this. Nobody talks about what happens there. You learn to be on their side, to do what they tell you to do.

See? See? That's a man and a woman. Try again. Are you listening? Take the chalk. Draw! Are you dumb or what? They want hips, waists, shoulders, boobs. I can't give them that. It could be dangerous. If I draw well, they will know something about me.

They talk with my mother in the waiting room. I see them complain to her. They talk about me, I am a disaster, I'm helpless. They don't like me. It doesn't work for me. I don't react to it. I don't improve. I get worse. She looks at me furious from the distance, she's disappointed. They are all angry. They understood very quickly that my denial was different. I'm hopeless, dangerous. I should not be there, I can damage the others, their progress. I know something the others don't know. They shouldn't know at their age. My age. They don't say that, but I know they feel it. I don't look my age. I don't come back. I am expelled, incurable. Hopeless. They don't take me to the doctors anymore.

Album 1

Mother   Sorry, but I don't have memories of these pictures. Of my relationship with him. Of the way we were together. They are strange pictures. Of unknown people. Of these two I see here. Their pictures. Not ours. Of two nameless people who are no longer us. I'm talking about the time when we met and were a regular couple in a provincial town, or during our honeymoon, dreamed of by all the girls who, like me, saved themselves for marriage. Something didn't work out from the first time. From the first night. It didn't work out for them, for these two that stayed together during the pregnancy till hatred and repulsion came in. The oblivion of this album. I see them now, in this picture. This one. They are embracing by the sea. His arm around her hips, around her low-neck dress of tiny flowers, tight on the waist and knees, typical of the fifties. Her short chestnut hair, blown by the sea wind that also inflates his dark color shirt like a balloon, unveiling part of his chest. The sea behind them, black and wavy. The sea in old black and white pictures. She smiles at the camera apparently happy. With a smile that announces what will come after. A kind of tension and pretense I also see here, in the wedding pictures. A fake and artificial smile hiding something I cannot define, but I can tell she's uncomfortable. She's stuck in the wedding gown, waving goodbye from the car surrounded by guests, by relatives. It's something I feel only by looking at these pictures of a wedding I don't recognize anymore. There is a lack of spontaneity in those moments when things are not pleasant for her, and she has to pretend. He's next to her, happy, truly happy. I can see him smiling in all the images, ignorant of what is happening to her.

I don't understand what was happening there. I know, but I don't understand it anymore. How did it come to that? To so much? Maybe the town, the pressure, the age, the convention. A mistake, everything was a mistake in them. However, the wavy sea, black, her chestnut hair, short, blown by the wind, his revealed smooth chest; deserved more. A destiny. One whole happy night that they didn't have. By stupidity? I don't remember. These are pictures that don't deserve to be kept. No one wants them. No one kept them. No one values them. They belong to no one. It's not us. We are no one. It's them! Two youngsters. Strangers on a beach, in a wedding, a long time ago. They are nobody's memories, nothing. It didn't happen, it was not real. It is not even past. It is not even memory. Because nobody remembers that. To be the past somebody has to remember. The beach, the wind, the shirt. It's nothing. Unfortunate photographs of two people that were not.

Therapies

Author   *Take him to another school, away from the neighborhood. Put him in a boarding school where his grandmother cannot reach him and nobody can spoil him.*

He   I am in second grade, middle of second grade. One day I don't go to class anymore. She doesn't wait till the end of the year, she pulls me out and puts me in a boarding school. It is a boarding school in the outskirts of the city. I am there from Monday to Friday. A school full of kids I don't know. Strangers. Of all ages. Where do they come from?

A school near the sea. They talk about the sea, about the wonderful school at the beach. The children say that if everything is OK, one day they will take us down to the beach. The school is on the hills. You can hear the beach down there. We can't see it, we just hear it. We feel it. The salt, the noise of the waves, the breeze of the sea. It's a place by the sea.

We live in beautiful houses that were confiscated from the bourgeoisie. Big houses with no windows or doors, rundown and full of bunk beds where the children sleep. I sleep in a bunk bed. From the hole of the window in my room, I can see a pine forest. I hear the noise of the sea. It is cold in the early morning. The oldest boys talk all night, they don't stop. They sit on their beds and smoke and talk. I listen to them, I don't quite understand what they talk about. In the mornings, we march in squads to the dining room and the classrooms. Military squads. One guide sings the steps while we march on the streets of that neighborhood that is the school. We march all the time. It's the only thing that works. The only thing that's well organized.

We wash in the courtyard, at the back of the house, altogether, outside. There's only one bathroom in the house with one big pipe of cold water, instead of a shower. You jump into the jet of water and quickly run outside, on the grass while another child jumps in. There is no soap or towels, just a strong pressure jet of cold water. You dry in the air, with your clothes. One teacher keeps an eye at the door and gives commands. *Hurry up. You get in. Hurry up. What the hell are you doing? Get out now.* He knows some of the kids and calls them by name. Others, like me, he has no clue who we are. He doesn't care. It's not his job. He doesn't know my name. Nobody knows my name there, not even the other boys. I don't know their names either. I am alone, in the squads, in the classrooms, in the dining room. Nobody takes me to class, or introduces me to any teacher. I'm not told what to do, or when or where to go. I get in the first class I see when I get to the houses where the classrooms are. I sit at a desk at the back and listen to the teacher without understanding a word. He doesn't care what I am doing there or who I am. A new one, he guesses, another one, who knows. I listen to the teacher and I don't understand a thing. Some kids know something and answer the questions. It is Chinese for me. It is only a matter of time. I don't want to be discovered or told off in front of the others. Next morning, I join a different class, with a different teacher and different kids. Then, one girl notices me sitting next to her and assures me that that is not my class. I ask her how she knows and she tells me my group is another one, I am from a different group. I don't know which one. I slip away from there when she insists on telling the teacher. I'm ashamed of not knowing which class I belong to. I'm ashamed of asking. I pretend to belong there. I try to be unnoticed. I will somehow understand. I will get used to this like the others. I have no notebooks. I don't take notes. I have nothing. I only have the clothes I'm wearing. I don't remember whether it is a uniform or my own clothes. I wear it all the time, every day, every week I'm there.

One day, I don't go anymore. My mother decides to take me out of there. Why? I don't know. They talk about corruption, teachers with girls, parties at the principal's office, scandals, reports. I don't know, but I know. I always know. I know what she avoids, what she's afraid of. She takes me out of there and puts me in another school. One more test, one more beginning. Therapy: Having a hard time, being hungry, being on my own, so far away, without contemplation. No consideration. I know the words they repeat around me. I know them and I make them not work. To cast myself aside, to hate everything, to wait. Do nothing to please her. Cooperating with that, with her, makes me sick.

I haven't finished second grade. It's still the same year, a lifetime, an eternity. She has her reasons, I know them, but I don't cooperate. She takes me from one place to another, with her, but far from her.

Mother   *Come.*

He   She takes me to those places, under surveillance. I hear her request:

Mother   *Make him work, make him fight, let him be one in the crowd.*

He   I'm always the new one, the one from the city, the weirdo, among weird children, among farmers, and violent teachers. The directors keep an eye on me to tell her and gain her. Among strangers. Far from home.

This time the school is near the sugar factory she runs at the southern part of the province. The 70s, the Ten-Million Harvest. She goes up, she climbs up. She becomes an important person.

I finish the year there with good marks. Despite the changes, the moving, the shuffling around. I should be smart, and not allow to be crushed. I know. It's my way.

I'm living in a house with a family of farmers with lots of daughters who take me in and treat me well. I sleep in a room at the back of the house, half built, in an iron bed with a thin mattress on top. I have breakfast with them in the wooden kitchen. Then, I walk to the town school. I immediately understand the town. I play with children from my street when I come home from school. One more, one less.

Sometimes she drives past the center of the town at top speed in her jeep. And when people see her pass they shout: *The captain, the woman captain, there she goes!* That's what they call her. Beautiful, domineering. She's a mystery, the heroine, the owner of everything. They soon start calling me *the captain's son.*

I don't see her till Saturday. She picks me up and takes me to my house, to my room. One room, in the city.

Politics

Mother   Politics for me? For my generation? I say it quickly. It was passion. A revelation . . . something overwhelming. It is not any longer, fortunately. Not now. Not for him. For him politics was a disgrace, the end, a disaster. It ruined everything there was before. Dreams. Life as it was. However, politics made me wake up. It made me fight the fate of being the woman he dreamed of, and all his family. It was a fate I was tied to like any other girl in that town, had the Revolution never triumphed at that moment.

All the passion I was capable of revealed itself back then like an epidemic, a broadening. And he, attached to the interests of his petit-bourgeois, well-off family, didn't even feel or understand. Just like that, so sad. It was an awakening that shattered the dream of becoming a good married woman, the obedient mother of the first-born son. Those dreams, that I had once longed for, that I had married him for, became instantly ridiculous with the Revolution.

He was reduced to nothing. A little man who sought happiness by means of family routine. All of a sudden, he stopped being the good catch all my friends envied me for, a guy from a good family, good looking, educated, with a future.

The Revolution was the place to experience freedom at a big scale. I gave myself to it, to politics, with such a thirst that cooled down all my passion for him, for a life with him. However, resigned and powerless, he would wait for me late at night to come home dirty, exhausted after long journeys of work I imposed upon myself with a fanatic happiness.

I can imagine his shame for not being able to control me, for having to take my place at home and being humiliated for what it implied in a small town where people know everything. He hoped for a normal life to return, for the madness to stop. He counted on it. He was in love. In love, not only with my beauty, that was outstanding, but also with my strength, the indomitable will, the dexterity and the surprising character I had. And maybe I don't have any of it anymore. There and then, he lost the game. He was unable to fight that spirit. Because, deep inside, he was too confused and fascinated as to firmly discourage me. And I hated that lack of determination, his weakness. *Your father's weakness, I used to tell you, accusing you of that dangerous inheritance.* Yes, I was a fanatic of determination, a fanatic of virility, of courage in life. And it's not that he lacked that completely. He was overwhelmed, surprised by the amount of strength, determination and courage I had.

I began taking on management positions with higher profile in the political spheres of the town. I became someone important, trustworthy, powerful, enchanting for all, even for him. A woman with power was something so unthinkable and inconceivable at that time, that it rapidly gave me an aura of attraction, a magnetism that I noticed and used for my purposes very cleverly. It was an effect that catapulted me quickly, astonishing everybody. A woman with power is stronger than a man with power. It bewitches, perturbs and disconcerts twice as much, all the more so considering the classic beauty that I was.

In less than two years, he became a man from another era, with no future, an example of a vanished world, a superficial boy from an annihilated and useless middle class, someone I was married to, who I had to get rid of no matter what.

1970—Ten Million

Therapies

He   Sugar cane fields burning. The harvest. She wants me to be there when they burn the fields. Yet another therapy. The fields burning for hours, during the night, during the whole night till dawn. Men fighting the fire, no time to waste, it's a combat, all together, gone crazy. *That will teach him, keep him there, he has to know how it is,* she said. Fire everywhere. Smoke in columns, black, up in the sky. Men on the sides of the trucks sweating all over, burned, black faces, stained, shouting, *what the hell is this boy doing here?* We sleep in the cabins of the trucks, surrounded by fire and smoke, keeping an eye on the fire.

Hunger, we are all starving. A piece of bread, a metal tray with rice, beans, water with sugar, I'm always hungry. I only see men with black faces, masks. I don't see real faces, clean, I can't see what those faces look like. Then they leave for other harvests. They disappear.

There's no time for resting. Morning comes and we are in the cabins, in the middle of the field. The ten million tons of sugar! Now, I see what therapy is.

Who's that? The Captain's son. The men murmur in the dark, around me, with black faces, with masks. *What is he doing here? He's helping with the fire.*

Album 2

Mother (*looking into the album*)   Yes, it's her. I guess. In the same recurrent picture. Always giving speeches in grandstands. Her finger to the air, her face lit up, facing attentive crowds who make her conscious of her natural skills. She's always wearing boots and a beret, surrounded by unknown people, optimistic, like an amazon, of a new age, defiant, amused.

These are funny photographs. She's having a good time. I'm sure she's having a good time. She's young. And she's free for the first time. She's herself. The one that was once. Authentic. In the zenith of her life. Happy. The one from those years. The one I really was. The one I cannot be anymore. Or wish to be anymore.

I can't stop thinking how entertaining the game of politics and the Revolution was for her, going away from a routine life in a small town (like in these pictures, but not now). And how boring it was before. Enjoyment, rhythm and speed broke something in her that made her get away from that first brief stage of her life. Her sight focused on big issues, transcendental issues, amusing, just or not, but definitely amusing, powerful, vertiginous, heady. Youth chooses vital intensity as the most interesting truth. Social justice has to be, above all, intense, fast, shifting, energizing, never boring or gradual. And she's young in these photos. She cannot walk away from this first connection with the Revolution, that is making her stay young, dangerously adolescent, until much later, when all of a sudden, she changes and leaves. When I leave. When I left. I guess.

Therapies

He   *You won't be robbed there.* My grandma says while putting clothes in my bag. Shirts, underwear, pairs of clean socks for each day of the week. *This is a real school.* She says while filling the bag. I have the feeling I'll be alright. I see the dorm buildings on TV, clean, large, luminous. Students wearing blue uniforms, a coat with a waist band and a buckle for the winter. A darker blue tie to wear when we go home. The buildings stand on concrete columns. They are modern, in the middle of the field. *A real school,* she mumbles.

He plays volleyball. I don't see him at first. He has pimples. His face is deformed by something that looks like leprosy. He sleeps in a bed at the far end. I don't look at him. He's quiet, invisible. He seems to be good at volleyball. Who cares?

I lose my sheets during the first week. I come back from class and they're not there. Nobody knows, nobody saw anybody. Nobody cares if I don't have sheets. Then the pillow goes. The socks in the bag are gone too. The five pairs for each day of the week. My grandmother's socks. I count each item of clothing over and over. I look for them in the bottom of the bag. Maybe she forgot to put them in, I'm not sure. Impossible. Then the underwear vanishes. The condensed milk too. The bread, the pencils, the notebooks. *Shock! Shock! Shock!* The bag is empty, flat on my locker when I come from class. It is worn out, ripped, open. It looks at me torn, dead, nothing inside. The world inside is now gone. Nobody knows, nobody saw a thing. Just like that. I learn that right there at once. This is it. This is it. Be careful! There are no socks for each day here. Nobody has so many socks here. Then, I don't have socks, underwear, food, notebooks. I only carry one folded notebook in the back pocket of my trousers, just to pretend I'm taking notes. I don't really do it. I just scribble. I learn and memorize the classes to pass the exams.

He has been robbed too. He sleeps with no sheets, naked or wearing the uniform if it is cold, on the dirty stained mattress, on the board of the bunk at the far end. He's not complaining. Complain? To who? Who would listen? Who cares about a thing? I know now. I've known for a long time, from the beginning, but I learn again the hard way, learn it for good, right there. There's nothing to say. Nothing to complain about, nothing to claim. Do something. Get away from this. There's no one. Nothing. There is a void out there, indifferent to you.

I try to steal a sheet to protect myself from the cold. He watches me doing it. He says nothing. He's strange, ugly. It doesn't matter if he sees me. He's quiet. He keeps silent, he doesn't denounce me. Nobody denounces anything.

I read. There's a library nobody goes to. Nobody gets in. I do. I go and get a book one day. Then I keep on going to read. To be calmed, alone in that place nobody goes to. A boring place, a nonexistent place. I read on the corridors too, at the back of the classrooms, in the fields, during the work in the fields. I read. Do something or nothing. I read there, bored. I read *The Red and the Black* over and over. The same book. That's how my reading started, my full-time reading. Because of *The Red and the Black*. But above all, because of Julian Sorel, the main character. Hated by the brothers in the sawmill, *it's me*. Reading a book on a tree, *it's me, another me*. Everything started with Julian Sorel. I look for more in the library day and night because of him. He's hiding up on a tree with a book from his brothers who throw stones at him. I become a full-time reader, in the classroom, on the central square of the school, in the nonexistent place.

The next year, the second there, he comes with his face clean. I can see his big eyes now. He is placed on the bed next to mine. He's very white. He gets these spots on his back that need to be cured with a potion. He can't get his hands to the spots and asks for help. I rub the spots on his back with a piece of cotton. My fingers get stained with the yellow potion that smells like iron or sulfur. It's something between him and me. The yellow stains on my fingers, my sacrifice. We do it when there's no one around. Sometimes in the bathroom, in the toilet. I am rubbing his back! It's a secret of necessity. He needs my help, I offer it to him. It's a forced complicity. He hates the spots on his back, like he hated his pimples. That's why he asks for my help, and agrees to hide away. He asks me to stay in the dorm when the others leave. I stay. Then he takes out the little bottle and a piece of cotton and we hide in the toilet. We lock the door and I heal him. While doing it, I see his eyes, they shine brown, big, they appear to me. I can see them now, not before.

Perhaps, it is the discovery of his features, his appearing face, the surprise to see what he has changed into; what makes me see his body, harmonious, pale, nude. The new face makes you see there is a body, a waist, two white feet, down there.

He approaches me. *What are you reading? A novel. What's it called?* The Red and the Black. *What for? What? Why are you reading it?* I don't know what to say. *Just because. I like it. What? What do you like? To read. Why? I don't know. Yes, you do, you know a lot.*

He shows me how much he ejaculates, the amount, he has the amount in his hand. He's proud of that. He asks how much I come. I tell him. He talks about women. He doesn't ask what I think of, he just tells me things, desires.

Then, I follow his volleyball skills. Now, I know what it is to be good at it, I learn it from him. Looking at him. Full time. I read and look at him playing full time. I don't do anything else. Just read and look at him. I notice everybody discovers him just like me. The girls, the tough guys too, the ones who steal, all fascinated by him. By his appearing new face that shows up in front of everybody and makes you see his pale, sweaty body, jumping and hitting the ball in the air and showing a smile that now you can see. I learn how to admire. It happens. For the first time. It blossoms all of a sudden. Admiration. Looking at him jump, fall, win. Every day, every week. I feel everybody's looking at him like me, all together, with me, pushed by me, by my eyes.

Every afternoon, in every match, in every victory on the volleyball court. I follow him everywhere, after class, to the dining room, during the break, to the fields. My time is his. I saw him before everybody. I helped him with the spots. His back shines now and it is my discovery too. Everybody is proud of him. They want him close. He's the best. But he doesn't use me, he doesn't step aside, he doesn't desert me. He has sheets now, nobody takes them from him anymore. I too have sheets because of him. He tells me: *You will do something*. He says that because I read, because he's impressed by the books, though he doesn't read.

Give him no privileges, let him be one of the bunch, let him look for his own place, let him learn what it is like. She always says. I finally understand what she means. I run away to the nearest town with him. We just wander around. Looking for food. I jump in the irrigation channels with him. I steal exams. We spit on the teachers' shit.

Are you alright? My grandmother asks. *At school, are you alright? Alright? Of course, I'm alright, grandma. With the piss and the shit in the dorms, the nerve of the teachers who don't teach anything, the promiscuity and the bullying around me . . . He's there . . .*

You look like brothers. The others say. He doesn't say a thing, but he's proud of us being seen like brothers. We learn what loyalty means. We hide away not to go to work in the fields, run away in the fields, under the rain, the sun. We eat oranges to fill our stomachs, share the soap, the clothes, the boots, the bad smells, the fever, the jokes. I learn nothing but that. I learn nothing but him. I have nothing of my own, a sheet, a dirty change of clothes for the week, *The Red and the Black*. The rest was stolen from me.

He was there.

The Last Summer

Mother   *Take him to his father's place and come back right away, I'm in a hurry.*

Father   They leave the city in the olive-green jeep at top speed. It's a long trip along the Central Road. They take the entrance of the hills, from where they look out over the town, the valley, the river. They pull up in front of the garden. He jumps down, bag in hand, and hugs me at the door, where I've been waiting shirtless, in shorts, with my arms open. I stroke his head, his hair. I bring him in to the slowness and twilight of my house. *You've grown up a lot this year! You are thinner,* I tell him. He's thinner every year, taller, grown up. Then, he walks around the bedrooms, the kitchen, the laundry, the aisles. He glimpses out the windows to the backyard full of hens, stones and rabbits in wooden cages. Frightened white rabbits with red eyes that I raise to eat. He looks out to the yard where there is a cold ditch with greenish water, full of slime, and frogs. I follow him around while asking him about school, the exams, his grades, what he intends to study. He doesn't understand. He cannot understand what it is, what happens. I take his sweaty shirt off and hang it on the back of a chair. I give him lunch and sit at the other end of the table to watch him eat. Quiet, smiling for having him there, again, another summer.

Father   *Aren't you hungry?*

He   *Yes.*

Father   *Eat.*

He   *You don't eat?*

Father   *I like watching you eat.*

Father   I can feel the despair of those moments. My despair, not his. I could leave the country at any moment. I know. He enjoys his summer. A summer with me. One more. He doesn't understand, he cannot understand.

Father   *I have a present for you. It's a surprise.*

Father   I always have presents sent in packages from Miami. My brothers, his uncles, my mother; have lived there for years and they send packages with stuff for those of us who stayed behind.

He   *What is it?*

Father   *I don't know, I haven't opened it yet.*

Father   I've lived alone in this house since my brothers got the permit to leave and left. Life is reduced to waiting. Since the permit to leave takes long, life goes by while waiting for a new start somewhere else. He comes on the established month, during the summer holidays. I have all the time for him, an unlimited time that I dedicate to him with the patience of a sentenced man.

He   *Balloons!*

Father   *Just that? Are you sure? I saw something else.*

He   *Chewing gum!*

Father   There are always balloons and chewing gum for him in those packages. I inflate the balloons that smell brand new, plastic, and tie them to cardboard bases so they can stand up on the floor as if they were tamed. They are long, smooth like rubber plants with dazzling new colors. I make him play with them all the time so he can make good use of them before he leaves. When he does, the balloons are still standing in a corner of the living room, a whole garden of balloons, waiting for next summer. *Keep them for me,* he says while covering them with a sheet and then leaves. There is no chance he can take them, they are clandestine balloons. There they are, on the corner of the living room, until little by little, with the days, they burst.

When the permit to leave comes, you have to leave at once, no matter the time, late at night or morning, or noon, and take the essential with you. No time to make phone calls. Calling the city by operator is difficult and slow, to say goodbye. This could be the last summer. The one before last, the one before that one perhaps. No one can know. Nobody knows how the mechanism works. The great mechanism of departure. My intense way of looking after him seems very normal to him, the right amount. It will never end. He doesn't understand. He can't understand. I do. That's why those days are ours, for the two of us, together. Walking freely around town, playing in the bushes in the backyard with the rabbits. Resting on the porch in the afternoons. Or in the darkness of the workshop where I work as a mechanic punished for having applied for my permanent departure permit.

At home, he takes a siesta with me, under the mosquito net, on the big bed. He uses real napkins to eat, and silver cutlery. He reads the comics I've collected since I was a child. *Lassie, Donald Duck, Superman . . .* yellowish—also clandestine—In full colors, in a box, his reading box. He doesn't know, he can't know.

We ride on a bicycle along the streets. I sit on the saddle and pedal, he sits on the crossbar within my arms clinging to the handlebars. The bicycle, he and me around the town, the heat. We look like a centaur. Mythological. Summer ends. It could be the last one, I fear it is the last one. Maybe not. We could have more. I don't know. Nobody knows. Inscrutably, the mechanism doesn't speak, it doesn't give hints. Only surprises.

He goes back to the city with his mother, to the boarding school. I have the feeling I won't catch up with him anymore.

Second Moment

Crowds and Power

Author   Memories of some months of 1980.

He   I hear my name on the loudspeakers, I need to present myself at the reception at once. When I arrive, I see my grandmother. Something must have happened that made her come to my school on a weekday. *Your mother doesn't know I'm here, we have to talk,* she says. We sit down at the parking lot, in the car she has rented to drive her from the city. Then, she takes out a letter from her bag, that a relative from the town has sent as an explanation. As an information on my father's acts. My father? What's the problem with him? They explain what has happened, what is happening, what could still be happening, what happened. I listen to her, but I don't listen, I don't understand what I am hearing till sometime after, even weeks. My grandmother reads the letter holding my hand.

In the letter, they explain there was an embassy giving political asylum to anyone. During the night, my father had traveled to the city on a truck, together with some other people from his town. They broke into the embassy. He was still inside, waiting for a permit to leave the country. A permit that *criminals*, *marginal people* and *traitors* that took refuge in the embassy were demanding.

My father?

The images of what is happening at the embassy are on TV. In the letter, they condemn what my father has done. *Unforgivable, an atrocity.* They write to give comfort to us, particularly to me, to his son. They urge me to be strong, to be fearless. They say I can count on the affection and support of whoever wrote that letter. I don't record the details of the story. Too many words, too much affection. Where does the affection come from? And the advice? I don't want any solidarity, I don't need it.

When my grandmother finishes reading, she says nothing will happen to me, I should be calm about this matter. *What matter?* I think. She says I shouldn't tell anybody. Much less at school. *It is important not to talk.* She repeats. *Nobody will harm you for this.* Who? Why? What is she talking about? She leaves frightened, crying. I come back to class. I don't know what to think. I really don't think about anything. Of course, I don't tell anybody what is going on. But, is it happening? They seem like alien events, from another world.

The TV channels continuously broadcast images of the occupied embassy full of people. They explain that the first people who broke in killed a security guard at the entrance. I can't stop looking at the images. I watch them and I can't understand what they have to do with me, with him. At school, the anger grows among the teachers and the students. There is no other subject during the daily morning ceremonies that week. We grow more and more heated while chorusing accusations. What do I think?

Or feel? I don't remember. I erased it. I echo each accusation and slogan along with the others. I become very angry at what I see, at what I hear is happening, *something beyond belief, unprecedented.* I am convinced and get upset with what is happening there, in the images, with the unpleasant sequences and faces. Faces so different to my father's. There's no relation. However, I know I should not talk. But I don't see any relation. I don't understand.

During the week, we are told we will parade in front of the embassy together with hundreds of students to protest against the events. I don't refuse to go. I don't pretend I have a high fever or a cold or any other symptom of a disease. I go. That has nothing to do with me.

On our day off, we take the buses. When we get to the scene of events in the city, we make up groups. We are given banners and flags. We slowly join the squad of people marching nonstop for days along the avenue in front of the embassy.

The anger grows. It becomes strong and energetic. People are chanting slogans. We hear loud political songs from speakers accompanying the parade like a soundtrack along with voices protesting on the procession. Some streets away from the occupied embassy, I start to understand my situation. I remember my euphoria for the adventure, for all that, for being there, in the parade. As we get near the embassy, people around me stop fooling around and change. I also change. Just when we are approaching the main entrance, the core of the event, the discomfort starts. My discomfort. I understand how exceptional and desperate the situation is. My father is in there, he can look out a window, see me pass, or I might as well see him. I'm outside yelling, cursing, accusing him. He's still in there receiving all the scorn. I am outside against him without him knowing. I begin to understand the situation. I am part of that massive crowd. I'm on my own, alone, helpless. Senseless. I'm being dragged there, forward, towards him, against him, hopelessly.

Just some meters away from the entrance, we can see some of the occupants on the roof. People around me start to yell with new and sudden fury. Once in front of the building, seen so many times on TV, a commotion overtakes the group around me, accompanied by much louder songs from the speakers. The songs generate a compact, deep and massive shuddering. And make us raise our hands and yell with a disconcerting fury. I yell too, unexpectedly, automatically. I yell over and over again what they all yell, what we're told to yell, what you have to yell there. In the few seconds it takes to pass the entrance, I anxiously look for my father's face among the people looking out the windows. I yell with the chorus and at the same time look for him fearfully, anxiously, I yell and look for him. The two things at the same time with a contradictory, unexpected and incontrollable impulse. Suddenly, I remember, I lower my hands, I stop yelling. It's a reaction no one around me notices or understands. Next, I remember I cry, for my father in there and me outside, for my yelling, for the disdain, for the emotion that brings us together and apart, for not being and being part of that. Distant and at the same time immerse in what is happening and shouldn't happen. Something I disdain and support. I cry. And my crying erases the last images of the façade of the embassy. The human river pushes us onward, towards reality. Then we try to find a way out and look for the buses parked on secondary streets. The noise. All the joking for finding seats.

The Banality of Evil

Mother   He arrives home excited. I've been waiting for him. Seeing him in such a state, I cheer him up. I feel relieved, I congratulate him and hug him. *Your father has done wrong, terribly wrong,* I remember I told him. *He didn't think about you, he thought about himself. He made his choice for him, not for you.* He had to understand the way he left him behind when he ran away. He had to be strong to face what his father had done, to face the irreparable damage caused. He nods. He understands me. I see he understands the transcendental moment we are living. *We have to define ourselves,* I tell him, *we have to be clear and not hesitate in a moment like this.* He agrees with me. At last! What a relief! I was afraid he didn't understand and would make things more complicated. But it's nothing like that. And I am happy. I praise him again. I hug him. I kiss him. I tell him I am proud of him, of his strength, of his character, of his courage to see the essence and the importance of it. He is moved by my words. I support him and tell him that we are right. He will understand and he should be confident in what he does. I remember the house was burning hot, the neighborhood, the people, for what was happening all the time, everywhere. It's a unique and definite moment.

I ask him not to go out, for safety reasons. *Everything is a mess out there. It's better to be isolated, rest and forget. It's better to wait for things to be clearer. It's your father, no one knows what they could think of you, what could happen.* He accepts. Understands. We are together in this, united for the first time.

He spends the weekend in his room, under my care. I'm watching the phone to make sure his father does not try to contact him, should he dare. Once he's sent home to wait for the departure.

From the news—we watch the news all the time—we know they are sent home first to be taken out of the country afterwards.

Those weeks are good for the two of us, I remember. He enjoys me taking care of him, attentive, next to him, not fighting like other times, on the same frequency. United. Like never before.

Little by little, the crisis ends, as well as the images and accusations on TV and on the streets. We come back to our previous lives. Then he goes back to school, to his classes. I return to my business, to work, to the problems that take all our time. My office requires all my efforts at a hundred percent, day and night, with no rest, no life. It is a sacrifice that can only be understood by the ones who know me and were there and know our life was like that.

He learned from relatives that his father left the country in a boat together with others like him. However, we don't talk about the departure and the details of his journey.

When and under what conditions. It's better like that. Turn the page and omit the matter, and the images that could be left. I'm not good at that either, at talking. I believe more in what oblivion fixes. The country forgets. And that's what he needs. His father left for good. An event with no return. With no solution. Something definite we don't have to deal with. Like death. *To leave like that, like he did, is like dying, disappearing. Period.* On the other hand, he doesn't look affected. He doesn't talk, he doesn't ask questions. He doesn't want to know. In a way, what he knows is enough for him. The little he knows is enough for him. I see him quiet, confident, satisfied, with no interests. That's the way it should be. Then, talk about what? What for? Was it raining when he left? Was it stormy or sunny? Was he in danger during his journey? It was simply a journey, a departure. A treason.

I stop watching the phone and eventually, I close the case. Until today, when I am asked to talk about it, to come back to that. What do I really have to say? How can I recall it? I can reconstruct some things, facts, perhaps some ideas that were at stake. However, they are ideas from the past, overcome, that I can only recall or dramatize for you now. And when you do this, they are not the great political ideas they used to be anymore. They are like ghosts of ideas. What I could say now is useless for what this play is searching for: To know what we were.

About this, one last thought and I exit this text. I maybe didn't act well. However, that was the person I was at that time, and I believed in that person. And I was backed up by the majority who believed that acting like that was just. The right thing. Moral.

There is no regret. It's a melodrama, a beautiful fiction: To regret really. When we regret, we are different already, and the past has no connection with what we are or think now. We are old. We don't see things the way we use to see them. We change our minds and move forward. To complain about what happened, to ask ourselves what it was or was not, what we did or did not; is silly. Because nobody listens to those demands, those complaints. There is no one to listen to them and do something real with them. We are not there. It is already too late when we listen to them, we are different. Complaining does not solve a thing. Justice does not exist, nor does the true reparation. It only occupies the present. To move forward, keep on going, to fight, to exist.

I am another person.

Journey Towards Myself

Father   He only goes back to the town after one year, with his grandmother, so I'm told much later. At the end of that visit, before going back to the city, they decide to stop by his sister's house. My other child, who used to live blocks away from me. They learn from her that the house is still empty, sealed since the departure. *You have grown up a lot,* she says. She tells me she told him when she saw him at the door. She told him just like I used to tell him every summer when he reappeared taller and grown up. She kisses him on the cheek and offers them lunch. They accept.

In a moment, after lunch, just when they are about to leave, very carefully, his sister starts telling them what happened when he returned home from the embassy. The events that took place the previous year, that he didn't know or didn't want to know or was not allowed to know. She tells him that when I left the embassy, instead of coming straight back home to wait for the departure, I decided, maybe because of fear, to spend those days with some cousins in a place nobody knew me. My cousins are in the same situation and that's why I think I will be safer there. Unharmed.

Next morning after I arrived in that house, some people had organized an event against us. Then, she describes what we know happens in those acts. Hundreds of people gather in front of a house and start to yell insults, slogans, to throw eggs, stones against the façade, the windows, the main door.

We are in the room at the back of the house, on the floor, on the corners, against the walls, in the dark. There is no electricity, the windows are shut, it is hot, terribly hot. Someone in despair suggests to go out through the back door, climb up to the roof to reach another roof and run away. No matter where we look, there are people outside waiting with sticks and stones shouting. We are under siege. The neighbors have besieged the house. They are in the backyard, in the aisles, on the roof. We come back in to the dark, to the ground, fearful of stones breaking the windows. We are hungry, there is no food since yesterday, no water. We can only wait for whatever to happen, with no consciousness, no reality, no time, full of fear.

He was scared, she tells him. *Can you imagine? It is important to see it, to feel yourself in there with him, and see it.* She didn't really say this, she told me she thought of telling him, but she couldn't. She felt pity for him.

The house is under siege for two days. They cut the electricity, the water supply, the phone service.

The day the cousins get the departure permit, people outside are warned beforehand. Since these people know they have to go out through the main door if they want to leave, they are waiting. When the father comes out, whom they don't know—All of them know each other, the ones inside and the ones outside, they are lifelong neighbors, and he is a stranger they don't know—they hit him on the face, on the ribs, they throw him to the ground with kicks, they raise him to the air, above the crowd's heads, they throw him once and again to the ground until he is almost unconscious, she tells him, like I told her before, what it was, what it is.

He couldn't leave with the cousins at that moment, she explains after a pause, a pause no one interrupts in that afternoon. His departure should be organized, according to the law, from his real address. Then, he is sent to his place in such a state to wait for his turn, she says.

She tells him that if she wanted to see him, she had to get in his house through the backyard, thanks to the help of a neighbor. Their father has, she says, broken ribs, broken teeth, the face completely swollen, bruises everywhere, on the chest, on the legs, he can hardly swallow. She has to bring something soft to him, like puree or something like that for him to eat, and it is not always possible to get into his house. She tells him their father tries to call him every day, obsessively, to talk with him, but the calls, one after the other, are not accepted by the operator. She says she was able to take the cage with the canaries at the end, because, as she points out, it was forbidden to take the furniture, any object, clothes, photographs . . .

In the town, however, the neighbors refuse in silence to make any act against their father, she says, nobody visits him, but nobody bothers him either. They leave him alone in his closed house the final days. When he leaves, he's sick, aching all over, but he makes the journey like that.

She told me that after she finished talking, after another pause, after having been sitting in silence, he said he had seen things on TV, or on the streets, the beatings, the yelling, the crowds, the running; he had seen that from a distance, in his neighborhood, in other neighborhoods, walking around. He said he had heard stories of things that happened to people before they left, but he couldn't connect that with his father. *Why?*

He   *I didn't think it happened. Not to him.*

Father   *How could you possibly think it wouldn't happen if you were seeing it?*

He   *I don't know. I don't understand.*

And he keeps silent, I knew afterwards.

I think that right now, he—the one who writes in New York, and kept on writing—tries to comprehend the *I don't understand* he had said to his sister then. And tries to remember what happened inside of him. But now, as he made his mother say, he's also another person and does not remember. It is strange to forget who you were, isn't it? Or why you were like that, that way you no longer recognize. He wants to remember, but he can't find himself, who he was, the one who does not ask questions, does not enquire, does not react, does not make the links.

He had been unaware and lost in his thoughts during those months waiting for his sister's story. I knew the story later on, years after, when it didn't matter. When it doesn't matter. I'm also another person, I know. An old man. An ordinary man who worked hard to find his way, here, far away. Someone who had to move on, erase and cut, like many others. Neither better nor worse a father than others. The one who runs away, the one who leaves things behind and the one who rebuilds himself. The one who did what he could.

What's the use of writing or performing afterwards? Now? What he could write or confess? What's the use of the truth afterwards? Now? What could be done with it now? With this text?

Dream

He   We leave. My grandmother doesn't speak. At the bus stop, I say I am to blame, and she is too. Both of us are guilty. She cries and keeps silent. She asks me, for my own good, for my future, to keep silent. I obey. I keep silent. We come back to the city in silence.

Then, I come back to the town, to my father's house . . . In dreams. I cross the garden, knock on the door, I call to him. I get impatient. I call out again. I shout. I wait for him to open up, sleepy, smiling, and lead me to the darkness of the living room. Sometimes he opens, other times he doesn't. Then, I stay outside. Cold, with my bag in my hand, at night. Always certain he won't open up, I'm still there, at the door, under the flashing lamp, no place to sleep, no place to wait for the morning.

Epilogue

Havana, 2012

Author   My father did not come back again. I didn't see him for the next thirty years. He's a senior now, about to retire. He raised other children and rebuilt his life. In exile.

Eventually, she also, my mother, disconcertingly, decides to leave. A difficult and long process that took years. To break with everything, with herself. But when the critical time arrives, she leaves. I say *she leaves*. Period. She leaves. She too. Too. Period. She lives abroad, on her own, she earns money. She's doing well in her business. They didn't see each other again. I'm talking about them, my parents. The two that once were young in a town. They never had to talk to each other again for some obscure issue about me. Their political views are quite similar now, they are only slightly different. When I've visited them recently, they've received me very kindly in their houses. I have met their families, relatives and friends. I have seen the places where their lives have built up—far from mine. They have taken me out around the cities where they live. In my trips, they have given me money, when I haven't had enough. I do theater, I travel with the theater, and theater does not make enough money. They have taken me out to dinner, we have talked and I have slept in their houses. I have thanked them for their attention and I have promised, before leaving, to write more often. Since it is possible, I receive emails wishing *Happy New Year, Happy Birthday*. And photos of their grandsons, granddaughters, nephews and nieces. From time to time, I find them on Facebook, I leave messages, greetings. It is expensive to call them, although it's better to write. It is simple to write *Hello, greetings, kisses, all the best, Happy New Year, regards and hugs for everybody*. To write is simpler. To talk is expensive. Impossible.

La razón blindada (Armored Reason)

Arístides Vargas

24th Street Theatre—Los Angeles, California

11 *La razón blindada* at the 24th Street Theatre, Los Angeles. Photo by Juan Tallo.

Snapshot
Grace Dávila-López

In the context of Encuentro 2017, *La razón blindada* (*Armored Reason*) embodies an example of international collaboration. Written and directed by Argentinian playwright Arístides Vargas, it exemplifies the intricate interlace of political themes and word-centric poetical aesthetics that have gained the author solid recognition in Latin America and beyond. This staging by Los Angeles-based Mexican actors Jesús Castaños-Chima and Tony Durán arose from their own deep personal interest in performing the play in Los Angeles. Vargas agreed to direct them in accordance to the rigorous Malayerba Actor's Laboratory (a collective theater method that emphasizes the actors' role in creating the staged performance of the text, as well as its meaning).

Although this version of the play was produced for a US audience, it emphasizes the original context in which it was written, as well as Vargas's debt of gratitude to Cervantes and Kafka's insight into the power of art and imagination, as stated in the program. Still, the actors made the play their own by incorporating personal elements, such as the evocative background music, references to Mexican cuisine, and visuals of the US–

Mexican border landscape and fence. Through exploration, they created their own corporal choreography. And, of course, their Spanish diction reinforces a deep Los Angeles Mexican referent. It was named "Production of the Year" by the LA Weekly Theatre Awards in 2011, and was well received on its 2017 return to the 24th Street Theatre in Los Angeles.

La razón blindada showcases characters that play other characters, who willingly or seemingly unwillingly transform themselves into the fiction they are trying to imagine or create. For the characters in *La razón blindada*, the simple act of imagining—thence, creating fiction—becomes a life-affirming and liberating force. That is probably, in its essence, the central idea of the play; and through different thematic emphasis and styles is also a form of common ground between most plays at Encuentro.

La razón blindada was staged during the pre-Convening schedule; only those participants that arrived early to Los Angeles were able to watch it. The play was invited to the festival as a substitute for a theater group that could no longer attend, and, contrary to other theater participants—and due to previous commitments—these Los Angeles actors did not participate in the general discussion sessions. Considering that *La razón blindada* is a very successful example of teatro en español, produced in the US, one would have expected for the play to have generated conversation among the participants about the plausibility of developing Spanish theater for the mainstream audiences in the US.

Most of the comments I heard about this performance were in line with previous ones: amazement at the high-energy acting and versatility of the actors. Some stayed in awe still trying to figure out the full meaning of the play, or the feelings the situations conjure. The most problematic commentary I heard, and which would have made an interesting post-performance discussion topic, came from a director who objected to the use of "blackface" on stage. It was a reference to a part where De la Mancha, in his embodiment of el Quijote, is trying to convince Sancho (el escudero/servant) to admit his ambition for "power." To challenge el escudero, De la Mancha forces him to accept an island populated with *negros*. This is a re-take on an episode from *Don Quixote*, where Sancho agrees to rule over black men, as long as he can profit from them. In Vargas's appropriation of el Quijote, el escudero advocates for the right of *los negros* to govern themselves, while emphasizing their virtues and his own inadequacies to rule over them. In this scene, De la Mancha transforms himself into three personifications of *negros*, while trying to simplify to Sancho problems faced by poor African countries. These caricaturesque personifications are created by De la Mancha by protruding his lips and speaking with an African accent. The intention was obviously not to make el escudero laugh; as a matter of fact, el escudero acts confused and surprised. The intention is not to imitate the oppressed African subordinates of the crown, but to present the stereotypical vision of *el negro africano* as created by the West.

Still, it is understandable that the image of a non-black man embodying a black presence may be shocking, especially in the current context of US cultural politics that tries to denounce social and racial biases. It is a complex topic that would have been interesting to discuss, as it would probably have led to an encuentro of contexts and sensibilities, and to one of those difficult conversations about what forms of representation are or are not acceptable on the stage. All this is of particular interest in discussing a play that calls for the need for imagination as a means to survive oppression and recover man's humanity.

WET: A DACAmented Journey

Alex Alpharaoh

Ensemble Studio Theatre LA—Los Angeles, California

12 Alex Alpharaoh's *WET: A DACAmented Journey*, 2017. Photo: Youthana Yuos.

Critical Introduction

Trevor Boffone

The May/June 2018 issue of *American Theatre Magazine* featured performer and playwright Alex Alpharaoh on the cover against a weathered adobe wall looking longingly to the side.[1] While Alpharaoh is alone on the cover, he is not the focal point. His T-shirt is. His plain royal blue shirt reads in white all-caps block letters: "IMMIGRANTS ARE U.S." A tattoo on Alpharaoh's left arm reads: "Los Angeles." In one picture, Alpharaoh foregrounds the import of the immigrant population to the United States and reiterates the fact that, despite being born in Guatemala, Los Angeles is the only home he has ever known. While the nation became introduced to Alpharaoh's work in this issue of *American Theatre* and through a subsequent national tour of his solo show *WET* in 2018–19 produced by David Lozano and Clyde Valentín, Alpharaoh was one of the artists at the Encuentro that audiences just could not stop talking about.[2]

Although *WET* was not originally selected to be in the festival, its inclusion was openly welcomed given the hostile political climate that undocumented people face in the United States.[3] While each play in the festival addressed pressing sociopolitical issues, *WET* took the representation of immigration issues to a new level. As an undocumented American who has been in the United States since he was three months old, Alpharaoh's solo show chronicles his life with attention to what he has had to go through to maintain his status in the US and gain legal residency after the Trump regime took power and complicated the plight of the nation's eleven million undocumented people, including Deferred Action for Childhood Arrivals (DACA) recipients. As Alpharaoh told his harrowing life story, the audience around me was filled with tears. Near the end, I thought to myself: "I'm the only person in the theater who isn't crying." Not a minute later, I was crying. Moreover, as I hung on every word, my heart raced with anticipation wondering if Alpharaoh would make it back to the United States even though the performer was in front of me and clearly had survived his harrowing journey. *WET* is that powerful.

In the LATC's intimate Theatre 4, Alpharaoh stood on a bare stage. Aside from a table, a chair, and a coat-rack, the space was empty. While the show certainly would have benefited from a more ambitious design, what was presented was more impactful because spectators had no choice but to focus on the performer. This added weight to the performance. Near the end of the show, Alpharaoh recognized the fact that he could walk out of the LATC and immediately be deported. Performing *WET* is a risk in and of itself, speaking to the difficulties of living one's true self while also having to self-police.

In an interview with theater critic Jose Solís, Alpharaoh explains how remaining silent about his immigration status was imperative growing up in Los Angeles: "I was told not to say anything, not to tell people I didn't have these elusive papers everybody had."[4] While he was forced to keep his citizenship status a secret for much of his life, in a powerful act and turn of events, the playwright broke this silence as he developed *WET* at Ensemble Studio Theatre, Los Angeles, performing the show in 2017 before taking the show across town to the Los Angeles Theatre Center.[5] As with most art-making, *WET* is Alpharaoh's way of working through the struggles he has faced because of the US's immigration policies.

As a critical one-man show written and performed by Alex Alpharaoh and directed by Kevin Comartin, *WET* fuses hip hop aesthetics and personal narrative to give voice to the challenges that undocumented immigrants face in the United States. The play tackles the idea of what it means to be "American" in all meanings of the word except for legally, on paper. Contrary to the DREAMers featured in *Deferred Action*, *WET* centers on Alpharaoh's personal experiences, demonstrating the difficulties that DREAMers face when navigating through the United States Immigration System. In nearly every way, the system is rigged against him; to this day, there is no path to US citizenship for undocumented people, even if they were brought here as an infant. The play shows the negative mental, emotional, and psychological affects that Anner must face to remain in his hometown of Los Angeles.

In the play, Alpharaoh primarily goes by the pseudonym Anner Cividanis to chronicle his story of living in the United States as an undocumented person since he was three months old. Adding a touch of theatricality, Alpharaoh alternates between three personas: Alpharaoh, Alex, and Anner. While Alpharaoh the character is a poet who gives voice to the inner turmoil undocumented immigrants face, Alex is a relaxed and collected man who shares vignettes about his struggles to remain in the US. Rounding out Alpharaoh and Alex, Anner is reactive and subsequently battles the intersections of rage and reason.

Throughout Anner's life, he combats the challenges of being undocumented in Southern California. A simple childhood trip to Sea World in San Diego was strictly forbidden since the short journey would involve passing through the border patrol in San Clemente on the way back to Los Angeles. While these vignettes mark Anner's early experiences, *WET* primarily focuses on his incredibly complicated experiences traveling back to Guatemala for the first time in order to gain a legal entry into the United States as a documented immigrant. The play shows the hardships endured as part of the refugee travel document, or advance parole. At any moment he could have been deported back to Guatemala, a country that he has only heard about.

Notably, Alpharaoh is the only member of his immediate family who is not a United States citizen and, although he has been protected under DACA and maintains the legal right to stay and work in the US, the Trump regime continually threw everything into disarray. For instance, when Attorney General Jeff Sessions announced on September 5, 2017 that the government would not be renewing DACA, Alpharaoh's present and future became uncertain.[6] Even though he had spent a lifetime dealing with the difficulties associated with lacking papers (i.e., birth certificates and a social security card), this newfound immediacy is where *WET* is able to find its greatest strengths. Through direct address, Alpharaoh implicates the audience. While this may be his story, we are all involved in some facet and must find ways to advocate for comprehensive immigration reform so that stories such as *WET* will be a thing of the past. Notably, this issue emerged in several shows at Encuentro such as *Broken Tailbone*.

Similar, to *Deferred Action*, *WET* is a testament to the power of live performance to ignite a conversation around contemporary social justice issues. As Alpharaoh stated in a *Café Onda* conversation with David Lozano and Karen Zacarías, the play is "educating people who may not know what it's like to be an undocumented American."[7] Even though DACA recipients have clean criminal records and are productive contributors to the US, they are often "categorized with drug dealers and thieves and murderers and people who came her to steal jobs and identities is kind of the rhetoric I'm trying to help change."[8] Immediately after Encuentro, I spoke with LTC producer Abigail Vega who emphatically told me that if we could get Alex Alpharaoh to perform in front of our change-makers at local, state, and federal levels then we would see a shift in the ways in which our nation's leadership views the undocumented population who have long lived in the shadows despite contributing to the nation's success. As a writer and performer, Alpharaoh holds the tools to make change a viable reality. His tale is a sympathetic journey that humanizes the experiences of undocumented people in contrast to the hateful rhetoric that is often directed at individuals whose immigration status remains in a constant state of limbo. As such, *WET* speaks to the power of Latinx theater as a tool for social change. Plays such as *Deferred Action* and *WET* are important conversation starters that trouble the notion of "common ground." While the Latinx community is unified in many ways, there are still millions in the Latinx population who are not afforded the privileges of citizenship. Moreover, in addition to the dichotomy between documented and undocumented Latinx peoples, there are also historic tensions between communities that receive refugee status and those that do not. Naturally, there are critical narratives and perspectives that have yet to be heard. As such, these are compelling stories that are still being written. Quite frankly, we don't know what will happen next with regards to the situation of undocumented persons living in the United States. The final chapter has still yet to be written even as the instances of inhumane deportations continue to rise. One thing is certain, theater such as *WET* speaks to what Latinx theater scholar Jorge Huerta calls "Necessary Theater." Perhaps now, more than ever, we need artists such as Alex Alpharaoh who are unafraid of putting themselves on the line for the sake of social change.

Notes

1. This issue of *American Theatre Magazine* focused on the plight of undocumented people in the United States with a particular focus on undocumented theater artists such as Amalia Rojas, Diego Salinas, and Alex Alpharaoh.
2. After seeing *WET* at Encuentro, Lozano and Valentín began working with Alpharaoh to further develop the show and produce the tour, which would ultimately be taken over by the playwright's agent.
3. After Double Edge Theatre's production of *Cada Luna Azul/Once a Blue Moon* had to withdraw from the festival due to logistical challenges, the Latino Theater Company filled the last-minute spot with alternating performances of two Los Angeles-based shows: *WET* and *La Razon Blindada*.
4. Jose Solís. "Perchance to Dream: DACA Recipients, Feeling Unwelcome in the Country They Call Home, Claim a Home Onstage." *American Theatre*. April 24, 2018. Accessed November 27, 2020. https://www.americantheatre.org/2018/04/24/perchance-to-dream/
5. *WET* was first produced by Ensemble Studio Theatre Los Angeles as part of the True Story Program, which helps facilitate autobiographical solo shows.
6. In March 2019, Alex Alpharaoh became a permanent resident/green card holder. He will be eligible to apply for US citizenship in March 2022.
7. Alex Alpharaoh, David Lozano, and Karen Zacarías. "Undocumented Stories Have Always Mattered / Las Historias Sobre Los Indocumentados Siempre Han Importado." HowlRound. October 15, 2017. Accessed November 27, 2020. http://howlround.com/undocumented-stories-have-always-mattered-a-conversation-with-alex-alpharaoh-david-lozano-and-karen
8. Ibid.

Interview with Alex Alpharaoh
Trevor Boffone

Trevor Boffone   Can you tell us briefly about your journey as a theater artist? What were the defining moments of your career leading up to Encuentro?

Alex Alpharaoh   I was twenty-four years old when I took my first acting class at Cypress College with Mark Majarian, the man who would become my mentor. However, my artistic journey really began when I was twenty-three. My daughter's mother left me. We were high school sweethearts and our daughter Aileen was a love child that came to us when I was nineteen and she was eighteen. Before I found my purpose as an artist, I was devoted to being a father, a spouse, and learning the ropes of psychiatric social work at the convalescent hospital we both worked at in Anaheim, CA. I had dreams of being an artist, but that reality slipped further and further away from me with each year that went by. I had to focus on being a provider, and hopefully earn a degree by going to community college part time. Being an artist was the last thing on my mind. Looking back on it now, I had given up on my dreams without really having tried. I had set unrealistic goals for myself such as making it by the age of twenty-five, having platinum plaques, making a million dollars, collaborating with all the great artists of my generation, and leaving the poverty I grew up in behind me once and for all. That was my only definition of success. Yet, I always felt that it was a foolish dream. For one reason and one reason alone: I didn't have papers. That fact held me back from even trying. I found safety in the familiarity of the little family I had created for myself. I figured that if I kept my head down and laid low long enough, eventually, hopefully, one day I would be able to have legal status in the country and maybe I could pursue music or even acting. So, at twenty-three, I was just trying to afford basic cable and an iPod. After Aileen's mom and I split up, I sunk into a deep depression that caused me to almost drop out of school. I almost committed suicide once and if not for my brother Gabriel coming home at the moment right before I slit my wrists, I wouldn't be here today. He stopped me and prevented me from taking my own life. The desolation, frustration, and emptiness I felt was more than overwhelming. It hurt to live and breathe. I knew taking my life was not and never has been the answer, but when you lose the little you have worked so hard to gain so early on in your adult life, that made me feel less than worthless.

I found acting in the fall of 2006 when I auditioned for my very first show, *Long Story Short* by Doug Cooney. That show saved my life. I almost didn't audition because I didn't know anything about being an actor. I didn't even know what a monologue was. I'm grateful I listened to that little voice in my head that spoke to me with the wisdom and kindness of highest self. I've learned to listen to that little voice that guides me. It guided me when I decided to pursue this work professionally and took a leap of faith by going back home to LA with no money, or job, or connections in the business. I listened to it when I applied for DACA for the very first time. Then again when I decided to leave in order to meet my ailing grandfather. I heard it clearly when it told me that it was OK to trust Liz Ross and share my journey with her. By then I was already involved with Ensemble Studio Theatre LA [EST/LA] as a regular performer for *True Story*, the monthly storytelling event where I developed parts and aspects of *WET*. When Liz offered me the opportunity to produce a limited run of *WET* at EST/LA, I didn't want to do it. Yet, it was that little voice that told me to trust that it would be OK and that sharing the story would serve a purpose greater than my own. After I agreed to a run, she asked Kevin Comartin to direct me. Kevin was responsible for helping guide and shape the first version of *WET* that was produced at EST/LA. That was also the version that was presented at Encuentro.

Boffone   As opposed to other shows in Encuentro, *WET* was a last-minute addition due to another production having to drop out. Can you tell us about your journey to Encuentro? How did *WET* develop and take on new meanings as you continued to perform against the backdrop of the growing uncertainty surrounding DACA and immigration reform?

Alpharaoh   *WET* was supposed to have been a limited, four-week engagement at EST/LA with the possibility of a two-week extension. I didn't expect it to do well at all.

As an artist, I tend to be my own worst critic. I knew the odds were stacked up against me. I was an unknown writer/performer, and immigration was not a topic that was being tackled by the theater community in Los Angeles. Thankfully, there was an amazing social media marketing team, along with publicist Judith Borne, who managed to get reviewers in to see the show on opening weekend. Those first reviews helped give the show legs. What gave the show a shot in the arm was on September 5, 2017, Attorney General Jeff Sessions announced that DACA would be rescinded. That weekend, the audiences began to flood in, prompting EST/LA to add the extension to the run.

On closing night of the extension, I was relieved to almost be done with the performances, but I was also sweating bullets because I saw that José Luis Valenzuela and Sal Lopez from the Latino Theater Company [LTC] were in the audience (yeah, I like to cheat and see who's out there). I have tremendous respect and admiration for both of them, as well as the rest of the ensemble of LTC and was privileged to have done my spoken word show *SP!T: A Tribute to Tupac Shakur* at the Los Angeles Theatre Center [LATC] back in 2012 when I was a member of Urban Theatre Movement and they were presenting *Short Eyes* by Miguel Piñero as a co-production with Latino Theater Company. It was an honor to have José Luis and Sal in the audience that night. I didn't get a chance to speak to José Luis or Sal after the show but I received a call from José Luis's son Fidel Gómez the Tuesday after the show closed. I'm friends with Fidel and he reached out to congratulate me on a successful run, and wanted to know if I was interested in having a conversation with his father about future plans for the show. It turns out José Luis had heard about the show from several people that work with him, including Geoffrey Rivas, who has always been a strong advocate and supporter of my work since he saw it at the LATC back in 2012. I met with José Luis, Geoffrey, and Fidel on Thursday of that week and José Luis offered me the opportunity to present *WET* at Encuentro. It was a dream come true for me. During this time, I began performing excerpts of *WET* for Human Rights Watch Student Task Force throughout Los Angeles middle schools and high schools. I didn't understand the importance of sharing my journey until those affected by similar circumstances began to share their journeys with me. I began to understand that I was and continue to be in a unique position. I have the platform and the ability to contribute to the amplification of our collective voices by taking charge and ownership of my own narrative so that others may do the same and shed light to this issue. By sharing my humanity and, in turn, allowing others to see themselves reflected in the DACAmented journey. All the while, I am well aware that my work permit will expire by March 5, 2019, unless I renew it, or there is change in immigration policy, whichever comes first.

Boffone   How do you balance the real world and the world of the play, Alex the playwright and Alex the performer? Is it even possible to separate the two?

Alpharaoh   I am, that I am. Balancing my artistry and real-life responsibilities can, and does, get difficult from time to time. The difference from when I play other characters in other projects is that I can put those characters away once I get off the stage or the director yells cut. I can't put Anner Alexander Alfaro Cividanis away. It is getting easier as time goes on to embrace those aspects of the journey that cause me fear, mainly, being deported to a country I don't know because I am openly sharing my status (or lack thereof) in the US.

Boffone   Bringing together a diverse group of theater artists from across the Hemispheric Americas, Encuentro sought to uncover what common ground exists between teatristas who have been divided by social and political borders. What did *WET* add to this conversation?

Alpharaoh   Teatristas are not limited or bound by borders, or policies, or ethnic background, or political affiliations. Art does not have a requirement when it comes to its expression. The human condition is what we strive to understand, live, and in turn, interpret through our presentations. You don't need a passport for that.

Boffone   Do you think there is common ground between Latinx and Latin American theater makers?

Alpharaoh   Of course there is. The Encuentro festival was a perfect example of how multi-discipline artists from all over the world can come together, united under a singular artistic language, and create work that can be enjoy by all peoples, regardless of language barriers, physical borders, or any perceived differences that often times create divisions that are not only unnecessary, but foolish.

Boffone   Do you think there are some aspects of common ground that are not shared across the Americas? In what ways do you think *WET* challenged this?

Alpharaoh   The Undocumented American experience is unique for various reasons. For we are American in every sense of the word, except on paper. We were brought here, often times without our knowledge, as infants or young children, and raised here without any knowledge of what it means to be a WET or "Mojado." The commonalities are shared with the cultures that make up our presence here. Regardless of what part of the world we originate from, we are viewed by everyone outside of the United States as Americans except for racist Americans. *WET* challenges the anti-immigrant establishment to find a deeper reason for not wanting us other than the tired rhetoric of not having come to this country the "right way." Right way meaning through a broken immigration system. The anti-immigrant establishment cannot accuse us of lacking assimilation or not properly contributing to the overall well-being of the country. It is a proven fact that immigrants, DACA recipients specifically, are some of the most contributing and respectable members of their communities. We have to be; we don't have a choice.

Boffone   One of the most powerful aspects of Encuentro involved having a diverse group of theater makers in residency at the Los Angeles Theatre Center for a month. How did this experience change your approach to art-making? What sort of conversations did you engage in?

Alpharaoh   I learned so much from every person that I worked with. It was interesting to be part of a group of artists that came from all disciplines and parts of the world. One individual didn't speak English, the other didn't speak Spanish. Most of us spoke some form of Spanglish, but we all spoke theatrics. Through gestures, body language, taking turns interpreting from English to Spanish and vice versa, we were able to create an organic piece of theater that was inclusive, authentic, and representative of every individual in our group. Ego was left outside the rehearsal room and love was the only language that mattered when we were creating our ensemble offering. My approach to art-making has been expanded by giving me tools rooted in increased active listening and community sharing. These are the building blocks to great collaborations. The conversations we engaged in were personal, vulnerable, painful, courageous, and sometimes, off limits. The level of generosity and willingness was refreshing and inspiring to say the least.

Boffone   Of all the plays I saw at Encuentro, perhaps *WET* was one of the most generative as it's a play that can lead to genuine social change. What do you hope audience gain from seeing *WET*?

Alpharaoh   What many audiences have already deduced: that they are watching an American story about an American who doesn't have documentation that says he's an American, even though he's lived in the United States of America for all but three months of his thirty-five years of life. To force him to live outside of the United States would be un-American. To force any of the over 800,000 DACA recipients and thousands of TPS recipients, and asylum seekers, and any/all immigrants that migrate to this country for a better life to leave because "we are full" is not what being an American is all about. Being an American is as much a mind state as it is a birthright. Throughout my journey of performances I have met many people that understand that being an American is more than just having been born within the United States.

Boffone   One of the most fascinating aspects of Encuentro 2014 was following the path of the artists afterwards. For some, the festival proved to be a career-changing moment in a number of ways. In what ways did Encuentro 2017 shift your approach to theater making? What have been the opportunities that have emerged following the festival?

Alpharaoh   Many wonderful connections and friendship were established through the Encuentro festival. Because of the festival, I feel I have been embraced with open, loving arms by the Latinx theater community, not just in Los Angeles, but throughout the country and the rest of the Americas. Since Encuentro, EST/LA and I have teamed up with ArtsEmerson, Cara Mía Theatre Company, and Ignite Arts, to bring *WET* to various cities throughout the country, including multiple cities in Texas and a run of the show in Boston. I am also in talks to possibly bring it to other cities like Chicago, New York, D.C., San Francisco, and hopefully back home to Los Angeles. It is my sincerest wish to perform the show in as many venues as possible, so long as there is a need for the story to be shared, and I am able to legally stay in the country while doing it. At the end of the day, the most rewarding thing I have received from participating in the Encuentro festival is that I feel that the artistic theater community, the Latinx Theatre community specifically, has embraced me with open arms and unwavering love. For the first time in my life, I truly feel that I belong. To have complete strangers come up to me and tell me that they would hide me and protect me if the worst were to happen to me because I have chosen to share my story is something that has brought many tears to my tears. Tears that are rooted in gratitude, because I spent so many years living in the shadows, and to know that the shadows I am standing under now are the shadows of the people that are choosing to stand with me, and in front of me because they love me, and they are choosing to protect me because they see me as one of their own.

WET: A DACAmented Journey

Written and Performed by Alex Alpharaoh

Production History

WET: A DACAmented Journey was developed and world premiered as a True Story production by Ensemble Studio Theatre/LA in 2017 at Atwater Village Theatre in Los Angeles. It received developmental support from CRITICAL BREAKS Residency Program at HI-ARTS, NYC in January of 2018, and the touring version was co-commissioned by Cara Mía Theatre, Ignite/Arts Dallas, and ArtsEmerson, directed by Brisa Areli Muñoz. The national tour played multiple cities and engagements in summer/fall 2018. *WET* was nominated for Best Solo Performance and Best Playwriting at the 2018 Stage Raw Awards, and received an Ovation nomination for Playwriting for an Original Play in 2018. The play won the LA Drama Critics Circle Award for Solo Performance in 2018. Festival participation highlights: Encuentro de las Américas Theatre Festival, Los Angeles, CA; Lincoln Center Education, New York, NY; HipHop Theatre Festival, The Kennedy Center, Washington D.C.; Destinos Latinx Theatre Festival, Chicago, IL; Sin Muros Latinx Theatre Festival at Stages Repertory Theatre, Houston, TX; PivotArts Theatre Festival, Chicago, IL; Visions and Voices Festival, Los Angeles, CA; No Boundaries Series, and Yale Repertory, New Haven, CT.

A bare stage. A few projections, some lights, and some sounds. A few props including a backpack, some documents, a wallet, a key on a necklace.

Alpharaoh   A shadow is shaded reflection of a person's purpose under the sun. Worthless if one is not considered a native son. Papa, reconsider taking off; don't run. Life stays hard after you're gone, plus mom can't raise a Don without a solid plan, see . . . she never learned to live without a man. "My brothers and sister can't look up to me!" "I don't have what it takes to earn a degree," is the lie that CREEK would recite whenever he was in sight, whenever his reflection stared back in mirror, angrily cuz he never thought Anner would make it to be here. My shadow is but a temporary indentation on the earth. My indignation is towards the decimation of my spirit through and because of being poor and wet. Cumulative in the tears and sweat, drunken regrets, constant upsets, that defeated my old man. If only my transcripts added up. If only my documents could be validated. My transparency is seen as conspiracy by those that would rob me of my identity, do y'all see the fucking irony? So when do I begin? When my breath stops and my corpse rots? When my dreams die due to missed shots? When my friends speak my name over comfort Chente lyrics and tequila shots: "he was a good man, whether you knew him or not." I grew up hearing whispers that this too shall pass but over thirty winters froze my heart till the dread began to outlasts, the feeling I used to get when I was a child: the feeling that anything is possible for me. And please, don't talk to me about a dream. Because Martin Luther King had a dream and now he's dead. Because Tecun Uman fought for a dream and now he's dead. Because I placed my faith in a fabricated DREAM and it filled my head, with worry and dread, watching others live and get ahead, while witnessing any chance of reform die instead. But I refuse to go silently into the night. Kicking and screaming; I will go out fighting. I will change my destiny or die trying. I will defeat the inner critic that would beat the greatest part of my truth, a truth buried deeper than the root of my sorrow. It's time for me to test these wings; flying towards my better tomorrows.

Alex   I need your help. I have reason to believe that our government is going to try to persecute me. The story I am about to share with you puts me in great danger. My name is Anner Alexander Alfaro Cividanis. My friends know me as Alex Alfaro. Artistically, I'm simply known as Alpharaoh. But what's in a name? I've been called many names throughout my life: Wetback, Spick, Beaner, Mojado, Illegal, Alien, Illegal-Alien, Mexican, Salvadorean, Honduran, Nicaraguan, Costa Rican, Panamanian, Dominican, Puerto Rican, Cuban, Filipino, Egyptian. A reviewer once referred to me as "The African-American Soothe-Sayer who told poems with a tragic twist." I've been called almost everything except for what I am: American!

Technically I'm Guatemalan . . . I say technically because I've lived in the United States my entire life. I am what you would call an "Undocumented American." I need you to help me find a way to adjust my status, quickly, and legally.

My first piece of documented proof of me being in the U.S. is in the form of my vaccination records from "La Clinica Medica Santa Fatima" on 8th and Alvarado Street. The stamp on my vaccination card reads February 1983. I was born October 1982, and if it wasn't for those few months between October 82 and February 83, my life would have turned out a whole lot more easier for me. Because growing up, I was constantly being bullied and made fun of by other little kids because I was always told that I needed papers but for one reason or another, I never got them.

Little Che   Anner doesn't have papers because he's a dirty mojado who doesn't belong here.

Little Popis   And then, and then . . . I heard that Anner can't come to our house, or immigration is gonna take everyone away to Mejico.

Little David   I heard you can get fake papers at MacArthur Park because that's where my dad and my uncle got theirs.

Little Che   Yeah, but Anner can't afford them because he's poor and his mom abandoned him, huh Anner?!

Little Popis   And then, and then . . . I heard that if Anner touches you, you become a dirty mojado too, and they can come, and take you away from your family forever.

Alex   What were these papers, and why were they so elusive? Could I get them at Staples? Did they really sell them at MacArthur Park? Why were these papers so important, and why did it seem that I was the only one that needed them but didn't have them? No one else in my family seemed to need them. My brothers and sister didn't need them, my cousins, nieces, nephews, aunts, uncles, none of my friends needed them either.

When you're undocumented in the country, there's a whole list of things that you can't do, such as: claim lottery winnings, radio caller prizes, get a library card, or a driver's license. You can't get an apartment because you don't have credit history because you need a social security number, in order to open a bank account which you're not allowed to have because you're not supposed to be making money without a work permit. You can't have utilities or property under your name, you can't apply for financial aid, or in-state tuition, you can't vote, although two million of us totally voted for Hillary. You can't travel internationally, and traveling domestically presents its own set of risks.

The first time it dawned on me that I was WET came when I was about nine or ten years old. My cousin Jewels approached me, and excitedly shared about her upcoming trip with Aunt Claire that weekend.

Jewels   Anner Anner Anner, guess what? Guess where I'm going on Saturday? It's better than Disneyland. It's better than Universal Studios. It's better than six flags! . . . Yes of course it's better than Knott's, Knott's sucks! I'm going to Sea World! And I was thinking, that because I've never gone before, I don't want to get lost, and since you're really smart, I'm going to ask my mom to bring you too. That way we can explore Sea World together.

Jewels *sees* **Aunt Claire**.

Jewels   Mom, mom, mom, mom, mom! I was just telling Anner, that we're going to Sea World, and that he should totally come with us.

Aunt Claire   Ay no! Dios me guarde! Como? No! (*As she makes the sign of the cross.*)

Ainer, mijo . . . Jew kenah go to da See Wurl. Jew no habit da paypers. En San Clemente dey aske forda paypers. If jew no habit, jew go back tu Guatemala.

Alex   I couldn't even go to Sea World, and now that I can go to Sea World, all the fucking whales are gone!

Beat.

Let's fast forward in time to June 16, 2012, When I was twenty-nine years old. President Obama, or "Brother Barry," as I like to remember him, held a press conference stating that he was going to enact an executive order that would grant a temporary reprieve of deportation to a select group of individuals, commonly known as the DREAMers. This executive order titled Deferred Action for Childhood Arrivals or DACA, would grant two-year work permits with the possibility of renewals.

Anner   This is it. This is my shot. If I can qualify for this program, I won't have to be homeless anymore. I won't have to live off of Nutri-grain bars and Gatorade. I could get a driver's license and drive without being afraid of getting pulled over and deported. I can get a real job, and not just do odd jobs from Craigslist. I can take of my daughter . . .

Alex   But first, I would have to meet certain set of criteria. All applicants must have:

Be under the age of thirty and have come here before their sixteenth birthday. I was twenty-nine at the time that I applied, and I've been here since I was three months old. CHECK!

Be physically present in the United States when the Executive Order was announced. I can prove that. On June 16, 2012, I performed my spoken word play that pays homage to my lyrical mentor Tupac Shakur, titled: *SP!T: A Tribute to Tupac Shakur* at the Los Angeles Theatre Center, very well documented. CHECK!

Have graduated high school, college, served the armed forces or currently be in college or active military. I can prove that. I've graduated elementary school, middle school, high school, college, and I'm even a certified clown. CHECK!

Register with the government—I can do that, I just have to come up with a list of the more than thirty places I had lived at by that time, cuz growing up poor sucks. CHECK!

And lastly, Not have any felonies, serious misdemeanors, or more than two minor misdemeanors on your record . . .

Alex   Shit . . . Cheeeeeeeck? . . .

See, what had happened was: it was the 2009 fall semester at UC Irvine, and the first murder in the history of the campus occurred, and no, I didn't do it. I'm hood, not stupid. There was this couple, graduate students, who were arguing in their housing unit. The husband, in a fit of rage, pulled out a gun and killed his wife while their toddler witnessed the whole thing. That night, the entire Verano Housing was on lockdown: police had the whole place blocked off and everyone was being checked before being allowed into the housing area. I had just gotten out of my last class, around 9:30 p.m., when I was stopped by Irvine P.D. They wanted to see my I.D. before letting me through. I wasn't carrying my student I.D. that day, Plus, the cops didn't believe that I lived there because, well, I look like this (point to myself). Even though I was carrying a backpack full of books and I was wearing sweatpants and a sweater that had the words "UC Irvine" on them. The officers offered to escort me back to my apartment, and if I showed them I.D., they'd let me go. So, I complied. On the way to my apartment, one of the officers kept whispering into his two-way radio. That same officer asked for my California I.D. After I'd given his sergeant my school I.D. Suddenly, then first officer's questions sounded like:

Officer

- Do you go by any other names aside from Anner Alfaro?
- Is Alex Alfaro a real name?
- How long have you been living on campus?
- How long have you been here? No not the school.
- Why are you here?
- Who pays for you to be here?
- Whose place did you take to be here?
- Have you ever lived on Ball Road?

Anner   Yeah.

Officer   Gotcha.

Alex   The officer went over to the sergeant and they briefly spoke in hushed tones. Then the sergeant approached me and said that there was a bench warrant out for my arrest. No Good Deed Goes Unpunished . . .

Beat.

See, what had happened was: in the beginning of 2009, I was working as a social worker at a psychiatric nursing home. One of my responsibilities was that of abuse coordinator, which meant that all claims of abuse came to my office and it was my job to resolve them. I was once informed by one of the patients who lived in the facility that his roommate was being beat up by his nursing aide. My investigation cracked open a case against an employee who had a long suspected trail of abuse at other facilities but for one reason or another, had never been caught. My findings were enough to have this man terminated, federal charges were brought up against him, and he was eventually put away for a very long time. That same year, I was nominated for California social worker of the year, it's as if I could do no wrong. Even the Department of Justice got involved. Special agent Judy with the DOJ came down to interview me, make copies of all of my documentation, and she even said that I was one of "the good ones." She also offhandedly stated that there was a slight chance that I might have to testify in court but that she strongly doubted it because the evidence against this guy was so overwhelming, that he'd be a fool to challenge it. Nonetheless, a few weeks later, I get a voicemail message.

Judy   Hi, Anner, It's Judy over at the DOJ. Listen, weird, but I think I might have made a mistake when I took down your information. Would you mind calling me back and giving me your full name, date of birth, and correct social security number? I can't seem to find you on the DMV database and I need to send you your court subpoena.

Alex   Shit. The gig was up. I had been working at the nursing home for almost ten years with a social security number I made up. And before people start with the whole rhetoric about stealing livelihoods, and taking people's jobs, and bad hombres, or any of that other ridiculous shit that's said about undocumented people, just stop. First of all, no. Second of all, I've never taken anything from anyone. Everything I have, I've had to earn. Lastly, I did what I did for one reason, and one reason only: I had an infant daughter to feed. So, I quit my job of almost ten years at the end of that week, and figured:

Anner   Hey, I dodged a bullet. I'll take the summer off, I'll live off of my savings while laying low until school starts in the fall. What's the worse that can happen?

Alex   I was booked at men's central jail in Santa Ana, California on one count of falsifying a government-issued document. The Department of Justice wanted to make an example out of me. They wanted to give me fifteen years in jail and then deport me. Lucky for me, I have these two great mentors Checker and Eugene came to my aid, paid for a lawyer, and since at the time I was a student with a GPA of 3.87 and had never gotten in trouble before in my life, my family was able to post bail for me for five grand (which I still owe them). Turns out, the Department of Justice didn't have a fake birth certificate to present in court BECAUSE I NEVER DID THAT. My attorney jumped on the opportunity and cut a deal with the Department of Justice. The DOJ agreed to dismiss the original felony charge in exchange for the following: Time served, an $1800 fine, eighty hours of community service, staying out of trouble indefinitely, two years of informal probation, and pleading guilty to one count misdemeanor of disturbing the peace . . . I was pissed!

Anner   Disturbing the peace? Disturbing the peace, Jeff? When the fuck did I disturb the peace? I was walking home from class, those motherfuckers harassed me, then disturbed MY PEACE!

Jeff   Anner, calm down! You want to get out of here don't you? Listen, this is how these things work. They're not just going to dismiss the charge and let you go. It's a give and take. If you fight this and take it to trial, you will lose, and then you'll really be screwed. This is a good deal. Take it. It's a minor misdemeanor, a low-level offense. After two years, I can have it expunged from your record. It'll be as if it never happened. Look, I know about your immigration status. I can empathize with you, my great-grandmother was an immigrant. If ever you get a chance to adjust your immigration status, you have a better shot with an expunged misdemeanor on your record than having been deported for challenging the DOJ, and more than likely having come back into the country the wrong way. You seem like a smart guy, Anner, take the deal.

Alex   I took the deal. Three years after the school incident, on September 5, 2012, I applied for DACA for the first time. I filled out the application, gathered up all of my supporting evidence and documentation, I saved for weeks, to get the $465 money order needed to process the paperwork, and then I waited for a few weeks until USCIS sent me notice stating that I needed to go to present myself at an immigration center. I've been avoiding immigration centers my entire life, and now I needed to go to one and submit biometric fingerprints and a facial scan for a background check. Well, I did it . . . Coming out of the shadows . . . and I waited, and waited, and waited.

For over nine months, my days were full of dread as I would call the USCIS call center at least twice a day to check on the status of my case. My evenings were full of anxiety as I would constantly check the USCIS website for updates on my case. Suddenly, one day, out the blue, I get a call from my mother.

Lucrecia   Mijo, you got some mail that came in, I think it might be your work permit. When are you going to come to the house to pick up your mail? This house is NOT a mail center!

Alex   And just like that, on May 1, 2013, I was granted DACA for the very first time, which meant that I now had a work permit. I could get a social security number, which would allow me to get a driver's license, which would allow me to get a job in my field of discipline, which meant that I could now take care of my daughter. At the age of thirty, my life was finally going to begin. What could possibly go wrong?

Alex   Election Night, 2016. Red state after red state is going towards the 45th as Aileen and I somberly eat our burgers at the unusually empty Johnny Rockets at Universal City Walk . . .

Anner   It's okay baby, it's still early in the night . . . shit . . . This guy might actually win the presidency. If that happens . . . I might end up getting deported.

Alpharaoh   If I have to go away to a place I never stayed, except for when I was a babe; with no collection of memory to be recollected; tossed out as if I were defective. How then would my departure be constructive, if my whole life can be relocated, decimated, dismantled; my woe deepens at the stroke of a pen. My livelihood should not have to depend on political trends, police are at it again. It'll feel like Poland in 1939, if I have to hide in attics and dens. Putting friends at risk due to mere association, I am the mirror of this broken nation. I am the keeper of its shame in the form of misplaced blame, for unrequited hate is required before the next heated debate, while I sit in a processing center amongst other sinners awaiting our transfer dates. I thought I saw light at the end of the tunnel, But it may be my turn to be told to go, turned away from the only home that I know. If I ask where to, their reply: "I don't know, regardless, you shouldn't have been here in the first place." Words spoken with conviction, dead eyes, and a straight face. Now my life can be null and void, I'm fighting thoughts of being paranoid, practical voice kicks in: Anner chill . . . things like this are always said for the win, it's politics. But these promises won't be blown away by the wind and forgotten. A whole platform was broadcast, soon the witch hunt will begin, which one of you brought the matches? My dreams can turn into a nightmare. For years I prepared for a worse-case outcome, so how come I was so surprised that DACA's demise came well before the next sunrise?

Alex   The day after the 45th won the election, I start figuring out a way to get a green card and establish permanent residency. Now, you may be asking, "Anner, why don't you just go down to the Social Security office and apply for a social security number and then go get a green card?" Because it's not that easy. I tried that, literally. It didn't work. My mom also attempted to adjust my status when I was twenty years old. She had just married a service man and had gotten her green card. She petitioned for me to get mine but I was denied for two main reasons.

The first reason was that I no longer qualified for adjustment as a minor because I was over the age of eighteen, being that I was a few months shy of my twenty-first birthday. All she could do was petition for me as an adult relative. What that petition did was put me at the end of a long line of people waiting for priority visa date through immigration's lottery system. Granting me a priority lottery date between 13–15 years, which is right around now. A lottery date wouldn't guarantee me a visa, only the opportunity to participate in the game. Each year the government gives 50,000 visas. Each year over 14 million people are eligible and apply. Only 3 percent of applicants get their green cards.

The second reason why I was denied was because I didn't enter the country legally. Mom and I weren't inspected at a port of entry by immigration. Mom smuggled me in, which meant that I was out. However, I did find a tiny loophole in the form of advance parole. Advance parole basically means you ask the government for permission to leave the country for a specific reason for a specified amount of time. Now, why is this important? Because in order for someone to adjust their status in the country and become a legal resident, the individual has to have proof of having been inspected and allowed into the country at some point in time in their lives. This is a Catch-22 for Initial DACA recipients. When the program first rolled out, only individuals that had not been inspected and allowed into the country by immigration could apply for DACA. Later on this was amended to include people whose legal status had expired. In order for me to adjust my status through my mother, I would need to have been inspected at some point in time. Inspection and admission is one of the key requirements for adjustment to permanent residency.

In theory, If I can leave the country and be allowed to come back in legally, I may be able to activate my mom's original petition and adjust my status upon return. If the adjustment request is granted, I can become a permanent resident within three to six months. After five years of permanent residency, I can apply for citizenship, and this nightmare will be over!

Now, is the process of applying and traveling with advance parole easy? Fuck no! First, they have to vet you. Run an entire background check and make sure you're not a murdering, gang-banging, drug-using, contraband-selling terrorist. Pretty much anything that would make you a threat to society. Second, you actually have to leave the country. Immigration doesn't care who leaves the country. Coming back is the problem. If for whatever reason you are not allowed back in, you are barred from re-entry for ten whole years. Third, let's say you do get advance parole, there's no guarantee that you will be paroled back in. Parole is at the sole discretion of the inspecting immigration officer. So if I get a racist, vigilante, "white supremacist," been punched for being a Nazi, well . . . let's just hope that doesn't happen.

DACA recipients were only able get advance parole for one of three reasons: humanitarian, educational, or business purposes. My only option is a humanitarian request. My grandpa is sick and dying. I've never met him, or at least, I don't have any recollection of him. So I call my cousin Lucy, that I know from Facebook, and ask her to help me obtain a certified letter from Grandpa's doctor stating the facts about his medical condition and a request for me to visit before he dies. Lucy says that she'll see what she can do and will get back to me soon.

A week after the 45th wins the election, I apply to renew my Guatemalan passport. It had been four years since I renewed my passport. I didn't have a need for it. I have a California I.D. and I can travel domestically with it. But if I get advance parole, I'll need that passport to go to Guatemala. The renewal shouldn't take longer than four weeks. It should arrive around the first week of the new year. If I get advance parole approved, I can leave and come back well before the 45th is sworn in.

Beat.

It took Lucy a little over a month after the election to get me the letter. She sent me rushed package dated December 26, 2016. The contents: A bookmark, a letter, and a certified document. The letter reads

Anner   Dear Anner, Here is the certified letter you requested. It says that Grandpa has end-stage liver cirrhosis with a life expectancy of no more than four months. It also says that Grandpa would like for you to visit him as soon as possible, so that he can meet you before he dies. Since you are a hospice social worker in America, he would like for you to make mortuary arrangements on his behalf. Cousin, I hope this letter helps. I don't have much, so I'm sending you my lucky bookmark. I know you love to read, so I'm sure you'll find a good home for it. We're all praying that we get a chance to finally meet you in person. With much affection, your cousin Lucy.

Alex   The certified letter is the last piece of paperwork I need in order to apply for advance parole. And on the advice of my attorney, I go down to the immigration offices in downtown LA in person, so as not to have to wait the approximate three to six months it takes for them to make a decision on your request. But see, I didn't know that. I didn't find out that a decision on advance parole takes up to six months until after I had sent in an initial request via mail, along with a money order for $485 that was non-refundable, and only after having fired my immigration attorney for not telling me I could have applied for this years ago. My new and wonderful attorney told me that I could get a decision within hours if I went in person and applied for emergency advance parole. So I did, and paid another $575 for that request because the prices went up after Christmas. After strenuous review of my documentation on January 4, 2017, I was granted emergency advance parole, which meant that I could leave the country for up to thirty days, with just one re-entry. The document was good from January 4 to February 3, 2017,

The very next day, I go to the Guatemalan consulate to pick up my passport. It's been about five weeks since I applied. Now let me tell you something about the Guatemalan consulate: I fucking HATE the Guatemalan consulate! Never in my life have I dealt with a more entitled, self-righteous, ignorant ass group of fucking—But I'm not there for that today! Today, I am simply there to pick up my passport. So I bypass the smug little man who hands out numbers that designate when you see a consulate agent, but he quickly gets in front of me, blocks my path, and asks me if I have an appointment. And I'm like:

Anner   Bro, chill, I don't need an appointment. I'm just here to pick up my passport.

Alex   To which he smugly replies:

Consular   Guwee don hav et. Guwee don hav et da pasaporte. If ju aply aftir Nobember ferz, guwee don hav et. Guwee don hav et da booklet for da pasportes. Com bag endo marz.

Alex   Endo marz? What the fuck is "endo marz"? I can't come back "endo marz" I have to leave and be back in the country before February 3. And just as I'm about to start cussing this guy out, he tells me that the consulate can issue me a temporary passport, so I'm like "Alright, give me that." But then he tells me that the passport is only good for being let into Guatemela but I won't be able to get back into the U.S. with it, so I'm like "what the fuck do I need that for then?" Then he goes on to explain to me that I could go to Guatemala with the temporary passport, and once there, I could go to the consulate office, take my receipt for the passport I paid for here, and they could issue me a new passport in Guatemala. So I'm like "Cool! Let's do that then." but then he asks me if I have a "De-Pe-Ee"? and I'm like, "What's a De-Pe-Ee?" And he's like "A De-Pe-Ee es nachuno I.D. car" and says that every person in Guatemala needs one in order to conduct any kind of official business. Of course I don't have a "De-Pe-Ee" because I've never been there. But then he tells me that won't be a problem, because the consulate actually issues DPI National I.D. Cards, and they only cost $15. Great! I have $15 bucks, hook me up! I fill out the application, submit it, along with a copy of my birth certificate and $15, and I ask the little lady on the other side of the counter how long it'll take for them print me my DPI after I took the photo. I figure if it's anything like a Costco membership, it should be fast. It's around noon time. I can have lunch in Atwater Village, then pick up Aileen from school in Eagle Rock, and by the time I'm done doing that, my DPI should be ready. But then the little lady at the counter gently nods her head "no" and tells me that they won't be issuing me a DPI today, and when I ask her when, she simply replied:

Consular   Endo Marz.

Alex   These people suck! I get on the phone with Lucy and tell her that there is a good chance that I won't be able to make it to Guatemala anymore, because right now, the risk of getting stuck in Guatemala with an expired passport is outweighing any potential benefit of me going down there. Lucy tells me that she has a lawyer friend that she can reach out to and ask for help, and that she'll get back to me in a few days.

It took Lucy ten days to get back to me. By now it's January 15, five days before the 45th is sworn into office. I'm supposed to leave and come back before that happens. It's also been over sixty days since I sent in my paperwork to renew my work permit, over forty days that my stupid passport hasn't come in, I've already used up eleven days of my advance parole, leaving me with just nineteen days before it expires. My opportunity to go to Guatemala and get my legal entry into my record is closing fast. Lucy tells me that her lawyer friend is pretty confident that I should be able to get a new passport if I can show up in person, bring both receipts, one for the DPI, and one for the passport renewal. He believes that should be enough for me to get a new passport but he's not sure because he's not an immigration lawyer, he's a patent lawyer. I'm not convinced. I ask Lucy if there is any way her lawyer friend can guarantee me a new passport once I get down there. I don't want to go to a foreign country, and get stuck because her patent lawyer friend had a "good feeling"

about me getting a new passport. Lucy says that unfortunately, neither she, nor her
friend can guarantee that. But she adds that both of them are willing to write
affidavits of support on my behalf. I'm still not convinced. That's when I decide
to ask my mom for her opinion.

Lucrecia   Ay mijo . . . I say you go. I mean, what do you have to lose? Look, I
already told you, I spoke to your brothers and your sister, and if anything happens, yo
te prometo que te traemos de regreso. We'll bring you back one way or another. Ay
Anner, I know the whole point of you going to Guatemala is so you can come back
legally, but what am I supposed to do huh? I can't just leave you stranded there. You
may have been born in Guatemala but you're an American, They'll eat you alive
down there. Ay mijo, why are you worried about Aileen? She's a strong girl. She'll be
okay. We're taking a short trip, she won't even have enough time to miss you. Mira, if
Lucy thinks you can get your passport, then it's worth a shot. All these years, Mijo . . .
All these years that you've been without papers; this might be your only chance. After
this time, you may not get another opportunity. Think about it Annercito. I promise I
won't leave you this time. I live with a lot of shame because of how I brought you
into this country. Pero yo era una niña. I was a girl in love with your father. I would
have followed him to hell, and I did; for you. But if I would have known that bringing
you over the way I did, would have created so many problems for you, I wouldn't
have done it. Hijo, yo te amo, del tamaño del universo. I know I brought you to this
country the wrong way, but I have faith in God, en La Virgen de Guadalupe y El
Señor de Esquipulas, that I can bring you back the right way.

Alex   In the beginning of 1983, fifteen-year-old Ana Lucrecia Cividanis left
Guatemala City, Guatemala with me as an infant, as soon as the money my father sent
her from Los Angeles arrived. It took us a little more than a month to make it to the
southern border. At the end of the first week, we got robbed. At the end of the second
week, we ran out of food. At the end of the third week, we were starving. Her breast
milk had dried up and she began feeding me water from any sources she could find:
lakes, rivers, streams, leaking faucets, broken water pipes: anything to quiet the
hunger cries. By the end of the fourth week, she was weak, and I had gotten sick. My
brownish complexion had turned clammy and yellow, and so had my eyes. Then one
evening, I woke up, looked up at my mom, and began to convulse.

Lucrecia   Annercito, hijo despiertate, tienes que respirar—Ayundenme!!!! Por favor
hijo, no te mueras, por favor respira hijo. Tienes que despertarte. Annercito, habre los
ojos—AYUDENME!!!

Alex   There was this woman who had just joined the journey. She too had just given
birth but had decided to leave her child behind because she felt the trek would be too
difficult for the child. I once asked my mother about this woman, and all she ever said
was:

Lucrecia   I don't even remember her name. I just remember holding on to your
lifeless body and praying to El Señor de Esquipulas y La Virgen de Guadalupe to save
your life. Then this woman took you from my arms and she blew life into your lungs,
and when you woke up and began to cry, she took your mouth and she put it to her
breast, and she fed you.

Alex   We eventually made it to the Tijuana San Ysidro border, but I was still really sick, and the coyote, he was very concerned.

Coyote   Mire señorita. The cross, it's very dangerous. If you go crawl through the sewers or go through the desert, your son, he is very sick and he might not make it. The people crossing with us are worried that if he wakes up and starts to cry, he might get us all caught. No listen to me, señorita. I have a plan, but we don't have much time. Give me the boy. I will buy him a new outfit, give him some Tylenol, and let him sleep in the back seat of my car. I will cross him over as if he were my own son. Señorita, please, this is the only way. If not, I am sorry, I cannot cross you.

Alex   Mom gave me over to the coyote and walked for miles through the dark, cold desert, tripping on barbed wire, and tearing a whole chunk of flesh off her leg. Now let me put something into perspective. My daughter is fifteen years old. I don't let her go to the corner store by herself. But here's fifteen-year-old Lucrecia; a child. Thousands of miles away from home, with no food, or money, or any real way to get back to her loved ones or even her father. Of course she was terrified. Not so much at the idea of getting caught. Because what if she did get caught? Her fear was what would happen to me. What if in her absence I got sicker and died? She eventually made it to the safe house in San Ysidro, and she found me asleep on a twin-sized mattress, wearing a brand new Mickey Mouse outfit. Somebody handed her a Big Mac. "Welcome to America."

Alpharaoh   I grew up hearing whispers about a revolution, immigrants with hopes and dreams in search of restorative solutions. Aspirations by adults that fought, through the fear and tension, better lives for their offspring was where they placed their intention. In spite of the factory raids, the language barricades, the disdain in the blue-eyed, white guy who underpaid and overworked my mother in the sewing factory, she was fired for not accepting sexual advances from the foreman with lustful eyes and gold-rim glasses, who called Mom a wetback, threatened to have her sent back to Mexico, but she's Guatemalan, as he grabbed her ass and pulled her close, he ripped her blouse and spoke: "C'mon mami, be a good girl, or I'll fuck up your world." The revolution isn't televised, yet well documented, on the hard, cracked lines of my father's blistered hands, rough and swollen from heavy toiling. He taught me how to use my pen as a sword, my words as a legion, that pledges allegiance, to clear-minded reason, to risking treason, all for speaking against an oppressive system.

Alex   Mom risked everything, including our lives to get us here. Now it was my turn, to risk everything, by going back to Guatemala, a place I've never known, in the hopes of being able to come back home.

January 25, 2017. The 45th signs an executive order that begins construction of the wall, and yes! Mexico is totally going to pay for it.

January 27, 2017. The day I'm supposed to leave to Guatemala, The 45th signs legislation that enacts the first version of the Muslim travel ban, and with it comes radical new language that makes the over 13 million undocumented people in this country immediate targets for deportation, for anything ranging from felonies, to major misdemeanors, to suspicion of crimes, and who knows, maybe even expunged crimes, like I don't know, DISTURBING THE PEACE . . .

6:30 p.m. That evening . . . I'm pacing back and forth in my apartment. I'm not sure if I should take this trip. If I stay, I'm putting my fate in the tiny hands of the 45th. But if I go, I'm putting my faith in God. So, I did what I always do in times of great turmoil; I turned to one wiser than me.

Anner   Aileen. Baby, come to the living room please . . . Aileen . . . hija come to the living room . . . AILEEN!!!

Aileen   What?!?!?! I already told you. Just go! Why do you keep asking me the same question when you know I'm going to give you the same answer?! Dad, this is our silver lining. You've been living with this dark cloud your entire life. If you do this, it can change our lives for the good. Forever. Don't worry, you won't lose me, Dad. You're giving in to your fear. You know why? Because you're going to come back. You're going to come back because this is your home, and you deserve to be home!

Grabs key.

Give me your hand. You gave me this key when I turned thirteen. It has the word FAITH written on it. This key will keep you safe. Promise me, promise me that you will give me this key back when you return on Wednesday. I know you're going to come back on Wednesday, Dad. You know why? Because it is our destiny. It is our destiny to work together at the Hollywood Fringe festival this year. So promise me that you'll give me this back when I see you on Wednesday. Promise me that you'll allow it to protect you.

Anner   I . . . I promise . . .

Aileen   I love you, Dada. I'm going to help you pack . . . Later, cuz right now I'm listening to Tupac.

Alex   Aileen eventually helps me pack. She puts clothes in a gym bag for me, while I call my mom and tell her that I'll be at her place by 8:30 p.m. I call my brother Gee and ask him to take Aileen to our sister's house in Murrieta. I call my sister Azucena, and let her know Aileen is on her way. Then I call my brother Junior and ask him to house sit for me while I'm gone the anticipated five days. Afterwards, I begin writing a detailed e-mail addressed to close friends and family, giving specific instructions in case something happens. There are three main points I make: 1. What to do with Aileen if I don't come back within a reasonable amount of time. I'm a single dad and she's been living with me for over four years. If I don't return, she'll eventually have to transition to living with her mom again, and that's going to be hard for her. 2. What to do with my personal belongings. I'm going to have to give up my apartment, turn in my car, put things in storage; basically deconstruct my entire life if I don't return. Lastly, how to turn me into a poster child for the unDACAmented movement by contacting my lawyer, advocate friends, and having my artistic community support me in this time of crisis. Hopefully making enough noise in the media, to help me get back home. At 8:30 p.m., I arrive at my mother's house and we put my things in the trunk of her husband's car and he drives us to LAX. As we approach the terminal, my mom turns around and says:

Lucrecia   Mijo, listen to me. If for whatever reason, you have the slightest doubt about this trip: Then don't go! Just turn around, call David, he'll drive you to your place, get in your car, drive to your sister's house, spend the weekend with your daughter, and when I return on Wednesday, we can talk about how you're going to pay me back for your ticket. So if you feel like you don't want to do this, you have until the door on that plane closes, to change your mind, OK, mijo? Because once that plane starts moving, you're in for a long ride.

Alex   Mom and I go through security, check in our bags, and we board the plane.

Anner   OK, you can do this, you can do this. Four and a half hour flight. That's like from here to New York. You've been to New York. You go to New York all the time. You were just there a few months ago. OK, you got this. Just breathe . . . Practice your Kriya, and remember your breath—WHAT? No, Mom, I don't want no water! Damn! . . . Always treating me like a little kid—(*To flight attendant.*) Can I have some Scotch please? (*To myself.*) Just breathe. Ignore her, ignore her, close your eyes, focus on your breath . . . (*Beat.*) What if the plane crashes like the last scene in La Bamba? What if this plane is full of terrorist? What if I get kidnapped because the people there will recognize that I'm not like a "real" Guatemalan, and they hold me for ransom and when my mom can't come up with the money to save me they shank me to death? What if I don't get a passport and I get stuck down there? . . . (*Beat.*) . . . Fuck! The plane is moving. (*To* **Lucrecia**.) Mommy, I change my mind. I want to get off the plane. I want to go home. I'm sorry I got mad at you and I raised my voice . . .Oh shit . . . Chill, Anner, chill. Just breathe, c'mon breathe. Don't hyperventilate or you'll pass out . . . Why is the white guy staring at me like that? He's probably a U.S. marshal and he's going to come over and put a bullet in my head because he thinks I'm a terrorist and then I'll fucking die on this plane. This trip was a bad idea. This is worst than my worst nightmare . . .

Alpharaoh   My mom never severed her marriage to Nery, she was scared of him because he used to beat her, promised her papers but would always deceive her. One evening, it was storming, I come home from school to find yellow tape around the entrance to the pad, a handcuffed dad, confused eyes, soaking wet from the rain, he wore a grin: but looked sad. I caught the last bit of description through the police radio receiver. Pops made good on his promise when he discovered that she was going to leave him. She took a chop to the throat with a meat cleaver. The same one she was using to make dinner for my little brothers: broiled beef ribs with sauce smothered, their favorite. He claimed it was an accident, the argument got too heated: there was immediate regret, a life-altering event. He found out she was cheating with his best friend prior to the incident. Afterwards, I become a ward of the state, never again see my sister. Later I heard she was raped while in foster care by her custodian: Lester LeFaire. That same year, she disappeared, the cops dug Lester's back yard and found her cadaver there. I can't protect her because I was placed in a home off of Manchester, off the 110, my best friend was killed in combat after 9/11. He took shrapnel from an IED to the head. He joined the Marine Corps to get off the crystal meth, the shit he was supposed to be dealing. I never practiced my craft, so I never got into lyrics, instead, I chill in alleys consuming and speaking to spirits. I got my girlfriend pregnant at nineteen, the baby was born dead, today she'd be fifteen, but she was made in my spitting image. One of my brothers became a chemist, at the oasis motel, he died in an explosion, took two babies and a junky who were waiting for a sale. My other brother's a schizo, who lives in a nursing home, medicated, he talks to himself, while he fidgets and roams. I never went to college, never graduated, never traveled, explored, so I never dated, never met the love of my life so my idea of affection is twisted, distorted, with this emotional currency, lust is all I'm afforded. No funeral provided, for my soul, no one's mourning. No more mornings . . . no one's morning . . . no good mornings . . . no good mornings—

Pilot   —Good morning, ladies and gentlemen, this is your pilot speaking. The time is 6:30 a.m. Please return to your seats, fasten your seat belts, and turn off all electronic devices. We will begin making our descent in about fifteen minutes. Welcome to Guatemala.

Intermission.

Alex   I look out the window of the plane and I see three beautiful volcanoes. Each with a bit of smoke coming out of them. Then my mom leans over and tells me that my father climbed the tallest of the three volcanoes when he was a young man. Then I realize that this is how the volcanoes communicate with each other. These volcanoes have been speaking this way for millennia. Suddenly, an overwhelming sensation of anxiety and nostalgia hits me all at once. I understand the anxiety, I'm definitely not in Cali anymore, but the nostalgia . . . that just catches me off. How could I possibly feel nostalgic about a place I have no recollection of. How can I have love and fondness for a country I never understood why my mother always cried for. A country I was always told was fiscally poor but rich in natural resources? That I was a descendant of a great Mayan people, but I've never met anyone that was eager to go back and stay there. Mother was right. Guatemala is a beautiful country, but it's not home, it simply isn't.

Beat.

Arriving to Guatemala was a huge cultural shock. It was the first time in my life that I had ever felt like an immigrant. The possibility of not being able to go back to LA and be with my daughter and continue my life's work, it fucked with me. I have to confess, I was afraid to love Guatemala. I was afraid to even like it a little bit. I didn't want to accidentally tip the universe's scale in the direction of me staying.

Alex   As Mom and I leave the airport terminal we're greeted by cousin Lucy, and her mother, my mom's little sister, Aunt Susy, rushes to hug me and says:

Susy   Hay, mijo, the last time I saw you eras una creatura, as I handed you over to your mother. I never thought I'd live long enough to ever see you again.

Alex   I gave Lucy a big hug and thanked her for everything she had done for us up until that point. She then drove us to my grandmother's house. There, I met my grandfather for the first time. The man that made this trip possible: Don Juan Francisco Cividanis. Needless to say that my first encounter with him was an awkward one.

Anner   Buenos dias abuelo . . . soy yo . . . Anner.

Alex   He was lying in bed and looked confused. He was squinting his eyes in an attempt to adjust his sight in the dim light. He had no idea who I was, until it hit him and he realized who was standing in from of him. He then got up as quickly as his 76-year-old body allowed him to, and towered over me at six feet two inches. He didn't know how to treat me and I didn't know how to treat him, so he shakily offered me his hand but went in for the hug instead. At first he stiffened up but after a moment he relaxed into it. Afterwards, he gently pushed me back, caressed the sides of my shoulders before giving them a gentle smack, and with tears in his eyes said:

Juan   Aaaaaaaaay . . . que muchachon tan grande . . . Mucho gusto de conocerlo mijo.

Alex   My grandfather is a witty old man who loves to tell stories, make fun of people, and brag about the knowledge he thinks he has . . . Yup, I'm his grandson alright! Afterwards we both go downstairs and I say hi to my grandma. I see Grandma often because she has a visitor's visa and travels occasionally to the U.S. For the next few days, I play tourist in Guatemala. I visit the hospital where I was born, the church where I was baptized at, and we go to the central market, the one that reminds me of the one back home in downtown Los Angeles. I also eat some of the most delicious Guatemalan food I have ever had in my life.

Alex   Monday, January 30, 2017. It's my third day there. It's also my father's birthday. I'm going to go see him later today, but first I have to try to get this passport thing taken care of. So Mom tells me we have to wake up at 5:00 a.m. because we have to be at the Guatemalan Consulate no later than 6:00 a.m., even though the place opens at 8:00 a.m. Then I ask my mom why we have to do all that, and she replies "Oh, you'll see." So Mom, Aunt Susy, Cousin Lucy, and I arrive to the consulate office at 6:00 a.m. and there's already a long line of people waiting to get passports and I'm like, "Where the hell do all these people gotta go to"? Cousin Lucy tells me that she has to go. She has to clock into work but will ask her boss for the morning off so that she may come back and try to help me. Mom, Aunt Susy, and I go stand in line and we wait. Two hours later, Mom and Aunt Susy are talking about things pertaining to their childhoods, and suddenly the line begins to move.

Anner   Shit . . . Where's Lucy . . . I can't do this without Lucy . . . She's the quarterback of this whole thing . . . My mom and my aunt Suzy are talking about things pertaining to their childhoods, and the line begins to move. I begin to panic. Lucy is nowhere to be found. Shit. I can't do this without Lucy . . . She's the quarterback of this thing . . . I can't talk to these people by myself . . . I know myself. I talk a lot, I talk too much. I'll fuck this up . . . No! Mom definitely cannot talk to them. She's self-righteous . . . She'll snap at them and then I'll get kicked out for sure . . . There's about thirty people ahead of me . . . Where's Lucy . . . I can't remember the name of the consulate person I'm supposed to ask for . . . Oh shit . . . I'm starting to hyperventilate . . . Oh LUCY YOU'RE BACK!!!! THANK GOD!!!

Alex   Lucy reminds me that I have to go inside myself and that I only have to tell them what we rehearsed at Grandma's house last night: That I am traveling from the US, I need to come back home Wednesday morning, and that I need a new passport to be able to do that, otherwise I won't be able to go back home. I tell her I have an idea. I tell her that I'm going to pretend that I don't speak any Spanish, and although she doesn't speak any English, she's going to pretend to be my interpreter. Lucy gives me a mischievous grin and is like, "Alright. Let's try it." By now there are two people in front of us, and suddenly the smug little man who gives out numbers for people to be seen by a consulate agent calls us forward. Lucy gets ahead of me and before she can say anything, A tired-looking lady walks up to us and asks us our business. Lucy gives the whole spill about me being from the States and needing a new passport in order to go home. But before Lucy can finish the lady sharply asks us if we have our "De-Pe-Ee." Which then prompts Lucy to pull out the receipt for the DPI, but then the lady goes:

Consulate Lady   No, no, no, no, no, no, no! If jew no habit da de pe ee, jew canna go in sigh.

Alex   I start feeling the dread and anxiety overwhelming me and before I can stop myself, my bourgeois American side comes out!

Anner   Lucy, what the hell is going on here? Don't these people know that we have very important business to attend to? I am hungry! And I need to see my father, before noon!

Alex   And is as if the 45th himself had spoken English, both agents quickly perked up, and quickly ushered us in, but not before the smug little man pettily said that there was no way we were going to get anything because we didn't have a DPI, but I didn't care. We were in! And that's all that mattered. As Lucy and I walk into the hallways of the government building another tired-looking lady stops us and asks us our business. Lucy begins giving the spill about how she's my interpreter because I don't speak any Spanish—

Consulate Lady Two   Como? Él no habla Español, ni un poquito?

Alex   I look this woman right in the eye and say

Anner   Un paquito?

Alex   And she gives me the most disgusting look any woman has ever given me. She snatches the paperwork away from Lucy, and she walks away. Lucy notices that I'm trying to control my anxiety attack and begins to rub my shoulder.

Lucy   Sana sana, colita de rana, si no sana hoy, sanara mañana.

Alex   The tired-looking woman comes back after a few minutes and asks Lucy if the transaction were originated in the United States. Lucy says yes and then the woman gives me another disgusting look, and walks away

Lucy   Sana sana, colita de rana, si no sana hoy, sanara mañana.

Consulate Lady Three   Anner Alfaro a la primera ventanilla. Señor Anner Alfaro a la primera ventanilla.

Alex   Now, I know they're calling my name to the first window, but now Lucy is all into the bit, and she's like (*English mock.*) "primera ventanilla." I get to the first window and the lady there asks me for my old passport.

Anner   My old passport? Sure, no problem. It's . . . right here . . . wait . . . where's my passport? . . . Fuck . . . where's my old passport—

Consulate Lady Three Aquí está!

Alex The woman looks at the old passport, then looks at me. Picks up a booklet, looks inside, then looks at me, and gives me a new passport! In that moment I completely forget myself. I run up to Lucy and in perfect Spanish I proclaim!

Anner Prima, me dieron el pasaporte, vamonos!

Alex But I'm petty too. So I walked up to the smug little man and tired-looking lady who gave us a hard time outside and I said

Anner "Muchas Gracias por todo. Pasen buen día."

Alex I'm feeling great! I'm practically halfway home! Now, I have to go see my dad. Mi papi, Nery Martin Alfaro, came to the United States when he was 19. He was studying to be a public defender back in Guatemala. I once asked him why he wanted to be a public defender if all the money was in being a prosecutor. He said:

Nery Annercito, nothing that you see here is of permanence. Only that which you feel but cannot see, that eternal. Aver mijo, you tell me: what's the point of gaining the world if you lose your soul in the struggle? What's the point of having gifts that God gives you, if you don't use them to help others? One day, we'll go back to Guatemala, and we'll do a lot of good with what we learn here . . .

Alex Dad never made it back to Guatemala alive. He died of a massive heart attack on September 29, 1998 at the ripe old age of thirty-five. I said goodbye to him a day before my sixteenth birthday. He became a simple car painter. But by the end of his life, my dad was a bad muthafucker with a spray gun . . . The way he glide his hand from side to side made him look like a composer to a symphony that only he could hear. He could do with paint what I aspire to do with words. He would get paid $3.75 an hour and make about $150 a week. He would save most of that money by living off of a single egg and a slice of bread per day, in order to save money for Mom and I to come over.

Beat.

Visiting Dad was nothing like how I imagined it. There was no closure.

Anner Hola, Papi . . . I made it! Your big boy is all grown up. How come you don't talk to me in my dreams anymore? I don't remember what you sound like anymore. I don't remember what you smell like but I hate the smell of car shops. Why'd you leave? I was fifteen years old, what the fuck did I know about living? You didn't teach me to shave, or drive, or take me to a ball game, or teach me how to be a good father. I remember when I was a kid, you promised me that we go would go back to Guatemala, but not once did you ever ask me if I wanted to come with you. Because of your selfishness I've had to live without papers my entire life. I spent my twenties living just like you did: scraping by for money, doing odd jobs, evading the police so that they wouldn't deport me for driving without a license. I lived in my car for six months once. I used to cash my paychecks at the meat market because it was the only place that accepted my school I.D. I was forced to quit my job once they found out I didn't have papers. Now I'm here. What am I supposed to do, huh? ANSWER ME!!

What am I supposed to do? Listen, I'm sure you're busy doing heavenly shit but, I need to ask you for a favor—And you know, I don't ask you for much . . . but . . . If you have any clout, at all, with anyone up there . . . Can you help me get back home? I just want to go home. I don't want to stay here. I want to go back to my daughter . . . (*Beat.*) I have to go—yeah, Mom's here too. I'm sorry it took me eighteen years to come and see you. Hopefully, it won't take another eighteen for me to come back to visit. Te quiero mucho, Papi. Take care of yourself.

Alex   That afternoon, it was as if a weight had been lifted off my shoulders. My appetite had returned. I was cracking jokes with my grandpa. I explained in as much detail my love and passion for acting to my aunt. Then, at 6:00 p.m, Eastern Standard Time, CNN reported that the Attorney General issued a permanent stop to the Muslim Travel Ban. But at 9:00 p.m. Eastern Standard Time, the 45th fires the Attorney General and installs an interim Attorney General that resumes the ban. I panic. I tell my mother that we have to leave as soon as possible. We cannot wait until Wednesday morning; we need to leave tomorrow morning, tonight if possible! Mom tells me that I'm being impractical. That we don't have the money to move our flights a day early, and that we should just wait until Wednesday. I tell her that we can't afford to wait. That the politics back home are literally changing by the hour. Right now there's a ban on Muslims. Tomorrow, there might just be a ban on Guatemalans! You know what she did then? She did what she always does when we get into an argument: she got on her phone, rolled her eyes at me, and walked away. I then turn to my grandmother and my aunt and continue my rant, saying how I'm sure Guatemala is a beautiful place but I gotta go. There is enough confusion at LAX that I may just get through customs inspection and be paroled back into the country because immigration agents will have other priorities than some random Guatemalan traveling with his mother— (*Sound of an e-mail notification.*) Ping Ping . . . I open up my e-mail: My mom moved our flight to the next morning.

We wake up at 5 a.m. once again. We shower, get dressed, pack, and begin our goodbyes. I give Lucy a big hug, my auntie a hug and kiss on the cheek, and I do the same for my grandmother. And just as we're about to get into the taxi, my mom yells out:

Lucrecia   ANNER!!!! We forgot to say goodbye to my dad!!!

Alex   Oh shit! I haven't said goodbye to my grandfather, the whole reason why I'm here. Even though I had just met him in the last seventy-two hours. We really bonded.

Anner   Buenos días Abuelito. No mas le quiero decir que ya me voy.

Juan   Ya se va? Pero si usted acaba de llegar.

Anner   I know, Grandpa. But I gotta go . . . It's my time to go . . .

Alex   This time, my grandfather took his time in standing up, with the patience of a man who has seen seventy-six years. He towered over at six feet two inches. He then gave me a strong hug, a man's hug. In that moment, something about myself that I never knew finally made sense. He made me feel like a little kid again. I felt safe, loved, and cared for. I hadn't felt that way since my papi was alive. I realized then that he was the only father I had left. He caressed my shoulders and smacked the sides of them, while firmly looking into my eyes as the tears escaped his. His voice quaked but for a second when he began to say:

Juan   Porte se bien hijo, que nada le cuesta. Échele ganas a la vida. Sea fuerte. Yo tengo mucha fe en Dios, que todo le va salir bien. Esta es su casa, para cuando usted quiera regresar, siempre será bienvenido. ¿Como es que dicen los gabachos? Ebri tin es ok!

Beat.

Alex   9:45 a.m., Mom and I are on a plane headed northbound for Los Angeles, California, Good ol' U.S. of A. Mom offers me some Scotch because she thinks it'll help me go to sleep, I simply say:

Anner   It's okay mom, I'm cool. Thank you though. I'm just going to drink some water, and watch a movie, OK?

Alex   By 11:45 a.m, the flight attendant announces over the loudspeaker that we need to have our customs and legal documents in order and be prepared for inspection. Mom and I get off the plane, hold hands, and begin to snake through a long path that leads to the basement of the terminal, where we see a big sign that reads "CUSTOMS AND BORDER PROTECTION."

Anner   This is it, Mom. If I can get through customs inspection. We'll be able to leave LAX together. If not . . . I'll be on the first flight back to Guatemala—

Immigration Agent   —Next! OK, we have an Ah-near-al-pha-row-psy-ba-dawn-ease and a La-cree-sha psy-ba-dawn-ease—wait a minute, you're an American citizen. What are you doing in this line? Oh, you're traveling with your son. How is your son traveling? Does he have a visa? He doesn't. Then how is he traveling? How are you traveling? Advance parole? One moment. (*Beat.*) OK, ma'am, how are you doing this fine morning? Do you have anything to declare? Did you bring any fruits, vegetables, or animals back with you? No? OK. What about money? Do you have more than $10,000 cash on you? No, OK, great (*Stamps passport and returns to her.*) Alright, Ah-near, let's see here. I want you to take your right hand and place your four fingers on the scanner . . . OK, now do your thumb . . . Repeat . . . Take your right hand, place your four fingers on the scanner . . . OK, repeat. Place your left thumb on the scanner . . . Try again . . . STOP SHAKING . . . OK, now I want you to remove your glasses, take a step back, so I may take a picture—DON'T SMILE! . . . OK you can put on your glasses and return . . . You ever been arrested before Anner? . . . Hey, AP!

Alex   As one immigration agent gives my passport and paperwork to another, my mother quickly interjects!

Lucrecia   Excuse me, sir, I'm an American citizen, and this is my son. We're traveling together and I promised him I wouldn't leave him this time. Mijo, please tell him that we came here together. Sir, please let me wait with him. We came here together, and I promised I wouldn't leave him again—

Anner   Mami. Listen to me, OK? I need you to do exactly what they're asking you to do. I need you to take my bag, and go downstairs. My friends and Gabriel are down there, OK? Don't cry, Mom, please. If I don't come out, my friends will know what to do . . . Mami . . . Everything is going to be OK.

Alex   She bows her head in defeat, picks up my gym bag, walks away and never turns back. I stand there and watch her, waiting until she disappears. Only then do I follow the immigration officer and sit where he asks me to. I close my eyes and say a prayer of thanksgiving, and I try not to think about my life. I try not to think about my daughter. I try not to think that this may be the last place of home that I will ever see again.

Alpharaoh   This is/ your heart/ speaking/ listen/ beating/ listen/ beating/ working/ over/ time cuz/ you don't/ listen/ flatline/ prema/turely/ don't die/ early/ Aileen/ needs you/ Aileen/ loves you/ you de/serve to/ see grand/ babies/ all your/ work done:/ acco/ laded/ this is/ weighing/ on me/ for a/ while now/ no more/ wild out/ be good/ to me/ be good/ to you/ and you'll/ see how/ your life/ played out/ die old/ live long/ because/ you do/ deserve/ to live/ happy.

Immigration Agent   Anner! . . . When was the last time you traveled outside of the country prior to this time?

Immigration Agent   What was the purpose for your travel?

How long were you gone out of the country?

What do you do for a living?

You go to school for that?

What school did you go to?

Do you have a copy of your advance parole? Let me see your advance parole.

Alex   He stamps the parole paper and keeps it, hands me my passport and tells me to go downstairs. I have no idea what is about to happen. I go down the flight of stairs and out of the corner of my left eye, I can see my mother in the distance. She gestures to me to see if everything is alright. I gently shake my head because I have no idea what's going to happen next. I simply follow the immigration officer and stand where he asks me to. A few moments later, I feel someone grab my hand . . . It's my mom.

Immigration Agent   Next! Passports!

Mom gives hers first. I give mine second. He looks at Mom's, and gives it back. He looks at mine. Examines it. Looks at it, then looks at me. Looks at it again. Looks at me again.

Immigration Agent   Uh . . . You made it huh?

Anner   Um . . . yeah? . . .

Immigration Agent   Welcome home.

Alex   Mom and I look at each other and walk the fuck out of there as quickly as possible. My friend Luis sees me, shouts "ALFIE!" and gives me a big bear hug. My other friend Jason hugs my mom and begins helping her with her luggage. Right before we exit the terminal, my brother Gabriel arrives. Gabriel is one of the strongest men I know, but it's also very difficult for him to show emotion. In that moment, I could tell that it was taking everything within not to lose his composure. He gave me a big hug and did something that he rarely does—he whispered that he loved me. Afterwards we all left LAX and I've never been happier in my life to leave the airport as I was that day.

Epilogue

Alex   It's been over a year since the 45th won the presidency; a year since I decided to leave for Guatemala with an expired passport, a temporary passport only good for being admitted into Guatemala, an emergency advance parole that was expiring in seven days, with no guarantee that I would be given a new passport once in Guatemala, or that I would be allowed to come back into the country. All of this under a travel ban that was designed to specifically target the Muslim faith and the immigrant community. My DACA was eventually renewed. It came in two weeks before my old one expired. I have legal presence and a sort of temporary protective status until March 2019. Although I got a legal entry on my record, I wasn't able to adjust my status. It seems that the petition that my mom originally filed for me in July 2003 had expired. Then, on September 5, 2017, exactly five years to the day when I first applied for DACA, the 45th's administration rescinded the DACA program, putting over 800,000, including my own, into limbo. The 45th gave Congress six months to fix the issue. Since October 5, 2017, 122 DACA recipients lose their ability to go to school, work, and provide for themselves and their families each day, making them easy targets for deportation. People like myself, whose only home has ever been the United States of America. My friends and artistic family at Ensemble Studio Theatre, Los Angeles were concerned about my safety if I shared this story publicly. But the fact of the matter is that none of us are immune. (Insert current events relevant to what is occurring now). Yeah, People are trying to destroy our country, but it's not us, the DREAMers . . .

Alpharaoh   Mi poesía es causa para alarma. Mis palabras son armas mentales para los juveniles con miradas largas, en búsqueda de versos saturados en verdades, descontados como perdidas en los rostros de nuestros padres, porque ellos son la generación que sacrificaron sus dones para que nosotros tuviéramos en donde, vivir, que comer, no sufrir, por eso, no hay que perder; el significado de sus ofrendas. Por favor, no se me ofendan, simplemente hablo la lengua que mis conquistadores me enseñan. cuando era niño, mi padre me hacía que le leerá la Opinión, su jefe los despidió por dar una opinión. Llego a casa, derrotado, humillado, porque aunque pidió perdón, un mojado que piensa es muy peligroso para el don. Estas formas de discriminación vienen en siclos cada siglo. Polizas racistas fermentan en un sistema opresivo, pero nosotros tenemos culpa también por no recoger un pinche libro. Tan ocupados recibiendo el mínimo, que se nos olvida que venimos de lo máximo, les conviene que nos detengamos, porque nos temen. no quieren tocar el tema, saben que somos la nueva primavera pero prefieren que vivamos en el miedo del infierno que el gobierno ha creado: un invierno eterno. Simplemente porque somos del otro lado.

Pero las líneas a nosotros nos cruzaron. A nuestras mujeres: violaron, los hombres: mataron, los niños: adoctrinaron: los españoles nos robaron nuestra lengua nativa, y ahora el gabacho racista quiere matar las raíces de nuestras familias. Como podemos romper la cadena de esclavitud si no sabemos que somos esclavos. Las claves están escritas en mi piel morena, pero se me a olivado. Tengo la llave de mi libertad en mi mano, pero si no encuentro el candado, de nada sirvió lo que mi gente aiga sacrificado.

Anner   Mi nombre es Anner Alexander Alfaro Cividanis. I am an American in every sense of the word, except on paper. I am a son to an American, father to an American, brother to Americans. I am an actor, writer, producer, director, poet, and friend. What I am not is your enemy.

The End.

Section Four

Music and Autobiographical Performance

Conjunto Blues

Nicolás R. Valdez

Guadalupe Cultural Arts Center—San Antonio, Texas

13 Nicolás Valdez's *Conjunto Blues*, Historic Guadalupe Theater, San Antonio, 2018.
Photo: Rojelio Garza.

Snapshot

Marci R. McMahon

Written by Nicolás R. Valdez and directed by Ruben C. Gonzalez, *Conjunto Blues* presented a character-driven solo performance piece about a young boy's relationship with his abuelo. Filled with the sounds of conjunto music, "the soundtrack of the Mexican American experience," *Conjunto Blues* offered Latinx, multi-ethnic, and multigenerational audiences a connection to the Mexican American experience through the intimate sounds of the accordion and the personal relationship of the main character El Musico with his grandfather, family, and artistic and cultural community in San Antonio, Texas. In the piece, Valdez performs a composite of characters, including his abuelo and his very first accordion instructor, Valerio Longoria Sr., a pioneer in the conjunto music scene in South Texas. With live accordion music by Valdez throughout the show accompanied by Luis Gonzalez on bajo sexto, along with documentary footage of conjunto musicians, academics, and aficionados, the show amplified conjunto as a form of cultural resistance and liberation in Mexican American communities in South Texas who were, in the playwright's own words, "struggling to define their own unique Americanism."[1]

Conjunto Blues tells a regionally and culturally specific story of the Mexican American working class through the conjunto genre, but the personal, familial stories of struggle and the conjunto genre itself connects the piece to a larger political story of Latinx migration and struggle; through conjunto, we hear the dramatic immigration of the mid-nineteenth century that brought the accordion to the Américas. With the word *Blues* in the title, along with the conjunto genre that fills the sound world of the piece, the performance moves beyond the Mexican American experience to tell the macro story of working-class Latinx experiences. As Valdez explains, "People tend to not give as much attention to conjunto, it's a very American experience just like jazz or blues or zydeco, and that's where conjunto blues comes from, it's a story about the working class, the working people, accordion music is working people's music at the heart of it and we've been singing the blues for a long time . . ."

The inclusion of *Conjunto Blues* at the Encuentro signaled the importance and continued legacy of Chicano teatro activist theater and activism to the larger Latinx theatrical landscape, particularly through the minimal staging of the performance, which emerges from the rasquachismo aesthetics that have come to define Chicanx teatro.[2] *Conjunto Blues*' intimate storytelling of working-class struggle is visually told through veladoras (candles) that light up and adorn the altar on the stage, a bar filled with shot glasses and bottles of liquor—a prominent set piece that El Musico stands behind throughout the show to speak directly to the audience, along with sets of boxes on stage where the accordion and bajo sexto sit and wait to be played.

Ultimately, *Conjunto Blues*' visual and aural storytelling of Mexican American working-class struggle at Encuentro de las Américas signaled not only the larger legacy of Chicanx teatro to Latinx theater but, in our current political climate of scapegoating Latinx peoples, offered diverse Latinx audiences in attendance the opportunity to connect to each other's communities and to activate together to combat anti-immigration.

Notes

1. Yatrika Shah-Rais. "Nicolas Valdez interview." KPFK Global Village. November 1, 2017. Accessed November 27, 2020. https://soundcloud.com/user-653554044/nicolas-valdez-interview-with-yatrika-shah-rais-on-kpfk-global-village
2. Presented out of the Guadalupe Cultural Arts Center in San Antonio, Texas, *Conjunto Blues* reflects a history of Chicanx teatro that can be traced to the carpas, or traveling tent shows in South Texas. Valdez, brings his musicianship of conjunto and deep artistic, cultural, and political knowledge of the musical form to the show, along with his twenty-year experiences in Chicanx teatro, including touring with Teatro Campesino during the 25th anniversary tour of *Zoot Suit* and appearing at the LATC's Encuentro 2104 National Latino Theater Festival, with Su Teatro's production of *Enrique's Journey*.

Excerpt from Conjunto Blues

Lights up on a living room center stage. There is an altar with an accordion sitting upright in its case. **El Musico** *is dressing for* **Abuelo**'s *funeral. This is another moment beyond the time and place of the play. He moves between all spaces breaking the walls between past and present.*

Image of sunset on the rancho appears on the back screen.

El Musico   On a little piece of property just south of San Antonio the sun breaks through the horizon and casts long shadows. It's Easter Sunday and the rains have finally returned filling the *arroyos* and *acequias* with cool green water. Water to cleanse and water to revive the parched earth. A resurrection on the day of resurrection. "Water is like prayer," Lina would say.

El Musico *collects* **Abuelo**'s *shoes at the altar. Moves to porch and adjusts his tie.*

Out on the *rancho,* the party's just getting going. The church bells have been replaced by the sound of nervous laughter as the little ones anxiously await to fill their baskets while men with big *bigotes* and big bellies unload lawn chairs, ice chests, and BBQ pits. They sneak *traguitos* from flasks of tequila while the women in long summer dresses exchange *chisme* between sips of ice-cold *cheves.* ¡No comadre! !Sí comadre! !Ay, ní me digas comadre!

El Musico *sits on the porch steps and thoughtfully puts on his shoes.*

Abuelo and Lina take a seat on the hand-made benches that hug the concrete dance floor. Standing on the trailer with its four flat tires, the conjunto begins to warm up. They shuffle through a litany of standards—*polkas, redovas, cumbias,* and *rancheras*; here a *chotiz,* and there a waltz. The *gritos* and *chanclazos* are in full swing and the music never ceases. The chemistry of memory sparks beautiful melodies almost forgotten in the sepia'd past. Together, musicians, dancers, and audience alike are transformed and uplifted. Resurrecting themselves from the traumas of the past and the tedious realities of daily life.

El Musico *moves to* **Abuelo**'s *bench and kneels before it like a casket.*

It will be the last time I see my *abuelos* together in their element, all charm and firm tenderness. Dancing together, like so many times before, cheek to cheek in an embrace that belies their bickering. Lina will pass first and Abuelo will follow less than a year later, just long enough to celebrate eighty-six years of a life well lived. I will speak at his funeral, and play the mournful music that he himself requested. And I will carry that responsibility daily—to honor his memory, my grandmother's memory and all my relations stretching back for millennia. I will remember and resurrect you daily.

El Musico *approaches the audience as if speaking at a funeral.*

History breathes on the rancho in April. The trees and the soil recognize that space created by families and music, conjunto in its purest form, before the *bailes de campo* moved to the *cantinas de vicio*. How do we progress and still preserve the values of past generations? Things change, inevitably, but what do we preserve moving forward? *Nuestros costumbres cambian.* We are constantly evolving. It's that struggle between preservation and innovation that keeps culture evolving, sometimes stumbling, but always moving ahead. *Adelante. Siempre.*

Tonight, however, tonight the beer is still cold, the accordions and *bajo sextos* are musing, and the sweet mesquite breeze carries our stories all the way home.

At the final moment of the story he puts on that hat and grabs the cane becoming **Abuelo**. **Abuelo** *takes a moment, turns, and gives his final bow.*

The End.

Broken Tailbone

Carmen Aguirre

Nightswimming—Toronto, Canada

14 Carmen Aguirre's *Broken Tailbone*, Nightswimming, Toronto, 2017. Photo: Erin Brubacher.

Profile

Trevor Boffone

While the Latinx population has been growing in Canada since the 1970s, they remain marginalized both at home and abroad. There is only one Latinx theater company in Canada: Aluna Theatre in Toronto.[1] Likewise, Latinx actors are rarely seen on Canadian stages. This representation does not reflect the demographics of Canada's urban centers. Moreover, Latinx Canadian theater has largely been left out of the conversation in the United States. While the 2013 anthology *Fronteras Vivientes*, edited by Natalie Alvarez, remains a valuable resource guide for the breadth of Latinx theater in Canada, these plays have not fully crossed the border. Canadian Latinx playwrights such as Guillermo Verdecchia, Marilo Nuñez, and Rosa Laborde remain largely unknown or undervalued outside of Canada. Even in US Latinx theater circles, Carmen Aguirre, the veritable First Lady of Latinx Canadian playwriting, is still not a household name despite her long list of accomplishments and powerhouse plays such as *The Refugee Hotel* and *The Trigger*.

Needless to say, the inclusion of Aguirre's solo show *Broken Tailbone* in the Encuentro de las Américas was significant. This marked the Latinx Theatre Commons' first meaningful engagement with Latinx theater artists in Canada.[2] Oftentimes, in conversations about Latin America and its diaspora, Canada is left out of the conversation despite being home to roughly half a million people of Latin American descent.[3] As Aguirre's theater work demonstrates, it is past time to bring Latinx Canadians into the fold. *Broken Tailbone* emphatically showed that there is common ground between Latinx Canadian artists and their southern neighbors; they just need to be given the opportunity to have their voices heard outside of their home communities.

Broken Tailbone was commissioned, developed, and produced by Nightswimming, a Toronto-based dramaturgical company that explores the boundaries of theatrical storytelling. Following a two-year tour of Aguirre's *Blue Box*, director Brian Quirt developed the concept that would become *Broken Tailbone*. At the end of the first act of *Blue Box*, the audience would join Aguirre onstage for a dance party. Quirt and Aguirre wanted to take this idea further and expand the world of a fully participatory dance party. Aguirre began by compiling her favorite dance songs: cumbias, merengues, salsas, boogaloos, sons, candombes, sambas, and reggaetons. Each song has a memory attached to it. Together, the score induces memories from Aguirre's adolescence, youth, and from the present.

As a piece of immersive, participatory theater, *Broken Tailbone* takes spectators into the hidden world of Latinx dance halls in British Columbia. Aguirre leads a Latin American dance lesson, interwoven with tales of her own experiences in these spaces, all from a leftist point of view. Naturally, these seemingly unrelated stories all emerge from the geopolitical reality of Latin America. *Broken Tailbone* explores the migration of Latin Americans into Canada in the 1970s as a result of military dictatorships and state-sanctioned violence. In addition, Aguirre reveals that dance halls were also filled with draft dodgers and hippies who had fled the United States in protest of the Vietnam War. As *Dementia*'s Moises battles the Aids epidemic in Los Angeles, California and *10 Million*'s Él deals with the effects of the Cuban Revolution in Havana, *Broken Tailbone* speaks to the challenges that the Latinx community has faced in their home countries as well as their new home: Canada. As refugees in a foreign land, Aguirre's Chilean family found solace through dance and the community building that dance halls provided.

Throughout the lesson, she explains the history of each dance form, the history of Latinx dance halls in Canada, and the geopolitical history of Latin America. Naturally, it's difficult to tell where each story begins and ends. As with Aguirre's identity, stories blur together to form a cohesive narrative. When DJ Don Pedro plays a new song, Aguirre tells the audience about the song, occasionally choosing lyrics to not only explain but to move forward the performance's narrative. These songs are not chosen at random. Rather, they are perfectly strung together to build a narrative soundscape taking spectators from Aguirre's parents' arrival in Vancouver in 1973 to the present-day climate that led to Aguirre breaking her tailbone. As the performance begins, Aguirre explains that *Broken Tailbone* is not simply the title of the show, but something she unfortunately (fortunately?) experienced. Through the seventy-five minute dance lesson, audiences earn the right to hear the story and learn just how someone breaks their tailbone.

Broken Tailbone interweaves Aguirre's family's history with her own adventures in Latinx dance halls. The political climate influenced the atmosphere and demographics of the space. Amid political conflict, different Latin American ethnic groups went to dance halls and entered a utopian oasis where disparate identity markers no longer mattered. Dance halls are where people come to socialize regardless of social or economic class.

By definition, they decolonize borders by creating a space where people from all cultures and generations interact. They just dance. Dancing unites them. Moreover, it is in the dance halls where Aguirre sets aside the trauma she experienced and finds relief as well as the growing acceptance of her sexuality and erotic power. The piece culminates with the final tale about having sex with a Cristiano Ronaldo doppelganger with whom, to spoil the surprise, she breaks her tailbone during the sexual encounter.

Notably, *Broken Tailbone* is not scripted. Rather, Aguirre has certain benchmarks that she must hit with each song to keep the narrative—and the lesson—going. While any particular performance of *Broken Tailbone* features a slightly different "script," the show is scored and Aguirre is in constant communication with DJ Don Pedro, who creates the shows soundscape and helps build the dance hall atmosphere. The songs evoke memories from which Aguirre inserts herself into the history of Latinx peoples in Canada. While many of the refugees from Latin America had little by way of material possessions, what they did have was a rich musical cultural heritage.

Yet, what makes *Broken Tailbone* most unique is how Aguirre builds an interactive dance lesson. *Broken Tailbone* breaks the fourth wall entirely. When audiences enter, there is nowhere to sit except for a few seats far to either side of the stage. Where rows of seats normally begin, there is simply empty space. It is clear that to fully experience the show you must be on your feet and ready to move. The audience stands on the makeshift dance floor.[4] There is no barrier between the performer and from the audience, both physical and verbally. In this way, Aguirre engages audience members, making them active participants in the performance. The show is both mentally and physically engaging. As a critical piece of participatory theater, *Broken Tailbone* fully engages each audience member in an interactive performance. In many ways, the spectators become the performers. Without audience participation, *Broken Tailbone* would not work. The show relies on participation at every level. Notably, participatory theater is still considered outside-the-box in the United States and, in conversation with the other shows at Encuentro, *Broken Tailbone* was indeed experimental. In the end, all audience members have a shared experience in which they collaborate together to build the world of the performance. Admittedly, as hypnotic as Aguirre is as a performer, for much of the show my eyes wandered around the dance floor to watch my fellow spectators dance. The show is as much about what Aguirre does as it is about how the audience reacts, making each performance unique.

When I woke up the following day, my body was reminded of the show. My muscles ached from dancing. While rubbing my legs and stretching, I relived *Broken Tailbone*. Even though our lives and identities may be disparate, in Aguirre's dance hall we are all equal. Perhaps more than any other show at Encuentro de las Américas, I wanted to talk about it with my fellow dancers the next day. Not only did I want to know what they thought about the show, but I was curious about how they *felt*. What did it feel like for them to have a "broken tailbone"?

Notes

1. Founded by Marilo Nuñez, Alameda Theatre Company in Toronto ran for ten years, developing and producing many of Carmen Aguirre's plays.

2. Latinx Canadian artists did attend the 2016 Pacific Northwest Regional Convening as conveners. There was no programming centered on Canadian theater making.
3. Alvarez, Natalie. Introduction. *Fronteras Vivientes: Eight Latina/o Canadian Plays*. iii–xxviii.
4. While audience members are encouraged to participate throughout the show, there are seats surrounding the dance floor for those who need them.

Interview with Carmen Aguirre
Trevor Boffone

Boffone   You've had a long and successful career as a theater artist. What have been the defining moments of your career leading up to *Broken Tailbone*?

Aguirre   It is very hard to come up with defining moments, as every moment along this journey referred to as a "career" continues to teach me so much. Having said that, I will mention a couple that stand out. The first was getting accepted into theater school. That was a big deal. It was an all-white faculty (still is) and there were only three people of color in the fifty-strong student body (that has changed). When I started theater school at the age of twenty-two I had the naive idea that systemic racism/white supremacy did not permeate the world of theater, a place I viewed as a kind of utopia. Within the first few weeks of my training I became aware that this was not so, that systemic racism/white supremacy can be more glaring in the theater than in other areas of society. A month and a half into my first semester, the faculty warned me that I would be cast as hookers and maids due to my race. Was I sure I wanted to continue? Although this revelation filled me with shame, I will always be grateful for my instructors' directness at the beginning of my artistic journey. That is when I decided to create my own work and tell the stories of the Chilean community in exile. I wrote my first play, *In a Land Called I Don't Remember*, at theater school, where it was also produced.

Boffone   While workshopping *Broken Tailbone* at the Banff Playwrights Lab at the Banff Center for Arts and Creativity, you noted how, even in the twenty-first century, it is still a political and revolutionary act for a woman of color to be on stage, especially in a solo show. Can you elaborate on how you navigate intersections of ethnicity and gender onstage?

Aguirre   The latest numbers gathered by Canadian Actors' Equity Association state that of all the people we see on professional Canadian stages, only 3.7 percent are women of color. Of that number, very few are in lead roles. Last year, a Vancouver theater critic released the following figure after watching over a hundred professional shows: 93 percent of actors were white. These findings are troubling, considering that most professional theater takes place in Canada's major urban centers such as Vancouver and Toronto, where half of the population is of non-European descent. It is also troubling because there are large talent pools of BIPOC actors in these cities. And I haven't even talked about content (two years ago, Vancouver's Arts Club Theatre Company, the second largest theater company in Canada after Stratford, with eighteen shows a year on three stages, announced a season which featured only two writers of color, for example). Within this context, it is absolutely a revolutionary act to see a woman of color taking up so much space on stage. One of the things that systemic racism/white supremacy does is banish people of color from public spaces. People of color are supposed to be cloistered away and, when in public, only be there to perform gratitude to the mainstream for taking up said public space. It is within this framework that *Broken Tailbone* happens. The play features a woman of color being unabashedly sexual, unapologetically making anti-racist, anti-capitalist, anti-imperialist, feminist pronouncements as she teaches the audience how to dance salsa and invites them to create the marginalized space that is the Latinx dance hall.

Boffone   As a participatory piece of theater, *Broken Tailbone* offered Encuentro audiences a unique opportunity to become part of the performance itself. What has it been like collaborating with new audiences each performance? How do you maintain a safe performance environment for yourself considering the roles of performer and spectator are blurred?

Aguirre   It is always a rush to create a new show every night with the audience. *Broken Tailbone* is structured improv; there is no script, but rather notes on story points that must be hit with each song (the playlist is highly curated and was chosen through a lengthy workshop process). It is absolutely necessary to make sure it stays this way because I never know what the audience is going to hit me with. We've experienced everything from an audience that claps and laughs and sings along and dances with joy to a loud heckler taking over an entire performance because he disagreed with my politics to my having to eject a super-drunk audience member because he kept yelling out lewd remarks in reference to my body and how I was moving it. In short, the play is not entirely safe for me, which is what makes it electrifying for both myself and the audience. It is a show where all performer/audience barriers are broken, making the work simultaneously accessible and confrontational, a delicious mix in the theater.

Boffone   What do you hope audience gain from *Broken Tailbone*?

Aguirre   To have fun, first and foremost. To honor their bodies in motion. To celebrate female sexuality. To learn about salsa, Latin American geopolitical history from a Marxist perspective, the history of Latinx migration to Canada, the history of the dances themselves, the history of Canada's Latinx dance halls, to create their own dance hall, which is what *Broken Tailbone* becomes every night. The audience digests the stories in a different way when they are dancing. If they were sitting in a dark room watching me tell these stories, they wouldn't experience them with their entire bodies. It is a delight to see fellow Latinx people nodding with recognition at the narrative, proud to see themselves represented. It is also a pleasure to witness anybody who has been "othered" take up the same space that I am taking, moving their bodies with abandon. For some, it is the first time they have danced in public.

Boffone   How did Encuentro inform the eventual world premiere of *Broken Tailbone*?

Aguirre   It was very informative because it taught us all the possibilities of what we might encounter. It was at Encuentro that the heckler took over the space. It was also there that the audience had big problems with my politics and let me know it, either by talking back or walking out. But it also showed us how much hunger there is for that kind of content. There were gasps of surprise and support. One man applauded simply because I used the word "indigenous." An entire audience broke into applause when I told off the American Dream. Young women would approach me every night to tell me how the show affected them: it was the first time in their lives that they had seen a woman of a certain age (I'm fifty) be so unabashedly and unapologetically sexual. It taught them about a woman's agency, and allowed them to celebrate their own bodies and sexuality. It also solidified for us that the heart of the show is my Uncle Nelson, and so for the world premiere the key design piece was an altar in his honor.

Boffone   What does performing this show mean to you?

Aguirre   It means that I get to facilitate a whole new group of people every night form a dancing community. It is very special to witness that moment of license and abandon.

Boffone   One of the goals of Encuentro was to create a platform for collaboration between artists from across the Americas. How did the Encuentro influence your work as a playwright and performer?

Aguirre   It was a remarkable experience to be around so many fellow Latinx theater artists. Encuentro influenced my work as a performer because I was able to see Afro-Peruvian Ébano Teatro's production of Lynn Nottage's *Intimate Apparel*. The play was a masterclass in acting: can you be this honest, this vulnerable, this rooted, this real? Similarly, working with the group I was allotted to, made up of theater artists from Los Angeles, Texas, New York, Australia, Cuba, Colombia, and Peru, was another masterclass in collective creation led by Jorge Merced, Associate Artistic Director of the Bronx's Pregones Theater. Over a three-week period we created a short play and I learned a great deal from my fellow artists about the art of giving.

Boffone   In Los Angeles, there was a lot of discussion about the notion of common ground between Latinx and Latin American theater artists. How does Latinx Canadians fit into this conversation?

Aguirre   We are the forgotten Latinx people of the Americas. Many people don't realize that there are Latinx people in Canada. This is because we are fairly new to this country. The first en-masse arrival of Latinx people to Canada was in the mid-1970s when Chilean refugees fleeing Pinochet's dictatorship arrived here. That's when my family and I came. In the late 1970s and into the 1980s and 1990s thousands of Central Americans fleeing the wars there landed here. In the 2000s Latin Americans have been coming to Canada as international students and to seek work, not necessarily for political reasons. Professional Latinx theater has only existed in Canada since the mid-1990s, starting with Guillermo Verdecchia's seminal, Governor-General's award-winning one-man show *Fronteras Americanas*. Those of us who were at the Encuentro really are pioneers of Latinx theater in Canada. We are working under different conditions than our colleagues. In the States, the Latinx population is huge, it is visible, it has been around for a long time. In Canada, we are still dealing with erasure and appropriation on a regular basis (white people playing us on our stages because theater companies don't seek us out, claiming we don't exist). Our Latin American colleagues are faced with different challenges, mostly around funding. The common ground between us is that for those of us in the North, we are all dealing with issues of white supremacy, erasure, lack of representation, lack of inclusivity. It continues to be about gaining space (this holds true for Ébano Teatro in Peru as well). The common ground we have with our Latin American colleagues is our history. Because we are new to Canada, and because so many of us came as refugees, we are intimately acquainted with Latin America. Most of us were born there.

Boffone   What makes the Latinx Canadian experience different? In what ways do you think *Broken Tailbone* upheld or challenged this?

Aguirre   Our experience is different because we are not indigenous to this land, unlike, say, the Mexican American population of the Southern and Western parts of the United States. We are recent arrivals and many of us fled our countries for political reasons. Our history in Canada is very short, therefore we are pioneers. *Broken Tailbone* upheld this in its content: my parents started the first Latinx dance hall in Vancouver in 1974, making them pioneers of the local salsa scene, and the piece is unabashedly left wing. That speaks directly to my identity as a Chilean refugee, which in turn speaks directly to the identity of almost all of the Chilean exile community in Canada. In terms of challenging the immigrant play that we had gotten used to seeing in Canada, *Broken Tailbone* doesn't perform gratitude to the mainstream, doesn't present the country left behind as inferior to Canada, nor does it present a "model" immigrant. The immigrant/refugee in *Broken Tailbone* (me) swears, has one-night stands, has left-wing politics, adores Chile and all of Latin America, and takes up public space in an arguably impolite way. Canada's Multiculturalism Act states that immigrant groups have the right to practice their culture in public. This "allowed" immigrants to have Chinese New Year and Diwali parades (historically, the South Asian and East Asian communities in Vancouver have been victims of extreme racism). However, the Multiculturalism Act is not anti-racist, but rather an effort to contain radical demands to end racism. In *Broken Tailbone*, I don't perform rituals of my culture so that the mainstream audience can see that I too am human. I challenge the mainstream audience by breaking stereotypes that may exist about Latin America and Latinas and invite the non-mainstream audience to see a more complex version of themselves on stage.

Boffone   Where do you see the future of Latinx theater in Canada? How do you fit into this picture?

Aguirre   I see more and more of us creating our own work, acting in non-culturally specific roles, taking up more public space. I don't plan on retiring anytime soon, so I see myself continuing to insist on doing my work, and mentoring those that are coming up.

Latin Standards

Marga Gomez

San Francisco, California

15 Marga Gomez's *Latin Standards*, 2017. Photo: Fabian Echevarria.

Snapshot

Isaac Gomez

Latin Standards (the only production not affiliated with a producing theater company featured at the Encuentro de las Américas 2017), is a one-woman solo performance comedy-driven play written and performed by Marga Gomez of San Francisco and was directed by David Schweizer.

A tribute to her father, the dynamic comic performer and songwriter Willy Chevalier, *Latin Standards* uses music, comedy, projections, and mixed-media to take us through Marga's journey as an artist, and the obstacles she has faced (and still faces) paralleled with the trials and tribulations of her father in his career while he was alive. The title *Latin Standards* refers to the songs that Mr. Chevalier wrote, many of which were recorded and made the top of the Latin charts, and most of which were soulful laments about the trials of love—a topic Marga all-too readily explores in great depth not just in this show, but in much of her stand-up. To give some context of the significance of her father, culturally, Willy Chevalier was very famous. A usual suspect around the likes of Celia Cruz, Tito Puente, and the first transgender celebrity Christine Jorgensen, he was most commonly known for his comedy and music, but often struggled with substance abuse—a topic Marga readily explores in *Latin Standards*. "I was afraid to see him old and wrecked from booze, cigarettes, and cocaine," Marga says. "I was scared to see him poor. Now I'm the age he was when he died and I can see he was beautiful always, with all his mistakes."

As she enters the space, Marga shouts, "*Mi familia, que tal?*" (translating to: "My family, how are you?"), channeling a ritualistic opening her father used use when starting each of his own performances; a ritual that held a strong resonance to its largely Latinx sold-out performance at the Encuentro de las Américas, in which this edition was featured. At the top of the show, Marga, a well-beloved stand-up comedian and performer with more than thirty years as a practitioner, invites her audiences into her thirteenth solo show using a stand-up comedy routine that changes based on the location of her performance, and the country's cultural context at that time (references made in Marga's performance in 2017 referenced heavily a post-election cycle reckoning with the state of our country and its future). This stand-up comedy lead-up culminates in a declaration to her audience that "this is my final farewell concert." How true the statement is will be determined as the years progress.

Although Marga oscillates between playing herself and playing her father throughout the show, the core of the story is about her father and where she sees herself in his mistakes, his triumphs, and his legacy—especially after his passing—and the legacy she leaves behind. Through Marga's comedy, she draws her audience in with memories of displacement, of reconciliation with her relationship with her father, and the all-too common disassociation/conflict Latinx people (artists, especially) face when confronted with white American consumer culture, especially in the context of ticket sales and press.

"You look angry." "I'm not angry, it's just my face. I'm Latina so when I'm happy, I look angry." The inclusion of *Latin Standards* in the Encuentro de las Américas emphasizes the significance of Latinx artists who identify beyond stereotype and expectation of what it means to be Latinx, especially from an American point of view. Marga's work explicitly and subversively interrogates the expectation of roles and identities in theater, television, and film for Latinas, specifically. We see her wrestle with the expectations of Latinas in her upbringing as the show progresses, and how she pushes against those ideals in her performance work as an out lesbian Latina. And, perhaps more importantly, *Latin Standards* is an emphatic declaration of perseverance, resilience, and love. "Don't let anyone tell you no," Marga recounts towards the end of the performance, a phrase heard from her father. "Don't let *anyone* tell you no."

Excerpt from Latin Standards

Written and performed by Marga Gomez

Latin Standards received its world premiere in January 2017 at the Under the Radar Festival at The Public Theater. The production was directed by David Schweizer and produced by Mark Russell. Following the world premiere production, *Latin Standards* was produced at the Encuentro de las Américas in November 2017. In January 2018, *Latin Standards* was presented for a four-week run at Brava Theater, San Francisco. It has continued with engagements at Borderlands Theater, Tucson; Movimiento de Arte y Cultura Latino Americana (MACLA), San Jose; Bronx Academy of Arts and Dance, the Bronx; American Repertory Theater, Cambridge; The Provincetown Theater; and more.

Latin Standards *is mainly told by Marga Gomez as herself in the present. The story shifts from New York to San Francisco. She also portrays herself as "Little Marga" and Marga 2012. Other portrayals include her mom, her father "Willy Chevalier," her ex-girlfriend, and a Latino gay bar owner.*

Marga (to audience)   My dad's career was hot for decades until Latino venues started closing. But my father, Willy Chevalier, never quit—like I'm doing tonight in my final farewell concert!

Sound of applause.

Gracias!

Eventually he picked up a side job at a restaurant to hold him over till his comeback. When it was slow he'd write jokes and songs on the guest checks. He always had a plan. He always knew somebody—who knew somebody who had a cousin in the Bronx with a bar and a stage. He kept grinding till he died in New York—too soon. Why do we call dead people the late, when they're really the early? Let's get this concert started.

Marga *moves to a microphone stand in the spotlight.*

The first Latin standard I'm going to do for you was never recorded. My father called it "Una Mesa y Dos Sillas." In English it means, a table and two chairs. But everything sounds better in Spanish. Yes?
Una Mesa . . . .

Marga *pauses dramatically.*

Just so you know—there's no band coming. No pianist. It's not that kind of concert. (*Yanks microphone out and bangs it on the stand.*) This microphone-fake! And I won't be singing any notes. This concert is for *real* music lovers who never want the song introduction to end. You're passionate and curious about backstory and minutia. This is for you: fans of patter, banter, and the NPR station musicologist whose song introduction is longer than the song itself. (*She pulls out an old guest check.*) Especially this song which my father scribbled on a guest check during his restaurant years. I'll do it in Spanish first and then I'll translate for our "English only" friends.

Una mesa y dos sillas
Que solas se ven
Porque tú no estás
Ni yo tampoco
Como un recuerdo de lo que fuimos
Tú y yo—pero ya no somos.

And then he wrote:
"Budweiser, coke, shrimp, chicken."

Not part of the song. But we performers need to multitask.

On the surface we hear about two lovers. They rendezvous at the same dive. Sit at the same table, same chairs. Then the affair ends and neither will return to that table or those chairs. Ever. This isn't another breakup song. It's a song about chairs, and the struggle to fill them. The main character isn't part of this heteronormative couple. My father is telling us what producers go through. Chairs aren't cheap. I know. I once bought twenty-five chairs to start a comedy night at a Latino drag club in San Francisco called Esta Noche. The year was 2012, the tipping point of San Francisco gentrification. Esta Noche was steps away from 16th and Mission, a corner that in 2012 could still scare white people. It scared my girlfriend at the time.

She was blonde and a lot younger than me. Young enough to believe I knew what I was doing. Until my gig at Esta Noche.

Marga (*as girlfriend, scrolling through phone*)   Don't do it, Marga. The yelps are awful.
"Smells like urinal cake and bleach"
"Keep your wallet in your front pocket."
Marga don't do it. Don't work at Ay-sta Noch-ay.

Marga (*to girlfriend*)   Esta Noche is a gay Latino landmark. It would mean so much to me.

Marga (*as girlfriend*)   Think about your brand! Where do you see yourself in five years. At Ay-sta Noch-ay? It's like soooo ghetto. (*Off* **Marga**.) I'm not even being racist. Everybody knows Ay-sta Noch-ay is full of drugs.

Marga (*to girlfriend*)   Please! Stop speaking Spanish. It's pronounced Esta not Ay-st-a! Not No- Chay. It's Noche. Try? No. Why can't you people pronounce—(*Off girlfriend.*) I'm not even being racist. That's just not true. There's no drugs there. They have signs everywhere that say NO DRUGS.

Marga (*to audience*)   It was a sunny afternoon when I walked into the dark empty bar. My eyes adjusted to all manner of seizure-inducing lighting, lasers, phasers, chasers. Esta Noche reminded me of the last dive my father worked. But instead of hot Latinas in halter tops there were posters of bare-chested hombres in jock straps plastered everywhere. Hanging over the happy hour table, I noticed a life-size oil painting of an Andy Warhol superstar—Joe Dellassandro. Naked! His pinga was pointing down at the pupusas.

Marga (*to bartender*)   Hola. Coke por favor. Perdóname (*Struggling with Spanish.*) Yo soy aquí por hablar con el owner, Manuel? Manuel me está expectantandole?

Marga (*to audience*)   The bartender threw me that Latino shade. Like when Latinos who can speak Spanish look down on us Latinos who can't. Never lending us a mano? His attitude would change when my comedy show became a hit. I didn't see enough chairs for all the audience I would draw and two chairs were broken. Minor details. It was all about the legendary Esta Noche stage. Gay Latinos built that tall narrow stage in the 1970s for Latina drag queens to show off their finery; wigs, jewels gowns and pumps—in a spotlight against a glittery curtain. I imagined my comedians showing off their Old Navy outfits up there in the spotlight, which unfortunately also lit up the toilets flanking the tall but narrow stage. The smell of urinal cakes was real. So . . . I'd buy lots of potpourri and twenty-five chairs. My father taught me you have to spend money to make money.

Bowing.

That was "Una Mesa Y Dos Sillas!" Gracias! The next Latin standard—you know what? I'm going to break another concert rule for you. I'm giving you the encore now. It's my father's greatest hit and recorded by the fabulous Trio Los Condes. Titled "En El Ultimo Escalon" it's about a marriage that's over. It's sad like all Willie Chevalier songs and follows his usual arc, the woman is cruel—the man? Good! All his songs were inspired by my mom. He's always the victim. And she's the dream.

Conclusion

Aquí estamos, we are here

Trevor Boffone, Teresa Marrero, and Chantal Rodriguez

As *Seeking Common Ground* demonstrates, the Encuentro de las Américas was invested in inviting a nuanced conversation between Latinx and Latin American theater artists and theater making. The ground here refers directly to Los Angeles, California, USA. The organizers of both the convening and the festival were all US-based practitioners, and while the event was framed as an international convening, its germinating focus emerged in the Northern Hemisphere. Our Latin American counterparts were invited guests. As such, the Latinx Theatre Commons asked participants to consider the following questions throughout the festival: What do we share? How are we different? What are the things that keep us apart? What can we each do through our art-making to create the world we want to live in and how do we get there? What can we do together that we cannot do separately? These questions also grounded the work of the small groups which met three times over the course of the convening weekend. In addition to discussing the work on the festival stages, the small groups also grappled with the nature of the festival and the convening, as well with communicating across a variety of regional, generational, linguistic, racial, and cultural differences.

Different from previous LTC convenings, the planning committee implemented small discussion groups that would meet throughout the convening.[1] This approach proved effective as the groups fostered community and made a large event feel intimate. Conveners were divided into twelve groups of around twenty members; each group was led by two co-champions from the LTC Steering Committee.[2] For many, the small group environment allowed conveners to process and reflect on the shows and convening conversations in a more personal environment. Small groups enabled conveners to build relationships and meet people they otherwise might not have connected with during the festival. To do this, the planning committee pre-assigned and intentionally grouped people together who did not necessarily know each other. Moreover, group members were geographically and linguistically diverse, from designers to scholars to playwrights and producers, and from early career artists to practitioners with over forty years in the field. Representing the diversity of Latinx and Latin American identities, many of the small groups were bilingual spaces in which the conversations transitioned back and forth between English, Spanish, and Spanglish. Notwithstanding, the small groups struggled at times with continuity; as festival artists were not always available or present, group demographics changed daily which, in some cases, hindered both group cohesion and advancing the conversation.

When the convening participants gathered for the final full group session, the small groups were asked to report out and share their reflections. The reports took many shapes including performances, calls to action, musical numbers, and more traditional sharing of takeaways. While the form of each group's presentation was as diverse as the groups themselves, all responded to several guiding questions: What common ground have you found? What differences have you explored? What has surprised you? What still needs to be said? Where do we go from here?

After four full days of encounters we collectively bore witness to how the convening was experienced by its participants. In many ways this session served as a version of the critique sessions of the TENAZ Chicano Theater festivals, but these responses not only highlighted questions raised by the festival productions, but also expanded to the experience of the convening, and of the LTC itself.

One group saw members wandering aimlessly around the stage to reflect the chaos and confusion of being at the event. Another group had members say what they bring to the conversation. Members then linked arms, creating the visual representation of a bridge; as they leaned forward, they showed us what support looks like. Other groups took a more traditional approach. One group posed dramaturgical questions about the convening. The questions included: What is a scholar? And what does scholarship look like? How do we, as a community of theater makers, talk about problematic work in a constructive way, keeping in mind that what might be problematic in the United States may not be problematic in other countries? What are the producers doing to make this festival as accessible as possible? Overall, how is success measured in the long term? Should there be a better balance between artistic and scholarly engagement at events like this? What is our responsibility to one another as artists, producers, educators, and students as we grapple with these questions?[3]

In addition to questions of representation, several of the groups offered provocations to the conveners to consider our responsibility to our politics as a community. How does the representation of issues like misogyny, racism, queerness, transphobia, and sexual violence on our stages inform field-wide dialogues on these topics? they asked. The impact of painful encounters was made evident in a public request to create intentional space to address harm, including micro-aggressions and triggers experienced during plays and panels. Several groups challenged the LTC to engage in more rigorous analysis about its own role in perpetuating societal issues, asking the collective "What work is needed to decolonize Latinx and Latin American spaces? How can gatherings like this contribute to the work of dismantling colorism in our communities?" Discussions about race, equity, diversity, and inclusion were prevalent among the small groups, and also spoke to the difficulties that groups faced when discussing these issues without a shared framework and analysis. A call for new, non-hierarchical models for panel discussions was also made.

Reflections on language also highlighted the challenges participants faced in not only accessing the convening and festival events, but also with communicating and understanding one another. A call to review the ways supertitles are used, translated, and placed in a production gave voice to many frustrations experienced while watching the festival shows. Additionally, as the first fully bilingual event for the LTC, concerns about only recognizing the English/Spanish binary revealed the limits of the convening's approach to language inclusion. Groups called upon the LTC to consider indigenous languages and sign language as a part of these convenings. The need for a dialogue about Spanish itself, and how US Latinx people are shamed if they don't speak it, was also raised as a major concern. Another potent topic was the exploration of the term "Latinx." While there were artists from the US and Latin America who expressed an uneasiness with the term for a variety of reasons, the idea that the term is a US imposition, a bastardization of Spanish, and the result of the children of Latin American immigrants being too far removed from their mother-tongue and culture, was a particularly painful and difficult discussion to navigate. The conversation highlighted key ways in which Latinx and Latin American identities must be understood through a specific history and context.

When one of the small groups declared, "How about all-gender restrooms?!," it was also a challenge to the LTC's use of "Latinx." In January of 2017, the LTC formally changed its name. In a statement published on HowlRound, the LTC Steering Committee stated, ". . . we have collectively decided to officially shift our name from the Latina/o Theatre Commons to the Latinx Theatre Commons. This change signals the beginning of our work toward being radically inclusive of those who do not identify as either 'a' (female) or 'o' (male). The 'x' includes everyone: those who identify as 'a,' those who identify as 'o,' and everyone beyond and between."[4] Ten months after this name change and public commitment to radical inclusion, the LTC was confronted with what it means to embrace the term while continuing to uphold gender binaries and heteronormative practices.

One of the small groups chose to create a devised performance of their experience at the convening. They ended by repeating in Spanish, English, and American Sign Language the phrase which grounded the experience for them—*aquí estamos, we are here*. In the presence of one another the festival artists and convening participants bore witness to joy and pain. As the phrase was repeated it became an intention to continue to be present for one another, even if the common ground we find is shaky.

During the final small group session, groups were tasked with responding to the following two questions: What still needs to be said? Where do we go from here? Indeed, foregrounding the participant experience at Encuentro de las Américas festival led to several tangible action items for the LTC.

For instance, the underrepresentation of Afro-Latinx and indigenous artists and convening participants at the festival necessitated a conversation about who is included and excluded from dominant formulations of Latinidad. During the "Current and Emerging Trends in Theatre of the Américas" panel, Paul Flores, a San Francisco-based playwright and producer, challenged us all to face the racism and anti-blackness inherent in Latinx and Latin American culture. He shared his experience with his current collaboration *Tenemos Iré* (*We have Iré*), a project which engages Afro-Cuban artists in an exploration of how spirituality informs their culture, and catalyzed it as a call to action for us to recognize the absence of Afro-Latinx people in the LTC and in the theater of the Américas at large. "Isn't the 'X' about inclusion?" he proclaimed.

In light of conversations around language access, gender inclusive practices, and anti-blackness, it was clear that there remained much work to be done. For the LTC Steering Committee, this prompted a nuanced plan of action to redress the issues. Championed by Emily Aguilar and Beto O'Byrne, the Anti-Racism Training committee facilitated two trainings in 2018 (in Chicago and Denver), requiring all active LTC Steering Committee members to undergo anti-racist training with The People's Institute for Survival and Beyond. These multi-day trainings were twenty hours in length, and they aimed to support the LTC in developing a shared analysis around race, class, and community organizing. Notably, these trainings were also the result of valid, long-standing criticisms from both inside *and* outside of the Steering Committee. The LTC's growth from 2014 to 2017 demonstrated that, as the organization grew larger, so too did the issues that could arise. With this, the LTC has become sensitive to those which had not gone to the foreground before.[5]

Coming out of the Encuentro de las Américas festival, the LTC began to confront how it was living its values, particularly the core value of "radical transparency." This introspection was largely prompted by lessons learned in Los Angeles in tandem with historic criticism and concerns of elitism and a lack of significant diversity within the Steering Committee. On April 15, 2018 a group of Steering Committee and Advisory Committee members met in Princeton, New Jersey to discuss the future of the LTC with the aim of providing recommendations to the larger Steering Committee.[6] Several of these recommendations were a direct result of Encuentro 2017, such as the need to be more intentional about including Latinx identities that had previously been left out of the conversation: "We recognized our programming gaps in the past and recommend the entire Steering Committee (not just recruitment and programming committees) prioritize and value the experience and participation of Afro-Latinx, indigenous, disabled, and queer people; designers, technicians, and critics; and advocate for language justice in our convenings."[7]

¿Adónde fuimos? Where did we go?

A hallmark of all LTC convenings is that they reignite a spark of connectivity for Latinx theater makers and scholars. The acts of collective gathering, debate, and celebration help to propel the movement forward. However, it is important to note that the experience of the artists at the Encuentro was markedly different than that of the LTC conveners. As this book has shown, especially the artist interviews, festival artists were able to dive deeper into larger questions of Latinx and Latin American identity, politics, and aesthetics in a way that festival-goers were not. Encuentro artists were in residence at the LATC for three weeks, where they developed relationships with the Latino Theater Company and the city of Los Angeles as their hosts, as well as with one another as artists. Their residency was one of creative and cultural exchange, and programming was tailored around artist-based discussions and workshops across those three weeks. Additionally, a large amount of programming took place in the first and last weekends of the festival with the Patas Arriba late-night micro-theater performances by LA-based companies, along with film screenings and music performances. This multi-week engagement allowed for a more immersive and interdisciplinary engagement than that of the LTC conveners.

True to the core mission of the festival, the broader dissemination of the festival artists' work is impactful to track. While many productions from the Encuentro 2017 have gone on to post-festival success, we would like to highlight a few. As a direct result of relationships formed between artists and companies at the Encuentro, Cara Mía Theatre Co. and Ignite/Arts Dallas partnered to co-produce a national tour of Alex Alpharaoh's *WET: A DACAmented Journey*, which saw the solo show performed at ArtsEmerson, Yale Repertory Theatre's No Boundaries Series, Southern Methodist University, University of North Texas, Cara Mía Theatre Co., Destinos International Latino Theatre Festival in Chicago, Sin Muros Latinx Theatre Festival at Stages Repertory Theatre in Houston, and Hi-ARTS in New York City, among other venues.

Following Encuentro 2017, Culture Clash continued to present their work at major regional theaters including *Bordertown Now* at Pasadena Playhouse (2018), and *Culture*

Clash (Still) in America at South Coast Repertory (2019) and at Berkeley Repertory Theatre (2020). Marga Gomez's *Latin Standards* has enjoyed many subsequent performances including at American Repertory Theatre's Oberon stage, The Public Theater's Under the Radar Festival, and at Segerstrom Center for the Arts in 2017; at Movimiento de Arte y Cultura Latino Americana (MACLA), Borderlands Theater in 2018; at Esparza Center, Provincetown Theater, and the BAAD!ASS Women Festival in 2019 to name only a few.

Vueltas Bravas' production of *Miss Julia* was subsequently presented at La MaMa in 2017, and at the Festival Iberoamericano de Teatro de Cádiz in 2019. Carmen Aguirre continued to tour *Broken Tailbone* across Canada. Following Encuentro, the show took its makeshift dance hall to Workshop West/Chinook Series in Edmonton, and The Clutch in Vancouver over the 2018–19 and 2019–20 seasons. Argos Teatro's *10 Millones* has also continued on to success both in the US and back in Cuba, with performances at the Miami Dade County Auditorium in 2017; The Family Theater at John F. Kennedy Center for the Performing Arts in 2018; and at the Bienal de La Habana in 2019. Organización Secreta de Teatros' production of *Quemar las naves. El viaje de Emma* had important repercussions. Thanks to the feedback received in Los Angeles, the company's creative process was reaffirmed, as they continue with interpretations of myths from antiquity. The Encuentro de las Américas opened the door for them to present internationally, and according to company director Rocío Carrillo Reyes, "Needless to say, for us as artists, it was one of the richest experiences of our careers. In 2018, I became scenic director of the Mexican Sistema Nacional de Creadores de Arte. In 2019 and 2020 we worked on *Las diosas subterráneas* (*Subterranean Goddesses*) based on the myth of Demeter and Persephone and addresses the women victims of sexual trafficking."[8]

In 2020, Peruvian company Ébano Teatro continues its mission to create and produce artistic projects with Afro-descendant actors as part of its goal to increase inclusion within cultural and creative industries. Alicia Olivares Robles, the company director, is working on a virtual and face-to-face First Scenic Arts International Encounter of Afro-descendent Women. The project seeks the visibility and recognition of black and Afro-descendent women dedicated to creative and cultural endeavors in Peru. Given the present historical moment, the company considers it essential to open more spaces and to create platforms where these women can tell their own experiences through storytelling, thereby finding representation and validation.

Several of the productions in the festival—*Dementia, El Apagón, La razón blindada*, and *Las Mariposas Saltan al Vacío*—could be considered revivals and they allowed audiences to engage with a historical trajectory of themes and approaches against the reality of the world in 2017. While these specific plays have not necessarily toured, the experience of the festival informs the new work they are undertaking.[9] Other connections and company trajectories are more intangible and are found in continued conversations, new works, networking and mentorship, and in ongoing reflections from these encounters.

As *Seeking Common Ground* illustrates, fostering dialogue and artistic exchange through cross-cultural encounters such as Encuentro de las Américas is important. Although relationships between Latin American, the United States, and Canada have historically been strained because of the legacy of colonialism and imperialism, there is power in pushing against the man-made geopolitical borders that seek to divide artists and communities across the Hemispheric Americas. There is power in finding commonality while understanding difference. There is power in art-making that stages these nuances which, as Diane Rodriguez proclaims in the Afterword to this book, can serve as "the coming together instead of the pulling apart."

Notes

1. Reflecting the organic nature of the LTC, small group leaders were given a loose framework from which to guide their groups. While some co-champions stuck to this script throughout the weekend, others adapted the guidelines to fit the needs of their leadership styles and the participants in the group. During the first small group session on November 9, 2017, co-champions led their groups through introductions, ice-breakers to encourage name retention and points of connection among the group, and intention setting for the weekend. Each participant was charged with identifying their goals for the weekend and what they hoped to get out of the experience. During the second group session on November 10, groups focused on things that had resonated so far and any instances of common ground that they had come across. In addition, groups were charged with identifying questions that had yet to be addressed at the convening. In the final small group session on November 12, groups reflected further on the convening, now having been together at the LATC for four days. From here, groups came to a consensus about their 3-minute share out during the final large group session.

2. Small groups included: Tango, led by Adriana Gaviria and Irma Mayorga; Bachata, led by Arlene Martinez-Vickers and Jamie Gahlon; Cumbia, led by Alex Meda and Armando Huipe; Salsa, led by Daniel Jáquez and Amelia Acosta Powell; Bossa Nova, led by Anthony Rodriguez and Tiffany Vega-Gibson; Samba, led by Teresa Marrero and Richard Perez; Bolero, led by Trevor Boffone and Diane Rodriguez; Mariachi, led by Mario Ramirez and Lisa Portes; Huayno, led by Chantal Rodriguez and Marci R. McMahon; Bomba, led by Elizabeth Nungaray and Emily Aguilar; Joropo, led by Beatriz Rizk and Carla Della Gatta; and Reggaeton, led by Olga Sanchez Saltveit and Clyde Valentín.

3. A full and detailed report of this session was written by Olga Sanchez Saltveit, and is published on HowlRound. We are indebted to her work in documenting this event. See, Olga Sanchez Saltveit, "Estamos Juntos / We are Together: Report-Outs from the Latinx Theatre Commons International Convening," November 20, 2017. http://howlround.com/estamos-juntos-we-are-together-report-outs-from-the-latinx-theatre-commons-international-convening

4. Latinx Theatre Commons Steering Committee. "Toward Inclusivity: A message from the LTC" HowlRound, January 18, 2017. http://howlround.com/toward-inclusivity-a-message-from-the-ltc?utm_source=e-Boletin%3A+February+2016&utm_campaign=2016+November+e-Boletin&utm_medium=email

5. For more on the Latinx Theatre Commons' current initiatives and programming, visit https://howlround.com/ltc

6. The Princeton meeting was limited in size due to funding constraints in tandem with the desire to create a hyper-focused conversation. Participants were chosen based on availability, years in the LTC, and experience in leadership positions on various committees. The intention was to create a cross-section of LTC's past and present in order to have a nuanced conversation with many distinct perspectives in mind. The meeting was attended by Emily Aguilar, Roy Antonio Arauz, Kevin Becerra, Trevor Boffone, Georgina Escobar,

Meggan Gomez, Brian Eugenio Herrera, Arlene Martinez, Alexandra Meda, Chantal Rodriguez, Olga Sanchez Saltveit, Abigail Vega, and Karen Zacarías. The meeting was facilitated by Lydia Garcia. David Dower, Jamie Gahlon, and JD Stokely from HowlRound and ArtsEmerson were also in attendance.

7. Latinx Theatre Commons. "Future Programming 2020–2023." http://howlround.com/future-programming-2020-2023

8. Rocío Carrillo Reyes, email message to Teresa Marrero, June 2, 2020.

9. During the COVID-19 pandemic, the Latino Theater Company and PRTT/Pregones made archival recordings of *Dementia* and *El Apagón*, respectively, available for live-streaming audiences.

Closing Reflections from the Latino Theater Company

As artists of the Americas, we are responsible for intimately examining our displaced narratives and reclaiming our voice. Through this Encuentro, we will not only better understand each other's narratives but also find the opportunities to build a joint narrative. To this end, we share our creativity and shine a light on both our differences and our commonality, embrace both, and reclaim our humanity. We make art that brings beauty and harmony to the world, work that questions and fights back, plays that give pleasure and bring laughter. Through theater, we celebrate our empathy, compassion, curiosity, and, moreover, we continue crafting a global, creative community.

> (José Luis Valenzuela. Excerpt from Artistic Director's Welcome from the Encuentro de las Américas festival program, 2017)

Evelina Fernández (Resident Playwright and Associate Artistic Director) There are still so many things to reflect upon three years out. One of the things that has stayed with me is the confusion about language by the Mexican and Latin American artists and their lack of understanding the loss of language and the cultural aggression we experience in the US as Latinx artists. They insisted that we should speak Spanish when English was our comfort language and there was unintentional "*pocho*" shaming that went on during the festival. However, there was an enlightened moment when one of the US artists, Nicolás Valdez, reminded everyone that "we are all speaking the language of the conquerors." His comment synthesized, for me, the essence of our common struggle and how far back it goes.

Another discovery was that the struggle of US Latinx theater artists compared to some of our Latin American counterparts is much more immediate and present within the field and the progress we have made in the areas of social justice, gender and racial equality are not yet shared by all of them. Unfortunately, there was not a forum for this discussion in the last days of the festival and I regret that to this day. I feel it was a missed opportunity for developing a deeper understanding of who we are.

And the last thing that made a profound impression on me was a general disconnect between the Latinx Theatre Commons Convening participants and sessions and the performing artists in the festival. There seemed to be a general unappreciation of the work by many LTC conveners which was very different from the general audience and, again, no opportunity to discuss why.

Encuentro de las Américas 2017 has been one of the highlights of our long history and we are especially proud that we were able to offer it with the help of our small, but amazing staff and artistic family.

José Luis Valenzuela (Artistic Director) It has become so much clearer to me now, three years later, the lack of understanding we have between US Latino and Latin American artists and audiences. We understand that there is a border but also there in an intellectual and cultural disconnect between us. There is a certain moral hypocrisy in the United States. We fill ourselves with moral values that we are supposed to uphold, and at the same time we as a country don't always adhere to those values. The responses to the work from the participants of the Latinx Theatre

Commons convening revealed to me a lack of understanding of the cultural context where the work was created, and for whom it was created. For instance, there was a misunderstanding about the use of nudity in one of the plays, and a claim of body shaming in another because a character was referred to as "la gorda" which for me meant that the work was not understood in its cultural context. The idea of the festival was to confront the idea of how theater companies in different communities create their work considering the needs, the language, and the cultural background of those communities. This needs a much more nuanced conversation that is not happening because we rule ourselves by certain values and we have very little understanding of other cultural experiences.

Also, the truth is when Latin American companies come to the US even in a Latino festival context, they often assume that the US is a white country in a way. This informs their expectations about audiences and the network of the American theater which Latinos don't often belong to because we have not had access to it. This is still the conversation in this country, how do we become part of the national conversation in the American theater? Even we as practitioners have a lack of understanding about that, and that is a major discussion that needs to happen. This conversation also needs to be expanded, which is a goal of the future Encuentro because we believe that we live in a global society and that culture and art are global and should not be relegated to isolated national discussions. It has become very evident how much we need this conversation and dialogue in order to be open as artists. To me, we need to talk about the hypocrisy of who we are as a country, and how we judge "the other" by the way we represent ourselves culturally.

Geoffrey Rivas (Associate Artistic Director)   We tried to create a safe environment for people to critique the work without taking offense, but I don't know if we achieved that because some people seemed like they were guarded or didn't want to comment one way or another. We aspired to create a place where we could critique each other's work at face value and not take it so personally. This felt different than what happened during the convening weekend since the critiques raised then were not from the festival artists' point of view.

José Luis Valenzuela (Artistic Director)   What we tried to do with the panels and artistic discussions was for people to talk about the work without a sense of competition which is often common in the US. To some degree, this became more difficult to do in 2017 rather than 2014 and I'm not sure I understand why. The idea of having this type of Encuentro was for it to be different from a festival where you see a play, you judge it, you go home. At the Encuentro, the idea was to discuss the work and try to have a better understanding of how and why the work happens in the artists' communities. There was supposed to be an expansive exchange of experiences rather than an absolute judgment of the work through by a narrow viewpoint.

Lucy Rodriguez (Associate Artistic Director)   I was very naïve, up until the Encuentro I did not realize the role that academia plays in developing a theater canon or determining what is okay and what is not okay, because I did not come up that way and I wasn't formally educated in theater. It came to a forefront during the Encuentro de las Américas. Who says what is "good theater," and who establishes that standard? I remember feeling that there were certain plays that I wasn't too sure about, but they were some of the biggest hits and I thought, "I'm the same way!" It has to do with our own personal aesthetic and who the theater artists are and who the audiences are that these artists were performing for originally. It was very interesting to experience what is good about something that I may not have seen originally, to see how people responded to certain things, and why they responded to those things, that was really eye opening for me.

Geoffrey Rivas (Associate Artistic Director)   I continue to reflect on the difficulties of crossing borders. It was particularly difficult for the companies from Colombia, Peru, and Cuba and the hoops they had to jump through to simply get an artist visa to travel to the festival. The political climate in 2017 continued to escalate under the Trump Administration and it significantly impacted not only the process for the festival but also for international artists and productions the company wanted to produce at the LATC after the festival.

Sal Lopez (Associate Artistic Director)   For me, one of the many takeaways is the resolve of Latino theater companies to do the work. Despite whatever circumstances you come from, the many obstacles and challenges that face so many in our community, we persevere. We make do "ahuevo." That is an impactful and impressive strength. It is good to cultivate and nurture these relationships with different companies and build on that strength. Certainly, the camaraderie and connection at the after-parties were something to savor. The panel conversations were insightful and the sharing of ideas was invigorating. To see, hear, and experience the uniqueness and different points of view, on and off the stage, the language, the music, the color figuratively and literally is another one of our strengths. The Encuentro format lends itself to creating the potential to strengthen, expand, and grow relationships among companies. The talent is undeniable, and the Latino theater community is still hungry. That is a cause for celebration. And that is the point, to celebrate this amazing endeavor.

Lucy Rodriguez (Associate Artistic Director)   The wonderful aspect about having an "encounter" with other Latino artists is that we learn so much from being in the same space, listening to each other, and experiencing each other's work. But there are also the encounters in more informal settings, going for coffee, enjoying the parties in our Grand Lobby or, escaping all the hoopla for a while and just talking with a participant in a quieter spontaneous meeting. I am so proud of the part Latino Theater Company played in this festival: we continue to develop as artists and to expand the definition of "Latino" and "theater," I also want to give a shout-out to our amazing administrative and technical staff without whom none of our artistic visions would come to fruition.

Afterword

Diane Rodriguez

In January, during the Chilean summer of 2018, I visited the Centro Ceremonial Mahuidache in a suburb of Santiago set below the great Andes mountain range as part of the Teatro A Mil Festival. On this site, the first nation Mapuche community had built a cultural center that included a gathering space with a round thatched roof and a dirt floor. We sat in a circle on the periphery of the inside of the structure. There were more than one hundred of us as we witnessed the ritual, western-style play and real-time cooking that was taking place in the center of the space. At the end of the presentation, we ate the bread and meat that had been prepared and cooked during the performance. The smell of the wet-patted floor, the food, the straw, the actors moving through the space with the awkwardness of non-performers but carrying the weight of their people and their mission, all made the experience electrifying. This *encuentro*, could have taken place in Canada, the United States, Mexico, Colombia, New Zealand, China, India, Morocco, or Malawi: any place where a group of people gather who are tied to the land, colonized by another nation, and re-affirming their place in the world through ritual and theater. It is the root of theater. Theatre at its most basic.

An *encuentro* is an encounter where you might meet someone or find something unexpectedly. Encuentro de las Americas in 2017 was such a convening in Los Angeles, California literally ten miles from the majestic Pacific Ocean. Festivals of this nature are akin to a treasure hunt. We have far too few of them in the USA. So much of the Western world uses theater festivals as a platform to see work from all over the world. You never know the gems you will find, the artists you've never heard of who have honed their skills and brought to the table an exquisite visual feast, or an emotional parable that quenches your thirst for a cathartic release.

Because of our ever-transforming world where with a click of a finger we are transported to another country, able to network with someone inside a screen thousands of miles away, or correspond in real time through many a digital communication platform, our world has become closer. However, mankind is on the move disrupting boundaries both physical and psychological causing a reaction based on fear to close the doors and lock them in order to protect the home country from an invasion that would affect the culture at hand.

As theater makers, we want this disruption. We want theater of a different language. We want a story that isn't ours but when we see it we own it. We want resourcefulness and inventiveness to go merrily hand in hand. We rejoice at the discovery, like middle school children in line for "Guardians of the Galaxy." It flies us out of our universe and into someone else's. And there, we find our sameness not our difference. Fear need not apply.

So, it was poignant and necessary to gather the tribe of Latinx theater makers from across the USA and Latin America to descend on the sun-drenched city at the edge of our once vast frontier. The lobby was abuzz with reunions, introductions, brief exchanges with the anticipation of more to come. This was the first time in Los Angeles where there had been a convergence of Latinx artists from the two continents of the Americas meeting to share work and ideas in a profound and intimate way. On the four stages and gallery space of the Los Angeles Theatre Center, we theater devotees flocked to see reimagined classics, new plays, solo shows, and ensemble generated work. We diligently observed the negotiation of themes and aesthetics that created a synergy that feed the conversation. We were all hungry for it and feasted on the work and the *plática*.

Not only were we able to see the performances but we were able to discuss the nature of the work, the context in which it was created, and meet the artists face to face. If only our US audiences throughout the country had the opportunity to take this deep dive, this extreme theater experience to heart. Gatherings of this nature are the future; a panoply of choices to see over two weeks, or a month. Choose a country to go to, experience their stories. Hear the cadence of their speech, their movement through space. I assure you that the border that separates us disappears, vanishes as if it never was and should never be.

El Encuentro de las Américas 2017 was a contemporary ritual gathering recalling the Centro Ceremonial Mahuidache. We found the unexpected, we surrounded and embraced the work as if we sat in a circle. The *Encuentro* was the coming together instead of the coming apart. It was an encounter of continents, our cultural plates accreting, and becoming one. The ancients from both the Americas and the continents to the east and west of us understood that we find our humanity through the ritual of gathering together to meditate and feast on the spectacle at hand. We did just that. Onward.

Notes on Contributors

Carmen Aguirre is an award-winning theater artist and author who has written and co-written over twenty-five plays, the #1international bestseller *Something Fierce: Memoirs of a Revolutionary Daughter* (winner of CBC Canada Reads 2012), and its bestselling sequel, *Mexican Hooker #1 and My Other Roles Since the Revolution*. She is writing an adaptation of Euripides' *Medea* for Vancouver's Rumble Theatre, Moliere's *The Learned Ladies* for Toronto's Factory Theatre, and a piece on Italian photographer Tina Modotti for Vancouver's Electric Company Theatre, where she is a Core Artist. *Reframed*, co-created with them, commissioned by The National Arts Centre, will premiere online in December. Her piece *Floating Life*, commissioned by Ontario's Stratford Festival, will soon receive its digital premiere. Carmen has over eighty film, TV, and stage acting credits and is a finalist for the 2020 Siminovitch Prize, Canada's most prestigious theater award. Carmen is a graduate of Studio 58. www.carmenaguirre.ca

Alex Alpharaoh is a Guatemalan-born actor, playwright, lyricist, spoken word poet, and solo performer from Los Angeles, California. Prior to Covid-19, he was on national tour with his autobiographical solo show titled *WET: A DACAmented Journey*, a story about what it means to be an American in every sense of the word except on paper. Alex is the recipient of the LA Drama Critics Circle (LADCC) 2018 Solo Performance of the Year award for his work on *WET*. As a formerly undocumented citizen, Alpharaoh believes in the transformative power of sharing one's truth and vulnerability, especially in the face of adversity. Alex currently resides in Los Angeles with his daughter Aileen, and is currently working on multiple projects, including an adaptation of Othello written in verse titled *O-Dogg: An Angeleno Take on Othello, WET: DREAMers, WET: South-Central American*, and writing his first memoir. www.dacamentedjourney.com

J.Ed Araiza works on multicultural, cross-disciplinary projects as a writer, director, and performer. A bilingual Chicano, he is a member of the SITI Company, the acclaimed experimental theater ensemble founded by Tadashi Suzuki and Anne Bogart. For more than twenty-nine years he has performed in SITI productions in major international venues. A playwright with seven original full-length plays produced, he has directed sections of 365 Days/365 Plays at the New York Public Theatre; *Voluspa* for the National Theatre of Iceland; *Savitri, Dancing in the Forest of Death* for the META Theatre Festival in Delhi, India (nominated, best production, best director); and *MEDEAstories*, his adaptation of the Euripides, at TeaK in Helsinki. His bilingual adaptation *Miss Julia*, based on Strindberg's *Miss Julie* has been presented internationally and at the LA MAMA ETC and the LATC Encuentro. Since 2013 he has been the head of the UCLA School of Theater, Film and Television's MFA Acting Program.

Trevor Boffone is the founder of the 50 Playwrights Project and a member of the National Steering Committee for the Latinx Theatre Commons. He is a Lecturer in the Women's, Gender & Sexuality Studies Program at the University of Houston. He is the author of *Renegades: Digital Dance Cultures from Dubsmash to TikTok* (Oxford University Press, 2021). He is the co-editor of *Encuentro: Latinx Performance for the New American Theater* (Northwestern University Press, 2019), *Teatro Latino: Nuevas* *obras de los Estados Unidos* (La Casita Grande Press, 2019), *Nerds, Goths, Geeks, and Freaks: Outsiders in Chicanx and Latinx Young Adult Literature* (University Press of Mississippi, 2020), and *Shakespeare and Latinidad* (Edinburgh University Press, 2021).

Rocío Carrillo Reyes founded Organización Secreta Teatro in Mexico City in 1991 along with a group of artists interested in experimentation and research. The group works with Carrillo Reyes as director of the company, while she also directs and works on lighting the works. Since 2018 she has been a member of the Sistema Nacional de Creadores de Arte FONCA, a national network that supports the cultural projects. Her company is known for experimenting with archetypal figures and reconfiguring them into contemporary contexts. They devise their work collectively, often challenging and expanding traditional definitions of the theatrical.

Carlos Celdrán is an award-winning and highly esteemed theater director, playwright, academic and professor, living and working in Havana, and presenting his work all over the world. Celdrán founded his company Argos Teatro in 1996, and has directed numerous plays by Brecht, Beckett, Ibsen, Strindberg, among others, has done much work for Cuban playwrights too, showing productions of local artists on multiple occasions. It is this fusion of different cultures that has helped Argos Teatro, one of Cuba's leading theater groups, to be acclaimed beyond Cuba's borders. The highpoint of the company's existence to date was its production entitled *Ten Million*, a piece written and directed by Carlos Celdrán himself. This piece won critical acclaim, and was performed both in Cuba and internationally. Their most recent works, *Misterios y pequeñas piezas* in 2018 and *Hierro* in 2019, also written and directed by Carlos Celdrán, have been likewise well received and acknowledged. Celdrán has been recognized with awards on countless occasions. He has won the Cuban Theatre Critics Award in the category of Best Staging more than eighteen times from 1988 to 2019. Beyond this critical acclaim, he has also won the recognition of his country and the world, receiving the National Distinction of Cuban Culture in 2000 and the Cuban National Theatre Award in 2016, UNESCO's ITI 70th Anniversary Medal and was the author of the World Theater Day Message in 2019. He has been part of the faculty of the Cuban Higher Institute of the Arts for more than twenty years, and the head of the Master's Degree course for stage direction since 2016. He received his Master's degree in 2011 from the Rey Juan Carlos University of Madrid, Spain.

Culture Clash 2020 marks the company's thirty-sixth-year anniversary as the most prominent Chicano/Latino performance troupe in the country, with works ranging from sketch comedy to powerful drama, to adaptations of Aristophanes and books for musicals. Founded in 1984 in San Francisco, Culture Clash is Richard Montoya, Ric Salinas, and Herbert Siguenza. This prolific group most recent plays include: *American Night: The Ballad of Juan Jose* for the Oregon Shakespeare Festival. Before the coronavirus shut down theaters worldwide, Culture Clash was enjoying a wildly successful run of *Culture Clash (Still) in America*. Currently, Culture Clash has made a very successful switch onto theatrical streaming platforms for La Jolla Playhouse and Center Theater Group.

Grace Dávila-López is an adjunct professor of Spanish at the Department of Romance Languages and Literatures at Pomona College. She specializes in Puerto Rican theater, and she has published in *Latin American Theater Review*, *Conjunto*, and *GESTOS*

(1986–2015), of which she was associate editor, and a founding member. She has also published articles on plays by Argentinean playwright Arístides Vargas, and the Ecuadorian theater group Malayerba. As a resident of Southern California, she is interested in the work of the Latino Theater Company, 24th Street Theatre, and the Los Angeles theater scene.

Carla Della Gatta is Assistant Professor of English at Florida State University. She has published essays and reviews, dramaturged professionally, and worked as a scholar and adviser for various theaters. She has been awarded fellowships from the Woodrow Wilson Foundation, the Folger Shakespeare Library, the New York Public Library, and the American Society for Theatre Research. Della Gatta received the J. Leeds Barroll Dissertation Prize from the Shakespeare Association of America for the best dissertation in 2016. She is the co-editor of *Shakespeare and Latinidad* (Edinburgh University Press, 2021). Her first monograph, *Latinx Shakespeares: The Staging of Intracultural Theatre*, is in process. It explores the intersection of Shakespeare and Latinidad through dramaturgical and textual analysis of cultural adaptations.

Evelina Fernández is a proud Chicana from East LA. She is an award-winning playwright, screenwriter, actor, and activist and she writes about the US Latinx experience. As a founding member of the Latino Theater Company, her collaborative artistic family of over thirty years, she has developed, written, and produced a prolific body of work using the company's unique artistic process and signature theatrical language and aesthetic under the artistic directorship of José Luis Valenzuela, including *The Mother of Henry* (LA Times Critic's Choice 2019, LA Drama Critics Circle (LADCC) Ted Schmitt Award 2019), *Premeditation* (Ovation Award Nominee) and LADCC Award for Outstanding Writing of a World Premiere Play for *A Mexican Trilogy*, published by Samuel French. Other LA Times Critic's Choice list; *Solitude* (2009), *Dementia* (2010). *La Virgen de Guadalupe, Dios Inantzin* has been featured in both the *LA Times* and the *NY Times*. In 2003, *Dementia* won the GLAAD Media Award.

Isaac Gomez is a Chicago-based playwright originally from El Paso, Texas/Ciudad Juárez, Mexico. His play *La Ruta* received its world premiere at Steppenwolf Theatre Company in 2018. He has received commissions from South Coast Repertory, Goodman Theatre, Actors Theatre of Louisville (Acting Apprentice New Play Commission), The Theatre School at DePaul University (Cunningham Commission for Youth Theater), Sideshow Theater Company, Steep Theatre, Albany Park Theater Project, and StepUp Chicago Playwrights. He is the recipient of the 2017 Jeffry Melnick New Playwright Award at Primary Stages, an inaugural 3Arts "Make A Wave" grantee, a member of the 2017/18 Goodman Theatre's Playwrights Unit, co-creative director at the Alliance of Latinx Theatre, a resident playwright at Chicago Dramatists, an artistic associate with Victory Gardens Theater, ensemble member with Teatro Vista, artistic associate with Pivot Arts, artistic curator for Theater on the Lake 2018/19, a steering committee member of the Latinx Theatre Commons (LTC) and a core producer with the Jubilee. He is a professional lecturer at The Theatre School at DePaul University and is represented by The Gersh Agency and Circle of Confusion.

Marga Gomez is a comedian, teaching artist and writer/performer of thirteen solo plays which have been presented nationally, internationally and Off Broadway.

Selections from Gomez's work have been published in several anthologies including *Extreme Exposure* (TCG Books), *HOWL* (Crown Press), *Out Loud & Laughing* (Anchor Books), *Contemporary Plays by American Women of Color* (Routledge), *When I Knew* (HarperCollins) and *Out of Character* (Bantam Books.) She was born in New York City to entertainers in the Latino community. At the start of the 2020 pandemic Gomez pivoted to adapting and presenting her work for livestreaming. She has been featured in online theater festivals from New York to San Diego, as well as a five week virtual run for Brava, SF where she is an artist-in-residence. She is a GLAAD media award winner and recipient of the 2020 CCI Investing in Artists grant. Her website is www.margagomez.com

Patricia Herrera is an Associate Professor in the Department of Theatre and Dance at the University of Richmond. Dr. Herrera researches US Latinx cultural productions, including visual art, performance, and museum exhibitions. She is the author of the forthcoming book *Nuyorican Feminist Performance: From the Nuyorican Poets Cafe to Hip Hop Theater* (University of Michigan Press, 2020). Her more recent public humanities projects include creating documentary plays, digital archives, and museum exhibitions about Richmond's history of Civil Rights, including *Nuestras Historias: Latinos in Richmond* (June 2017) and *Made in Church Hill* (2015) at The Valentine Museum. Her next book project, *Sonic Latinidades: Latino Theater in the 21st Century,* explores the centrality of sound to Latina/o performance.

Lillian Manzor is Associate Professor of Modern Languages and Literatures and Hemispheric Caribbean Studies at the University of Miami and Founding Director of the Cuban Theater Digital Archive (www.cubantheater.org). She is series co-editor of Sualos, published by Havana's Editorial Alarcos and Miami's CTDA Press. She is widely published in Latin American and Latinx theater and performance studies. She has co-edited *Latinas on Stage, Teatro cubano actual: dramaturgia escrita en los Estados Unidos*, and co-authored *Cuban Theater in Miami: 1960-1980* (http://scholar. library.miami.edu/miamitheater/) and *El Ciervo Encantado: An Altar in the Mangrove* (http://ciervoencantado.tome.press/). She is finishing a book titled *Marginality Beyond Return: US-Cuban Performances and Politics*. Her research has been funded the Andrew W. Mellon Foundation, National Endowment for the Humanities, American Council of Learned Societies, Ford Foundation, and Rockefeller Foundation. As a community engaged scholar, she has fostered US–Cuba cultural dialogues through theater and performance since 1993.

Teresa Marrero is Cuban-born and Los Angeles-raised. Marrero currently holds the position of Full Professor in the Spanish Department at the University of North Texas, specializing in contemporary Latin American and Latinx Theater. Besides writing scholarly essays, she also pens short fiction, plays, and performance commentaries as a theater critic. *Second-Hand Conversations with Irene*, a fanciful encounter among three women, one of whom is the renowned Maria Irene Fornes, earned second place in the Arizona Theatre Company's 2021 New Play Contest; it was also selected by Dallas' Undermain Theatre for its 2020 Whither Goest Thou America Festival of New Play readings. Her Spanish language play, *La Familia*, appears in *Teatro Latino: Nuevas Obras en los Estados Unidos* (New York: La Casita Grande, 2019).

She co-edited *Encuentro: Latinx Performance for the New American Theater* (Northwestern University Press, 2019) with Trevor Boffone and Chantal Rodriguez, and the landmark anthology *Out of the Fringe, Contemporary Latina-Latino Theater and Performance* (Theatre Communications Group, 2000) with Caridad Svich. In Argentina, she published a collection of short stories entitled *Entre la Argentina y Cuba, cuentos nómadas de viajes y tangos* (Corregidor, 2009). She is a member of the American Theatre Critics Association and writes for www.theaterjones.com

Marci McMahon is a Professor in the Literatures and Cultural Studies Department, with affiliations in the Gender and Women's Studies program and Mexican American Studies program, at the University of Texas Rio Grande Valley. Her research and teaching interests include US Latinx literature, cultural studies, theater and performance; gender and sexuality studies; sound studies; and American Studies. She is the author of *Domestic Negotiations: Gender, Nation, and Self-Fashioning in US Mexicana and Chicana Literature and Art* (Rutgers University Press, 2013). Her publications appear in *The Chicano Studies Reader: An Anthology of Aztlán*, third and fourth editions; *Aztlán: A Journal of Chicano Studies*; *Chicana/Latina Studies: The Journal of MALCS*; *Frontiers: A Journal of Women's Studies*; *Journal of Equity & Excellence in Education*; and *Text & Performance Quarterly*. She is currently work on a second book that explores the relationship between aurality and citizenship in US Latinx theater and performance.

Noe Montez is Associate Professor of Drama and Director of the PhD In Theatre and Performance Studies at Tufts University where he also serves as core faculty in Latinx Studies. He is the author of *Memory, Transitional Justice, and Theatre in Postdictatorship Argentina*, which considers how theater, as a site of activism, can produce memory narratives that change the public's reception to governmental policies on human rights violations. Noe also co-edits the journal *Theatre Topics*, which engages in the theory and practice of theater curriculum, pedagogy and performance. He has been published in a variety of peer-reviewed journals, serves on the executive committee for the American Society for Theatre Research and with the Association for Theatre in Higher Education's Latinx, Indigenous, and the Americas group.

Carlos Morton has over one hundred theatrical productions, both in the US and abroad. His professional credits include the San Francisco Mime Troupe, the New York Shakespeare Festival, the Denver Center Theatre, La Compañía Nacional de México, the Puerto Rican Traveling Theatre, and the Arizona Theatre Company. He is the author of *The Many Deaths of Danny Rosales and Other Plays (*1983), *Johnny Tenorio and Other Plays* (1992), *The Fickle Finger of Lady Death* (1996), *Rancho Hollywood y otras obras del teatro chicano* (1999), *Dreaming on a Sunday in the Alameda* (2004), and *Children of the Sun: Scenes for Latino Youth* (2008). A former Mina Shaughnessy Scholar and Fulbright Lecturer to Mexico and Poland, Morton holds an MFA in Drama from the University of California, San Diego, and a PhD in Theatre from the University of Texas at Austin. Morton has lived on the border between Mexico and the United States since 1981, teaching at universities in Texas, California and Mexico. He is currently Professor Emeritus of Theater at the University of California, Santa Barbara.

Chantal Rodriguez is the Associate Dean of Yale School of Drama and an Assistant Professor Adjunct of Dramaturgy and Dramatic Criticism. From 2009–16 she was the

Programming Director and Literary Manager of the Latino Theater Company, operators of the Los Angeles Theatre Center. In 2019 she co-edited a volume of Yale's *Theater Magazine* dedicated to Latinx Theatre, with Tom Sellar. Together with Teresa Marrero and Trevor Boffone, she co-edited *Encuentro: Latinx Performance for the New American Theater*, published by Northwestern University Press in May 2019. In 2011, the UCLA Chicano Studies Research Center Press published her monograph, "The Latino Theatre Initiative/Center Theatre Group Papers," which was nominated for three Latino Literacy Now International Book Awards. She is a member of the Latinx Theatre Commons Advisory Committee, and the National Advisory Board for the 50 Playwrights Project. Chantal is a graduate of UCLA where she earned a PhD in theater and performance studies.

Diane Rodriguez (June 22, 1951–April 10, 2020) A celebrated member of the Los Angeles theater community, Diane Rodriguez was an actress, director, playwright, and producer. Her career began in 1973 when she joined Luis Valdez's El Teatro Campesino. She went on to become Associate Artistic Director for Center Theatre Group, and worked with theaters and artists across the country as well as internationally; President of the Theatre Communications Group Board; and to receive recognition from President Barack Obama. She was also a cofounder of the ground-breaking comedy troupe, Latins Anonymous.

Gina Sandí-Diaz is an Assistant Professor of Latinx Theatre at California State University, Fresno. She is also an actor, director, and applied theater facilitator born and raised in San José, Costa Rica. She has a PhD and an MA in Theatre from the University of Kansas, and a BA in Performing Arts from the Universidad Nacional de Costa Rica. Her areas of expertise are Latinx Theatre and Performance, Theatre for Social Change and Applied Theatre.

Nicolás Valdez is a Texas-based interdisciplinary performance artist and cultural arts educator who has been writing and producing original theater for over twenty years. An accomplished musician, he began studying traditional Conjunto music at the age of nine, and at thirteen, was the youngest founding member of the Guadalupe Cultural Arts Center's youth theater company, Grupo Animo. Nicolas's theater credits include a national tour with Teatro Campesino's 25th Anniversary production of *Zoot Suit* and Su Teatro's production of *Enrique's Journey* at the Los Angeles Theater Company's 2014 Encuentro De Las Américas. His original one-man show, *Conjunto Blues*, which documents the Mexican-American working-class experience through Conjunto accordion music, was featured at the LATC's 2017 Encuentro and has toured throughout the Southwest. He is a member of Los Nahuatlatos who have released two full-length albums, *Tierra Sin Fin* (2017) and *Jamás Inquietos* (2018). Nicolas continues to perform around the country, holding workshops, and finding creative ways to empower youth voices.